SEVEN TROUBADOURS

THE CREATORS OF
MODERN VERSE

SEVEN TROUBADOURS

THE CREATORS OF
MODERN VERSE

by JAMES J. WILHELM

THE PENNSYLVANIA STATE UNIVERSITY
PRESS
University Park and London

Standard Book Number 271–00099–6

Library of Congress Catalogue Card 79–84668

Copyright © 1970 by The Pennsylvania State University

Printed in the United States of America

Designed by Marilyn E. Shobaken

for

Thomas G. Bergin

que.m tramezes la contraclau

PREFACE

Since this book has been written for nonspecialists desiring basic information about this relatively uncharted part of world literature, I have tried to keep the text as simple as possible, relegating questions of a particular nature to the end notes. I have not included the original Provensal texts, since those who cannot read the language would merely be disturbed by their presence, and those who can read it will find the texts readily accessible. Questions concerning my translations are often discussed in the notes unless the point is essential for understanding the poem.

The translations themselves vary from the simple and intentionally folksy ones of William of Aquitaine to some more elaborate samples which approximate the rhymes of the originals. In almost every case, rhetorical flourish has been sacrificed for closeness to the letter; I have felt that it is better to be prosaic than to stray far from the original. I have often tried to employ alliteration as a unifying device. I owe many thanks to Stephen G. Nichols, Jr., who examined the translations closely; in places where I stray from accepted readings of the text, the choice is mine.

Since I have already touched upon this area in a previous work, I have tried to avoid duplication as much as possible. As a result, I have omitted Bernart de Ventadorn's famous "When I see the lark flying," and, in fact, my entire discussion of Bernart accentuates his poetry rather than my commentary. Those who desire a more detailed consideration of the Provensal language's relation to Latin and of the role of Ovid in the troubadour tradition may find these matters discussed in my book *The Cruelest Month: Spring, Nature, and Love in Classical and Medieval Lyrics* (New Haven: Yale University Press, 1965).

I must here acknowledge my debt to the work of modern historical writers like Richard, although I have also consulted

7

the chronicles wherever possible. These seven troubadours are not meant to emerge as identifiable historical personages with the clarity of a Pier della Francesca portrait, but to cohere as poetic voices, with an emphasis on temper and style.

In the spelling of names I have tried to select the form sanctioned by general usage or the one which is most manageable for English-speaking people. I have used modern French place names, except for the names of some castles; chroniclers and ecclesiastics often appear with Latin names; most names for other people are Anglicized. In Biblical citations, I use the Revised Standard Version for quotations in the text and the Vulgate for notes.

Foremost among those whom I must thank for assistance is Thomas G. Bergin, whose gracious consent in granting me a private tutorial during my studies at Yale launched me on the road to writing this book. Kurt Lewent, who taught me Provensal at Columbia, was also an invaluable help. Angel Flores proved most generous in his extension of permission to reprint translations which have appeared in his anthologies (specific debts are covered in the notes). Others who assisted me in ways professional or personal are Frederick Goldin, Alfred Kellogg, Wilson Randolph Gathings, Richard Sáez, Raymond J. Barry, Conrad Waldstein, and Jean Hakes Witherwax, who never let me forget that these poems were written to be sung.

Livingston College of Rutgers University

CONTENTS

13   WHERE DID THEY COME FROM?

1
21   DUKE WILLIAM IX OF AQUITAINE
The Whole Medieval Man

2
61   MARCABRUN
In Scorn of Love

3
87   JAUFRE RUDEL
The Ecstasy of the Flight, The Agony of the Fall

4
107   BERNART DE VENTADORN
The Master Singer

5
131   THE COUNTESS OF DIA,
OFTEN CALLED BEATRITZ
"The Sappho of the Rhone"

6
143   BERTRAN DE BORN
War, Wit, and Morality

7
173   PEIRE CARDENAL
The Last of the Patricians

197   THE TROUBADOURS AND MODERN SONG

205   NOTES

225   INDEX

SEVEN TROUBADOURS

THE CREATORS OF
MODERN VERSE

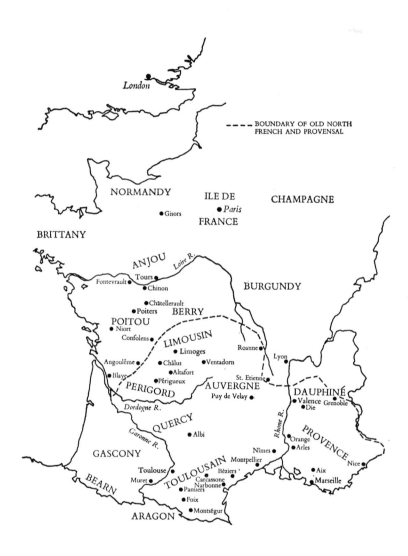

London

BOUNDARY OF OLD NORTH
FRENCH AND PROVENSAL

NORMANDY   ILE DE   CHAMPAGNE

●Gisors   ●Paris

FRANCE

BRITTANY

ANJOU   Loire R.

Fontevrault●   ●Tours   BURGUNDY
    ●Chinon

●Châtellerault

●Poiters   BERRY

POITOU

●Niort

Confolens●

LIMOUSIN

Angoulême●   ●Limoges   Roanne●
    ●Châlus   ●Ventadorn   ●Lyon

●Blaye   ●Altafort
    ●Périgueux   St. Etienne●

PERIGORD   AUVERGNE   DAUPHINÉ

Dordogne R.   Puy de Velay●   ●Valence   Grenoble●
    ●Die

QUERCY   Rhone R.

Garonne R.   ●Albi   PROVENCE

GASCONY   ●Orange
    Nîmes●   ●Arles
    Montpellier●
Toulouse●   TOULOUSAIN   Béziers●   ●Aix   Nice●
Muret●   Carcassone●   ●Marseille
    ●Pamiers   Narbonne●
BEARN   ●Foix

    ●Montségur

ARAGON

WHERE DID THEY COME FROM?

To many people the mention of troubadours suggests a medieval chorus, a group of guitar-strumming minstrels singing plaintive songs to a highborn lady, or perhaps a solitary figure strolling down a sunlit lane in Gascony or Anjou. One imagines pale, swooning ladies waiting for adulterous assignations on castle balconies. According to this picture, the poetry of the troubadours is socially oriented; the poets, except perhaps for Bernart de Ventadorn and Jaufre Rudel and one or two others, are faceless. The poetry is important for only two reasons: first, it is the earliest "modern" poetry; and second, it provided through its praise of women and love valuable social benefits that were brought to fulfillment by later generations.[1] As for the individual poems, they all sound the same; they are sweet but bland, repetitious reworkings of the few basic conceits that can be neatly summed up in the phrase "courtly love."[2]

It is to counter this widespread misconception that I have titled this work *Seven Troubadours*. The book is not about The Troubadours En Masse or Courtly Love Motifs, but about seven distinct lyric voices of the twelfth and thirteenth centuries. Naturally, like many poets of the same period, these writers have something in common. They share what might be called the Christian-secular heritage of the High Middle Ages. If scholars of the nineteenth century coined the term "courtly love" to describe this poetry, the drift in modern criticism is away from this thorny phrase.[3] The difficulty lies primarily in the word "court." It is true that secular poetry was written under the protection of wealthy nobles; the first troubadour himself was a duke, the leader of one of the most brilliant courts of his day. However, the phrase obscures the important fact that the poetry has markedly Christian overtones; it cuts the literature off from the dominant spirit of the age, which was religious, and is thus too restrictive.[4] In picturing this age, instead of seeing *The Idylls of the King* as a background or hearing the music from Wagner's *Tristan and Isolde* as an accompanying refrain, we should be aware of the vigorous, moving strains of Gregorian chant. Poitiers was never Camelot, nor was Ventadorn Neuschwannstein.

Once the poems have been read, the whole romantic picture dissolves, for the troubadours are in no way as sentimental, safe, and humorless as many scholars and artists have made them.[5] Some of them are quite dull, it is true; but so are the second-rate writers of any age. One must simply look for the exceptional. Thus only seven troubadours are presented, not the whole tradition; although these seven are by no means the only ones worth reading.

When troubadour poetry is good, it excels for reasons far greater than "creativity for the first time after the Dark Ages" or "evolution of the emancipation of women" or "first formation of the modern romantic sensibility," to quote a few standard interpretations. The real secret of the Provensal genius is wit, metaphysical wit the like of which was perhaps equaled only in the *Carmina Burana*, where Church Latin was adapted directly for secular ends.[6] The Provensal language is an offshoot of Latin, and thus the ambiguities inherent in the church-court or religious-secular correspondences extend directly into the Romance descendants. These ambiguities, with their enormous possibilities for creating metaphysical fun, can be pointed out best in discussions of the poetry itself. One of the saddest comments to be made about nineteenth-century scholarship must be that the great Romance philologists such as Diez, Jeanroy, and Anglade read about earthly ladies praised with all the idealized rhetoric reserved for the Virgin, yet never smiled.[7] Not only does the language present ambiguities, but the same music was used for both Romance lyrics and Church hymns, and the opening bar of Bernart de Ventadorn's "When I see the lark moving" (*Can vei la lauzeta mover*) is that of the *Kyrie eleison* of the *Cum jubilo* Mass.[8] Yet the poetry took precedence over the music, which was often shifted from piece to piece, perhaps with accompanying changes of tempo as well as of tone.

We should not, however, treat the troubadours as if they were all Augustinian mystics transferring divine epithets directly to earthly lords and ladies.[9] Duke William of Aquitaine was not St. Bernard of Clairvaux, although the two men shared the Platonic-Christian ethos of the day, a world spirit that stressed the correspondences of things. While Bernard wrote traditional praises of Our Lady, William wrote to his own, voicing in an original fashion the ego of lyric expression for the first time in the post-classical world.

The very name "troubadour" (*trobaire*) stresses the concept of originality. The Provensal word goes all the way back to the ancient Greek word *tropos* (a turning; often a turn of thought or figure of speech); it was then adopted by the Romans as *tropus* (metaphor). In the Middle Ages, the Latin word came to be used in ecclesiastical circles as a short, formulaic phrase in Gregorian chant or as a dramatic bit inserted in the religious service.[10] This very learned usage was accompanied by a more popular development. In the streets people used the Vulgar Latin verb *tropar*, or, as voiced in Provensal *trobar*, to mean "to find." The word used to describe the poet is thus related to the "tropes" of Latin rhetorical handbooks and of Christian sacred liturgy; but the emphasis, as is apparent in modern French *trouver* and Italian *trovare*, is upon discovery, invention, creativity.

Neglecting this concept of innovation, many scholars have gone searching in Celtland, Arabia, or Bulgaria to find the origin of troubadour verse. Ignoring one thousand years of Christianity and the unmistakable interplay of holy and profane rhetoric, ignoring the fact that both Ovid and St. Augustine were read in the schools by the well-educated troubadours, and ignoring the fact that the Provensal poets probably knew no language except Latin and the nearby Romance tongues, these people looked for a place where earthly ladies had been praised in song. Had they bothered to cast a serious eye upon the earlier Latin literature of France, England, Germany, and Italy, they could have found women in courts being praised in very elaborate, formal diction that mirrors the *Ave, Maria* tradition of the eighth, ninth, and tenth centuries. But these poems were not really explored until Reto R. Bezzola compiled his multivolumed work about the court poetry written after the fall of the Roman Empire.[11] This early secular poetry is actually quite different from the Provensal in spirit because it is deferential and obsequious, composed by a patronized poet to a highborn benefactress whom he respects greatly but does not love; still, the corpus does provide the kind of clear-cut evidence that many people will unquestioningly accept.

Let us look for a moment at one of the most popular theories about the origin of Provensal poetry to see what can be salvaged

from it. The French scholar Gaston Paris, for one, suggested
that the entire troubadour tradition was an outgrowth of a
secular instinct that is manifested in some popular songs and
dances which have survived simply because they were written
down.[12] One sample is the lively *A l'entrade del tens clar*:[13]

1. At the onset of the shiny time, eya!
   To start again with joy anew, eya!
   And to rouse up jealous husbands, eya!
   The queen would like to show
   That she is full of love.
   Go away, go away, jealous ones!
   O yes, let us, yes, let us
   Dance all together, together!

   . . . .

3. The king is coming from somewhere else, eya!
   To break our dance in many parts, eya!
   For he's all in a dither, eya!
   That someone might snatch away
   His April-capering queen.
   Go away, go away, jealous ones! . . .

4. But she will never allow it, eya!
   For she doesn't want an old john, eya!
   No, but a lusty young bachelor, eya!
   Who knows exactly how to comfort
   A very savorous lady.
   Go away, go away, jealous ones! . . .

5. A man who sees her dancing, eya!
   And enjoys her gracious body, eya!
   Might well in truth exclaim, eya!
   That the world doesn't know her par,
   Our reigning queen of joy.
   Go away, go away, jealous ones! . . .

Fresh and effortless though this poem may sound, it still bears
the trace of learned composition in the neat structuring of its
stanzas, the repetition of the cry *eya* (which appears in Christian

hymns), and the polished rhyme scheme. Furthermore, the basic drama here, involving a jealous husband, a beautiful woman, and a lusty young bachelor, is essentially the time-honored triangle of adultery. One can find it in the more sophisticated troubadour poems, as well as in Ovid, with the poets replacing the bachelor.[14] The casting of the woman in the role of the May or April Queen, with overtones of both the classical Venus and the medieval goddess Natura, strikes one as the work of a very self-aware medieval "pagan."[15] Similarly, in terms of chronology, this allegedly simple anonymous dance poetry appears at the very same time as the artistic love songs, and there is no broad corpus to indicate priority for the so-called "popular" works (was the stylized troubadour verse conversely "unpopular"?).

We should not be tempted to believe that that mysterious creative force known as "the people" had a fresh, active tradition running counter to or beneath that of the court.[16] There is no such self-conscious division among the classes of medieval society. The aristocrat's manor included serfs and domestic servants in a cosy microcosm. When parties were held on spring holidays, the whole castle reverberated with joy, and everyone danced to the music. The Queen of April in the poem, for example, is obviously aristocratic. A work of art cannot be attributed to an untutored, proletarian hand simply because it is fresh and anonymous. This theory bears the imprint of Zola and Balzac and those revolutionary French writers who strongly influenced the scholars of the nineteenth century who in turn were opening the way to the poetry. Instead of trying to seek some kind of temporal priority for the simpler works, we should link them with the main tradition, where they fit in quite neatly.

We might, however, note that the spring opening for the troubadour love poem obviously owes something to the actual song and dance of spring celebrations, and that the pagan roots of these rites are undeniable.[17] The dances took place in the squares around the cathedrals and castles, not inside them. Yet the minute that one starts searching for pagan examples for this rhetoric, either he finds Ovid lurking in the background, or else nothing. The sad thing about such dance poems is that there are so few of them in Provensal; in North French literature, the tradition was far more vigorous.[18] But even there, as in England, the popular creations waned when they came into touch with more sophisticated productions. That indefinable thing called freshness in art is all too evanescent.

The world of southern France in the eleventh and twelfth centuries was one which was awaking from a long literary slumber. Just as the Provensal poem often bursts forth with a shaft of spring sunlight, singing birds, budding flowers, and green-growing trees, so the external world was flowering in church and court alike. In southern France, the Platonizing spirit was reinvigorating Church expression, especially in that lively work *On the Totality of the World* by Bernard Silvestris, in which Natura, second only to the Triune God in many artistic representations, again commanded the world to know the miraculous ways of birth.[19]

This impulse to create is really all that one needs in order to explain the evolution of Provensal poetry. One does not need to know what was going on in Spain or in North Africa to account for the phenomenon. If poets there were writing one or two centuries before William of Aquitaine, they still were not writing in his stanzaic patterns and rhyme schemes, which descend from Ambrosian hymnology, nor with his own Ovidian-original sense of humor.[20] The Arabic poems are richly sensual and decidedly homosexual; the troubadour poems are neither, for Provensal sensuality usually turns out to be either suppressed or presented realistically as sex, and there is not a sign of homosexuality in the poems, except possibly for the masculine names for the ladies, a feature which will be discussed later on.

Southern France in the eleventh century was alive, as alive as the dancing bears and wailing flutes and jangling lutes and jumping jugglers and mimicking clowns who entertained before and after the songs were sung. The atmosphere around the Provensal poems stressed *joi;* our word "joy" is probably too religious still to capture the deliciously vulgar flavor of the word, which also meant simply "fun." Heresies were brewing, crusaders were moving, castles were rising, schools were expanding, and poetry was flowering also.

In selecting these seven voices to represent the entire troubadour tradition, I have followed the general taste of modern anthologists, emphasizing those who possessed distinct personalities and who at the same time help to communicate a sense of an unfolding tradition. Aside from Marcabrun, I have ignored the dark singers of *trobar clus* simply because, with the exception of Raimbaut of Orange, the mystery of their verse evaporates once it has been translated. Ezra Pound, who used his own great gifts as a poet, has shown us what can and cannot be done with an obscurantist like Arnaut Daniel. Pound's English versions abound with verbal and metrical wizardry, yet in the long run one is tempted to ask that fatal question: Why so much art?[21] Each of the seven represented here has left the world a sufficient body of work from which we can draw very distinctive features; admittedly I have not supplied space for some very good poets—Cercamon, Peire Vidal, Cabestanh—because the corpus is not as exciting as some of the individual works. I have followed a chronological scheme in presenting the poets in order to suggest the movement from fruition to decadence, and have begun in the logical place.

1

DUKE WILLIAM IX
OF AQUITAINE

The Whole Medieval Man

We are fortunate enough to know a great deal about William, the ninth duke of Aquitaine, the seventh count of Poitou, the earliest known troubadour. His character, as described by the chroniclers of the period, accords perfectly with the role of the first known secular poet of the modern world. He was vigorous, brash, amorous, and proud—thus possessing the characteristics needed to dispel the mists of anonymity that shroud much of earlier medieval poetry.

One of the most succinct portraits of William is contained in his vida or biography appended to the songbooks:[1]

> The Count of Poitou was one of the greatest courtiers in the world, and one of the greatest tricksters of women; and a good chevalier in arms, and grand in his woman-handling [dompnejar]. And he knew how to compose well and to sing; and he went for a long time through the world to deceive the women. And he had a son who took for wife the Duchess of Normandy, from whom he had a daughter who was the wife of King Henry of England, the mother of the Young King, of Lord Richard, and of Count Geoffrey of Brittany.

Here in the rambling style of medieval prose the writer seizes upon William's poetic powers and amorousness, but is noticeably skimpy in describing the historical importance of a man who owned more land than Philip I of France. Obviously the writer of this biography abstracted his information from William's poems and from some half-understood bits of genealogy; beyond this he contributes nothing.[2]

We can learn much more about the Duke from the pages of medieval chronicles. William, the ninth ruler of the dukedom of Aquitaine, was born to a powerful family of lords who had extended their sovereignty over Poitou, Guyenne, Limousin, and Périgord.[3] The domain bequeathed William in 1086 upon the death of his father thus stretched from Poitiers, which is usually considered a northern French city, into that vast area of southwest France known to the Romans as Aquitania. In his own lifetime William extended his control even further than his father had, to the county of Toulouse, although he later lost those lands. The dukes of Aquitaine named Guilhem, from Germanic-Frankish Willehalmi, displayed much of the pomp and magnificence, as well as the fractiousness, that we are accustomed to associate with Renaissance nobility. The historian Bezzola notes that: "Among all those Williams who preceded him, we could not find a single one who had that masculine crudeness, that somber and violent nature, that cold cruelty, those fits or that fanaticism which their neighbors to the north, the counts of Anjou, for example, manifest."[4] The best symbol of the dynasty is the splendid city of Poitiers, which, even now when it seems more like a museum than an actual place of residence, is studded with brilliant churches like the Baptistry of St. John (dating from the fourth century), St. Hilary (originally eleventh century), St. Radegonde (begun in ninth century), and the especially impressive Notre Dame la Grande and St. Porchaire, which were constructed largely during the twelfth century, the great period of troubadour florescence. From the time of the ancient tribes of the Picts, for whom the city of Poitiers and county of Poitou are named, through the Roman period, which is still remembered for its amphitheater and baths in the capital city, and finally during the Merovingian and Carolingian times, this section of France remained a bastion of culture, absorbing Celtic, Latin, or Frankish customs and converting them into new, uniquely realized art forms. The place was right.

As for the people, behind William's poetry one senses a world of shiny furs, prancing horses, glittering women, and constant social events. The friends to whom William addresses many of his poems are not the crude communal bread-breakers suggested in the word for companion, com-pan-ho; instead, they seem to show a sophisticated taste which is more typical of a select secret society than of a brawling medieval hall where a Frankish overlord entertained his vassals. True, William's companions shared his dangerous military exploits against Turks and Moors, but they also seem to have possessed the "counterkey" that the Duke mentions in one of his poems, the ability to fathom the strange new world of poetic creativity in which William made the first bold foray.

This ninth Duke of Aquitaine entered the world under most inauspicious circumstances, which were almost a forewarning of his own romantic misadventures. In 1067 his father, Duke William VIII, who was far more widely known as Gui-Geoffroi, then aged forty-five, took as his third wife the youthful Audiart (Audéarde), daughter of Duke Robert the Old of Burgundy.[5] The Church's disapproval was vehement.[6] After the baby William was born on October 22, 1071, Gui-Geoffroi was apparently forced to declare his marriage morganatic, for Audiart seems to slip away from the scene.[7] Then, except for a brief and none too successful skirmish against the Spanish city of Barbasto, the Duke spent the last fifteen years of his life in relative tranquility.[8] He even undertook the task of completing the work of the abbey of Montierneuf, which had been begun in 1069. He was finally buried there in a magnificent tomb containing a statue of the earthly lord at rest with his dog.[9] The construction of this monastery was obviously a gesture of reconciliation with the Church. At any rate, upon his death, Gui-Geoffroi left his son a large and prosperous realm that might well have been the envy of many a king.

William was only fifteen years old when his father died at the castle of Chizé on September 25, 1086.[10] The situation was thus somewhat perilous, for the "bands of Gascons and men of Anjou" whom William himself mentions in a poem concerning the plight of his own young son might easily have swarmed into Poitiers in an attempt to seize power.[11] The fact that they did not offers convincing proof of the strong, yet equitable control wielded by Gui-Geoffroi. From the days of Ebles Manzer in the latter part of the ninth century, the house of the counts of Poitou had managed to restrain the unruly barons within its borders; now, in a time of crisis, they reaped their reward.[12]

Because of his youth, William soon acquired the nickname "the Younger," or in Latin, *Junior*, an epithet used to distinguish him from his father in documents of the time.[13] Although this name is almost never used in literary scholarship, where William is referred to by title and number, it does have a special significance, for if one can isolate any outstanding phrase from William's poetry, it is *joi e joven*, "joy and youth." Even inimical chroniclers add that William was called "witty" or "merry," as if these manifestations of the joy of life were an integral part of his name.[14] The two qualities lie at the heart of Provensal expression, for the troubadours' enemies are old age, seriousness, somberness, and morality as preached by the literal-minded. Furthermore, even in his forties and fifties, William carried himself with some of the fun-loving abandon that one customarily associates with youth.

In his adolescence William seems to have been too much under the control of his mother and his counselors to have shown many signs of his later character. The young Duke was being helped during the early years of his reign by powerful nobles such as Boson of la Marche, Geoffrey of Taunay, and Hugh of Lusignan, and by prelates like Geoffrey of Vendôme, who was usually one of his staunchest defenders.[15] Another of his early associates was Bishop Peter II of Poitiers, toward whom he later held very different feelings.[16] Unquestionably, Audiart played a major role in her son's early administration, for she begins to emerge from the shadows where her husband apparently kept her. Her name is frequently found on public documents showing her presence at the establishment of monasteries and at other religious ceremonies.[17]

The steady calm of William's early years of rule was ruffled only by periodic squabbles over ecclesiastical offices, occasional usurpations of Church property, and the problem of succession after the death of Boson of la Marche. Yet during the last decade of the millenial year, western Europe suddenly began to hum with new life and reawakened activity. Times were prosperous, and life was not at all as dark and dreary as we have come to imagine existence in those "Middle Ages." As the Moors pressed harder to widen their holdings in southern Spain, and as the Seljuk Turks threatened the very tomb of Christ in Palestine, the Christian world suddenly rebounded with a surge of indignant wrath that it had never quite vented before. The lure of long, exotic pilgrimages was further intensified by the hope of material gain. In 1088 Count William of Toulouse, one of the most influential rulers in southern France, ceded his lands to his brother, Raymond of St.-Gilles, and went off to spend the last five years of his life in the Holy Land.[18] In 1095, Pope Urban II, traveling northward into France, summoned the Council of Clermont in Auvergne, where he issued his fiery and unforgettable exhortations to the nobles to wash themselves in the blood of the Lamb.[19] The Pope journeyed through the county of Poitou in 1096 and did the ducal family the honor of consecrating the monastery of Montierneuf, the beloved project of William's father.[20] One of the great lords who answered Urban's call was Raymond of St.-Gilles, the recent heir to the countship of Toulouse.[21] Taking the cross, Raymond IV left his holdings in the hands of the Church, which acted as guardian for the properties of all crusaders. As a result of his sudden fervor, a vast stretch of rich and tempting land near the southern frontier of William's domain lay totally unprotected. While other Christians were devoutly turning their faces toward the East, the Duke gazed south.

Actually, the attraction of the Toulousain was intensified by William's marriage in 1094 to Philippa (also called Mahaut or Matilda), the daughter of William of Toulouse and earlier the wife of Sancho Ramírez of Aragon.[22] After her Spanish husband was killed while besieging Huesca on July 6, 1094, Philippa was obviously anxious to get out of Spain, which was being ravaged in battles between Christians and infidels; she was also probably unsure about being welcomed by her uncle Raymond, since she was in a quite logical way the proper heir to her father's holdings. Fortunately, Duke William was at this time looking for a suitable mate and Philippa answered the need perfectly, for her birth and potential claims made her an equal to the haughty Poitevin. As soon as Raymond departed for the Holy Land, Duke William was offered the perfect opportunity for claiming what he considered his, since he obviously did not acknowledge Raymond's claim to the lands. Marching against only token opposition, the Duke "annexed" the southern dowry of his wife and, quite surprisingly, escaped without any official censure—at least for the time being.

With the county of Toulouse in his grasp, William amused himself with those medieval skirmishes that seem more like games than serious combats. He joined William Rufus of England in a brief encounter with Philip I of France. But when, after July 15, 1099, Jerusalem fell into the hands of the crusaders, western Europe was swept anew with an almost fanatic desire to drive all of the infidels out of the Holy Land and even the nearby realms of Arabs and Turks.[23] This time the canny Duke succumbed to religious fervor, although the spirit of adventure and a hope for spoils possibly accounted for some small part of his zeal. Despite his rich possessions, William had trouble raising the money to finance the enormous undertaking. At first William Rufus, who was ever anxious to annex lands through mortgage or sudden usurpation, promised to underwrite the Aquitanian campaign.[24] But when the English king was struck down suddenly in a hunting accident, Duke William was forced to sell the county of Toulouse to Bertran of St.-Gilles; he thereby created new trouble over the territory, which was finally lost again to the houses of St.-Gilles and Barcelona.[25]

At about this time in 1100, an event described by Geoffrey the Fat took place at Poitiers which sheds light on William's relationship with the Church. Pope Paschal II was holding a council to excommunicate Philip I because of his notorious affair with the enchanting Bertrade de Montfort, the unfaithful wife of William's neighbor, Foulques the Rough of Anjou:[26]

> When this excommunication had been accomplished, William, Duke of Aquitaine, who was present—an enemy of all shame and holiness—fearing that he might have to suffer a similar rebuke for similarly guilty deeds, enraged with frenzy, ordered all those present to be stripped, beaten, and killed. And when his attendants started to do this, the pontiffs and abbots began rushing here and there and, in order to cling to their lives in this world, struggled to find a safe hiding-nook. But Bernard and Robert d'Arbrissel, who were at the council, those stern defenders of justice, those champions against all iniquity and injustice, while others were fleeing in a cowardly way, held their ground, fixed and unmoving.

This excerpt from *The Life of the Blessed Bernard of Tiron* doubtlessly shows a strong clerical bias against a powerful earthly lord, but it also dramatically illustrates the conflict between church and state that often existed in William's day. It further shows that, even before leaving on a crusade, William had something of a reputation for being an adulterous lover. It also sets up the struggle between William the Duke and Robert d'Arbrissel the great preacher—a conflict that we shall have cause to mention later, for the eloquent orator was probably winning over William's wife to churchly deeds at the very same time that the Duke was making one of his few great acts of a clearly religious nature.

In the spring of 1101, the crusaders assembled in the fields below the sturdy walls of Poitiers. The chronicler Ordericus Vitalis tells us that William "collected a huge army from Aquitaine and Gascony, and swiftly undertook the road of the holy pilgrimage. This man was bold and courageous (*probus*, used here like Provensal *pros*, its descendant), and extremely good-natured, outdoing even the funniest of his comic actors (*histriones*) with his many pranks and jokes (*facetiis*). It is said that 300,000 armed men followed his standards when he left the borders of Aquitaine behind."[27] It is interesting to note how Ordericus cannot resist mentioning William's wit and his propensity for dramatic performances, even in a context where such information is somewhat irrelevant; it is obvious that one could

not think of the Duke without thinking also of his "acting."
But Ordericus tends to exaggerate anything factual, and Ekkehard of Aura, who actually took part in the movement, albeit a
very limited part, gives a more plausible figure: "from Aquitaine,
where William of Poitou was foremost, was a throng of more
than 30,000 men in leather corselets."[28]

Yet William's group was only a fraction of the entire mass
that broke in three successive waves over the mainland of Asia
Minor in a movement so ill-fated that it never really acquired a
name beyond "the Crusades of 1101." The first segment, stem-
ming largely from Lombardy, was led by the Archbishop of
Milan, Anselm, a Turpin lifted from the lines of Old French
epic.[29] With him came other Lombards anxious for plunder
and glory: Count Albert of Biandrate, his brother Guido, his
nephew Otto Altaspada, Hugh of Montebello, and a host of
others. They swarmed around the upper reaches of the Adriatic,
down into the valleys that lead across the Balkans to Constantinople, creating such a foul reputation for rapine and pillage in
their passage through Bulgaria that the Byzantine Emperor,
Alexius Comnenus, who had still not quite recovered from his
shock at the behavior of the Christians on the First Crusade,
ordered them to remain outside of the city's gates until they
could undertake the journey through Asia Minor.[30] Alexius
shrewdly tried to induce the Lombards to set out immediately,
but the crusaders held back, waiting for reinforcements to arrive
from Germany and France. The Emperor answered by cutting
off supplies and, as Albert of Aix tells the story, the Lombards
in retaliation clambered over the walls and went so far as to
invade the grounds of the imperial palace, where they slew one
of the Emperor's prize domesticated lions.[31] At this point the
Bishop and Albert of Biandrate forced their followers back,
and Alexius, quivering at their audacity and probably not a little
surprised at their easy invasion, acquiesced. Ordericus makes the
story even more dramatic by having Duke William take part in
the storming of the barricades and by having the Emperor set
out lions and leopards to defend his paralyzed capital, but the
Byzantines were less languid than the Roman Catholic historian
allowed, and the Duke of Aquitaine was not yet on the scene.[32]

It was now late in the spring of 1101, and the Lombards
began pressing southward, waiting at Nicomedia for the next
part of their group to join them: this segment was composed of
Germans under the leadership of Conrad, who was constable to

Henry IV of the Holy Roman Empire, and there was also a group representing Frankish interests under Count Stephen of Burgundy and the aged Count Stephen Henry of Blois, who, as Albert notes, was "led on by his penitence," since he had ingloriously run away from danger during the First Crusade, and his wife Adela would not let him forget it.[33]

At this point a name suddenly reappears: Raymond of St.-Gilles, the former Count of Toulouse, uncle of William's wife Philippa and once the owner of that vast county that had passed into the safekeeping of the Aquitanian.[34] In a situation where the adjective "Byzantine" refers to more than the inhabitant of a city, Raymond was indeed a shifty character. In the First Crusade he had proved to be a stalwart friend of the Byzantine throne, probably because he was realistic enough to see the necessity of having an established power in the East to assist fledgling governments and also because he fully recognized the strategic position of Constantinople for keeping land routes open, so that the mercenary Italian states would not reap a windfall from sea traffic, as they later did; yet because of this attachment and eccentric personality factors he was distrusted by his own colleagues, Godfrey, Tancred, and Bohemond. Now, having lived a while in the East, Raymond knew the terrain like a native, and the crusaders eagerly petitioned him to assist them. Ordericus, who blurs the picture by putting Duke William into it, has Raymond answering: "By the grace of God, I have labored long to capture Jerusalem and now, broken by old age and many a toil, I just want to enjoy a little peace and quiet."[35] This analysis of Raymond's psychology is undoubtedly right, for the former Count of Toulouse did not want undue involvement in the new cause and certainly he did not want to cross Asia Minor, where the routes were technically open, but the Seljuk Turks and Danishmends were constantly a threat. Raymond finally granted the request on Alexius' special plea, and the first wave of crusaders set out to win glory in the name of God.

Disaster tracked them from the first. Instead of sensibly pursuing a direct overland course, the Lombards in the group disobeyed Raymond and the Franks by veering toward Anatolia, where they hoped to rescue the great hero Bohemond, who was being held captive by the Danishmends. The Seljuk Turks started tracking them down as the unruly masses toiled in the hot early summer sun through scorched territory that had still not recovered from previous onslaughts. The Christians did manage to reach Ankara, and they did find some crops to pillage, but the Turks, moving cautiously under the leadership of their Sultan, by poisoning wells, stripping orchards, burning fields, and emptying cities, lured the bands of crusaders deeper and deeper into the barren waste. Almost all of the older chroniclers believed that a deal had been arranged between the offended Emperor Alexius and the Turks, with Raymond acting as the executor of the disaster; modern historians like Runciman tend to do the opposite, romanticizing the age-old villains and vilifying the crusaders.[36] It is far safer to assume that all of the major participants acted for selfish motives.

Actually Raymond clung loyally to his Christian compatriots, even when they were encircled and besieged in the familiar fashion of the American pioneers and Indians; he sneaked away only after a number of others had defected, and then he had to be rescued by Stephen of Blois and Conrad.[37] Upon his return to camp, however, seeing that the game could only end in loss, Raymond fled in the night and returned to face down a somewhat frigid Alexius.[38] Most of the vast group were slaughtered, although the rich and the important did manage to get away: Stephen of Burgundy, Stephen of Blois, Conrad, and the Bishop of Milan. They returned in sullen disgrace to Nicomedia; Bishop Anselm died soon after, but some of the others appear again in the Holy Land, after having reconsidered and taken the longer, more expensive, but more restful journey by sea.[39]

The second group of soldiers of God was a much smaller unit led by Count William II of Nevers, a man who immediately became famous because of the way he forbade his fellow crusaders from devastating the passing countryside.[40] He followed hard on the heels of the first group, hoping to join forces with them for better protection, but alas! on the hot, dry plains north of Heraclea and far from the verdant valley of the Loire, he ran into Sultan Kilij Arslan marching freshly in triumph with hundreds of slaves in his entourage. The Turks, who had strategically picked away at the larger army by bits and pieces, now simply overwhelmed this smaller group. Count William fled to Germanicopolis, a Byzantine garrison, where he was subsequently bilked of the remnants of his possessions and forced to flee half-naked to Antioch, where he at last reclined in the hospitality of the munificent Tancred.[41]

The third and last group contained the impressive soldiery of Duke William, accompanied by Hugh the Great of Vermandois. The Aquitanians traveled eastward into Germany, where they were joined by contingents led by Duke Welf of Bavaria and then by Ida, the Margravine of Austria, who in her youth had been much celebrated for her beauty.[42] Their group was one of the least orderly to pass through the rather unfortunately positioned land of Bulgaria. After some indiscretions at Adrianople, they arrived at Constantinople, where they lingered for a while as guests of Alexius.[43] The timing of their arrival and departure was especially unfortunate, for the two previous groups were already on the road, and no news of disaster had as yet drifted back to the city. As a result, this third contingent left the storied towers and domes of Byzantium with assurance that most of the route was already cleared before them. They passed through the hospitable countryside south of Nicomedia, up over the hot central tableland of what is now Turkey, encountering at first ruined villages and despoiled gardens and, finally, the slings and arrows of the advanced guard of the Sultan. Yet they pressed on. It was early September and the heat was frightful; some of the crusaders were at the breaking point from lack of proper drinking water; at last Heraclea loomed in view, with its crystal river beckoning beyond the town. Albert of Aix is the only historian to give us anything approaching adequate details:[44]

> From here they went down to the city of Heraclea, where the rushing river, so long hoped for with great fervor, would suffice for all. But the Sultan . . . and the princes of the Turks with their endless supplies and weapons suddenly were there for a confrontation with the unwary pilgrims on the other shore, and they prevented the men and horses and cattle from getting to the water by a hailstorm of arrows from bows, until at long last, worn out and totally exhausted, the Christians could not summon the strength to endure. And so after a very long, very heated and savage combat, carried on in the depths of the stream and on both shores, all of the Christians in a body took to flight and were cut down in an unheard of massacre by their heathen pursuers.

Welf fled, William fled, but the Margravine Ida was perhaps not so lucky. We do not know exactly what happened to her, but if she did not perish in the struggle, as Albert suggests, then perhaps she was carted off to a distant seraglio where she gave birth to an earthly Messiah, as various Arabic legends had it.[45]

At any rate, the Duke of Aquitaine escaped with his skin, and probably little more. He apparently stumbled through the hills with a few companions, finally finding refuge in one of the villages governed by Bernard the Stranger. From there he passed quickly to Antioch, where, despite his soiled credentials, he was received magnificently by Tancred, who seems to have welcomed anyone who came along. There in Tancred's rather opulent court the Duke languished for a time, although it is extremely doubtful that he spent his time learning Arabic or Turkish poetry or music. There too he met some of the other stragglers of the ill-fated crusade, and he appears to have made peace with Raymond of St.-Gilles (if indeed there was any real difference between them), for the Duke probably helped Raymond conduct a later successful siege of Tortosa.[46] Raymond himself had been jailed by Bernard the Stranger and turned over to Tancred, who released him on the pleas of the crusaders. The Aquitanian seems to have regained whatever dignity he needed and, with whatever crusaders survived, pressed on for the ultimate goal of every pilgrim, the Holy City. They arrived in Jerusalem in time to celebrate Easter of 1102 under the auspices of King Baldwin.[47] Soon afterwards, the Duke, feeling that his career as a swashbuckling crusader had been fulfilled, decided to go home. By the end of October 1102, thanks to favorable winds and a fleet ship, he was resting again back in the rolling hills of Poitou.

Ordericus Vitalis, who describes this segment of William's life in memorable terms, is certainly more reliable for affairs in France than for events in the Holy Land:[48]

> The Poitevin duke, having finished his prayers in Jerusalem, with certain other companions [consortibus] returned to his own property; and because he was merry and sophisticated [lepidus], after he was once more ensconced in prosperity, he publicly, before kings and magnates and Christian assemblies, many a time recounted the miseries of his captivity in rhythmic verses [versibus] with funny measures.

This passage is priceless for its information: it proves, even if there were a doubt, that William was both a poet *and* a performer; it shows that poetry was not in any sense restricted to courts, but was heard and enjoyed by clergymen and by laymen alike, as well as by nobles and commoners; it demonstrates that poetry was a living art form, not something imported or esoteric, and that people freely gathered to hear works recited; it suggests an established tradition of secular verse and song before William, but since we are not told whether the Duke sang in Latin or Romance, we cannot deduce the existence of earlier troubadours.[49] Some day perhaps we will know much more about possible links between Romance secular song and the poems sung by Celtic bards and Germanic *sceops*. If Ordericus can be trusted, William's poem must have been a mock-epic; certainly his misadventures were funny when compared to the actions of Roland, Waltharius, Charlemagne, or whatever other folk heroes still lived on in Poitou from the Roman, Celtic, Pictish, and Germanic past. At any rate, one can be fairly certain after reading Ordericus' words that the people were reacting to the Duke's native wit and private life, not to new "Arabic jazz" or "sufi mysticism" or any other esoteric import that would have brought an outcry from the already highly prejudiced chronicler. Only modern critics seem to be *that* inventive. Although a few people have disputed the historical authenticity of the passage because it mentions the Duke's captivity, we cannot be certain that William was not captured for a brief time. It is a bit extraordinary, however, to think that he would have sung about such an indignity. But William was sophisticated and bold; had he not been, world literature would have been much poorer.

In the meantime, Philippa had ruled the widespread domain of her husband during his absence, and seems to have conducted herself with aplomb.[50] Yet the Duke's wife was also employing her new-found freedom for her own ends. Obviously opposed to her husband's gay, fun-loving attitude toward life, she surrounded herself with churchmen, especially Robert d'Arbrissel, the orator who was now very widely known for his startling ideas about women. In an age when women were sometimes shuffled around like pawns, Robert treated them almost as men's superiors. His biographer Baudri tells us that the preacher selected a woman named Petronilla to preside as the chief abbess over his famous monastery of Fontevrault, where men and women lived together in separate cottages, but full equality, in idyllic bliss.[51] Robert was rumored, for example, to have tested his piety by having women lie beside him on a couch or even spend the night in his bed. The gossipmongers of the day obviously made much of his conduct, and he was reproved by the usually temperate Geoffrey of Vendôme:[52]

> You allow, they say, certain women to live with you in a far too familiar way, with whom you very often speak intimate words, and you do not even blush to sleep with them and among them very often at night. . . . If you are truly doing this, or if you have done it, then you have certainly invented a novel, unique, but quite fruitless kind of martyrdom. You have acted presumptuously against all reason if on any occasion you have lain with women whom you have stolen from the world and should be using to pay God.

Yet it was never proved that the golden-tongued preacher had indulged in a single licentious act. He won over some of the most beautiful women of his day—for the Church. During the next thirteen or fourteen years Philippa continued to live with her husband, although William was obviously untrue to her. Finally around the year 1116, when she was unable to bear the tension any longer, she removed herself to Fontevrault, where she died a few years later, not long after the passing of her friend Robert.[53]

The years after the abortive crusade seem to have been something of an anticlimax for William politically, although he did his best to enliven them. In 1106, for example, he promised to escort the young Foulques, son of the beautiful Bertrade, back to his father, Foulques the Rough of Anjou; the young man had been staying with his mother, who was still the mistress of Philip I.[54] Yet William kidnapped the young man and refused to turn him over to his father or to the French king unless some strategic fortified castles were handed over to Poitou. Despite the threat of war from these two formidable opponents, the Duke held out and won his castles. Finally in 1113 Bishop Peter II of Poitiers, the Duke's former friend, pronounced the long-delayed excommunication for the invasion of Toulouse and for the Duke's general licentiousness.[55]

By the year 1115 William's conduct was notorious. Leaving Philippa in one of his many residences, William began a long affair with the wife of Viscount Aimeric I of Châtelleraut. This woman seems to have borne the exciting name Dangerosa, but

William, with his playful fondness for invention, apparently called her Malbergion or Maubergeonne, the same name which was given to a tower at his castle in Poitiers.[56] In 1119 at the Council of Reims there occurred an extraordinary event that, unfortunately, is related only by Ordericus: "Meanwhile Hildegarde (or Audiart), the Countess of the Poitevins, proceeded in with her livery about her, and in a high, clear voice she eloquently unraveled her complaint, which the entire council attended diligently. She said that she had been abandoned by her husband, and that he had taken as his illicit partner in bed Malbergion, the wife of the Viscount of Châtelleraut."[57] The nickname seems to be confirmed by Radulfus de Diceto, who said of the year 1112: "William the Count of the Poitevins chose a woman of ill repute whose name was Amalbergun over his own wife."[58] The question of the identities of Malbergion or Dangerosa or any of a number of other mistresses whom the Duke obviously entertained matters little, but one is rather intrigued about the mysterious Hildegarde-Audiart who claimed to be a wife of William; did he marry after Philippa's death, which took place before 1119, or had he already been married before he took Philippa as wife back in 1094? There is reason to believe, from remarks made by both William of Tyre and Bertran d'Argentré, that the Duke had, perhaps in the late 1080's, married Ermengarde, daughter of Foulques the Rough and Audiart of Beaugency (she would thus have also used her mother's name, as many women did).[59] This self-willed woman later married Alain Fergant, the Duke of Brittany; after his death she joined that long line of famous beauties who followed the footsteps of Robert d'Arbrissel; yet unlike her counterparts, Ermengarde did not rest long in the monastery. She crops up again in secular life in a way that is richly suggestive of the close relationship between the two spheres. She may well have been the mystery figure at Reims, for obviously a woman of her strong, ironlike temper was hardly the right match for the Duke, yet naturally she would have resented any successor to her seat of honor. At any rate, in 1121 William went so far as to arrange the marriage of his own son by Philippa, William, who had been born in 1099, to Aénor, or Anor, the daughter of his mistress from her previous marriage. From this match came the celebrated Alianor or Eleanor of Aquitaine, the last ruler of the independent house of Poitou.

Despite his adulterous life, William accomplished many deeds which won him praise. He supported the building of numerous abbeys and monasteries, especially the pilgrims' asylum at Montmorillon, and he was unstinting in his support of Montierneuf. With a few notable exceptions, he remained on excellent terms with the prelate Geoffrey of Vendôme, who addressed him as "praiseworthy leader of a life which God has honored above all others in this world in beauty of body, and may He make you, who are 'fairest of the sons of men' (Psalms 45:2), like Him beautiful and mighty in Heaven."[60] Moreover in 1120 William rushed away to take up his second crusade, this time assisting King Alfonso the Battler of Aragon against the Moors.[61] This crusade, unlike the previous one, was a rousing success: William came home laden with trophies and praise. During the last years of his life the Duke was friendly with most of the important prelates in his territory, and when he died, apparently of normal causes, on February 10, 1126, at the age of fifty-four, he was buried with pomp and circumstance, like his father, at Montierneuf.[62] He was succeeded by his eldest son, William the Toulousain, tenth duke of Aquitaine, who governed only eleven years before dying suddenly while on pilgrimage to the famous shrine of San Juan of Compostela in Spain.[63] The son was followed by Eleanor, whose marriages, first to the King of France and then to the King of England, marked the end of Poitevin autonomy.

The most famous and complete portrait of William comes from the hand of William of Malmesbury:[64]

> There lived then William, the Count of Poitou, a foolish and shifty man who, after leaving Jerusalem . . . returned to loll in the slough of every vice, almost as if he believed that the universe ran by chance, and was not governed by providence. Furthermore, coating over his little bits of nonsense with a certain superficial charm, he passed them off as wit, distending the jaws of his audiences with chuckling. Then too at a certain castle called Niort he built some little houses, almost like monastic huts, and wildly proclaimed that he would found an Abbey of Whores. And he sang that he would establish this girl or that one, whom he named, all from famous brothels, as his abbess, his prioress, and his other officials.
>
> Also, when his legal wife was driven away, he carried off the wife of a certain viscount, whom he lusted after so much that he vowed to engrave the image of the strumpet on his

shield, saying again and again that he would support her in battle just as she did him on the couches [*in triclinio*].

When he was denounced and excommunicated by Girard, the Bishop of Angoulême, and ordered to put aside his illegal love, he said, "You can curl back that hair receding from your forehead before I'll repudiate the Viscountess." The joker said this to a man whose skimpy bits of hair required no comb. Similarly, when Peter, the Bishop of great holiness of Poitiers, charged him freely and began to excommunicate the disparager openly, William, seized with a violent rage, pounced for the prelate's hair and, waving his drawn sword, said, "Now you're going to die unless you absolve me." Then indeed the prelate, pretending to be terrified, begged for a little chance to speak so that he could follow faithfully through with what remained of the excommunication. And thus he suspended the Count from Christianity, so that William would not dare to associate nor even to speak with another soul, unless he came to his senses in good time. Thus, having completed his assigned duty as he saw fit, and thirsting for the trophy of martyrdom, the Bishop extended his neck. "Strike!" he said. "Strike!" But William, now grown contentious, bore his customary humor to the fore and said, "Indeed, I hate you so much that you're unworthy of my hatred, and you're never going to enter heaven with these hands as your servants."

In fact, a little afterward, poisoned by the viperish hiss of that whore, William cast his opponent into a sinful exile in which Bishop Peter, concluding with a blessed end with many great miracles performed, showed the world how gloriously he would dwell in heaven. When the Count heard these tales recited, he could not abstain from his customary insolent sarcasm. He proclaimed openly that he much regretted that he could not have speeded up the death a little bit, so that the blessed soul would render him all the more thanks, since it was because of his rage that the heavenly business had come to so successful a conclusion.

It is an easy matter to relate this bitter, religiously slanted portrait to the poetry of Duke William. For example, the following poem sounds exactly like the sort that William of Malmesbury would call "little bits of nonsense coated with a certain superficial charm":[65]

1. I'll write a poem, then take a nap,
   And then go stand in the sun.
   Some ladies are really misguided;
   I know which ones:
   Those who turn the love of a knight
   Into grief.

2. A lady commits a mortal sin
   If she doesn't love a faithful knight;
   And if she loves a monk or a priest,
   She's very wrong;
   It's right that we should burn her
   At the stake.

3. In Auvergne, that side of Limousin,
   I was cruising all alone on the sly;
   Then I found the wife of Lord Guari
   And Bernard's too.
   All they did was salute me simply
   By St. Leonard.

4. Then one of them said in her dialect,
   "God protect you, sir pilgrim;
   You're a man of excellent breeding,
   I do believe;
   We see far too many fools around
   In this world."

5. Now hear what I said in reply:
   I didn't say this and I didn't say that,
   Didn't mention a stick, not a tool;
   All I said was:
   "Babariol, Babariol,
   Babarian."

6. Then Lady Agnes said to Lady Emma:
   "He's just what we're looking for.
   For the love of God, let's put him up!
   He's a mute.
   He'll never be able to tattle about
   What we do."

7. The one covered me up with her mantle
   And led me in to her bedroom fire.
   Listen! It was all pretty nice:
   A fire nice and warm,
   And it made me feel good to get heated
   Up by her coals.

8. They gave me some capons to eat,
   And listen! I had more than a few,
   With no cook or scullion hanging around—
   Just us three.
   The bread was white, the wine was choice,
   And the pepper hot.

9. "Sister, I think he's a sly one;
   Dropped his speech just for our account;
   Let's bring out that big red tomcat
   Right this minute.
   That'll loosen his tongue in a hurry
   If he's fooling."

10. Lady Agnes went out for the beast;
    It was big and had long mustaches.
    The minute I saw him come in,
    I was scared;
    I almost lost all of my courage
    And my nerve.

11. After we ate and we had some drinks,
    I shucked off my clothes as they asked.
    And they brought up that cat behind me—
    That evil thing!
    And the one dragged him along my flank
    Down to the heels.

12. Then all at once she pulls that cat
    By his tail, and does he scratch!
    They gave me more than a hundred strokes
    In just that time;
    But I wouldn't have moved an inch—
    Till brink of death.

13. "Sister," said Agnes to Emma,
    "He's mute, and that's for sure!
    Let's get him ready for his bath
    And a nice, long stay."
    I stayed there a good eight days or more
    In their oven.

14. And I ————d them this many times:
    One hundred and eighty-eight.
    And I almost fractured my straps
    And my gear.
    And I'll never be able to tell you
    My later pain.

15. No, I'll never be able to tell you
    About that pain!

Granted that the poem does not show a very high level of sensitivity: the wit is more that of the barracks room than of the court, but the work is still very highly stylized in the original Provensal. It is written in fourteen stanzas with a two-line *tornada* (return or refrain), which, in this case, merely repeats the last two lines of the fourteenth stanza. The rhyme scheme is *aaabcb*, which utilizes the simple monorhyme or heavy repetition in the beginning. This rhyming process tends to refine and modulate itself in later troubadour poetry; because of the almost primitive stress of similar sounds, William's poem resembles the anonymous, rollicking popular songs, although the Duke was in no way faceless or nameless. But "popular" though the poetry may sound, a random thumbing through the *Analecta Hymnica* reveals a hymn of morning praise which contains the iambic dimeter beat that evolved into William's eight-beat accentual measure.[66] A hymn on the advent of God at vespers shows a four-line stanza with one rhyme repeated throughout the first stanza (*aaaa*), thus illustrating the religious parallel in assonance.[67] Henri Davenson has noted one of many stanzas contained in a famous manuscript of the Monastery of St. Martin (in Périgord or Limousin) which offers in Latin a direct religious comparison for the Duke's strophe:[68]

In laudes Innocentium,	A
Qui passi sunt martirium,	A

Psallat chorus infantium:	A
Alleluia.	B
Sit decus regi martirum	C or A
Et gloria!	B

PROVENSAL

Farai un vers, pos mi sonelh	A
E.m vauc e m'estauc al solelh.	A
Domnas i a de mal conselh,	A
E sai dir cals:	B
Cellas c'amor de cavalier	C
Tornon a mals.	B

Here we have an almost exact duplication of rhyme, meter, and stanzaic ordering. Need we go wandering blindly through Andalusia or Arabia the Blessed for a less significant model written in a language totally impenetrable to most western Europeans of the day? The monastery of St. Martin was in direct communication with St. Martial of Limoges and St. Gall of Switzerland, where poetry and music had flourished in the tenth century. If we need to bother with origins for troubadour poetry, we can find them exactly where they ought logically to exist, at home.

The poem itself is a *fabliau* or little story (from Latin *fabula* with diminutive ending, "little tale"), which usually turns out to be an off-color anecdote. Undoubtedly the plot is funny, for the gist lies in the male deception of the female to get what the female actually wants to give: the deceptions cancel each other out, just as the hundred or more strokes of the cat are repaid on the bed: an eye for an eye. One has the fun of savoring some earthy realism combined with suffering in the agony before the act and the pain that closes the poem. We thus get a carnal parody of a communal act of love, complete with the bread and the wine, along with a Passion to make the service of Amor "come out all right." It is an extravagantly parodic poem, and not at all typical of later Provensal verse. It is, in fact, more clearly akin to the North French tradition, which contains a wealth of fabliaux, as well as narrative poems of a more serious nature. Yet, since Poitiers is itself very close to being a North French city, and since we have every reason to believe that William had to learn some of the language of the majority of the people whom he ruled, it is perhaps natural that we should find certain elements in his work that do not recur in later poetry.[69] Still, William's strong personality and his early appearance in literary history probably explain his "primitiveness" far better than does any theory concerning ethnic origins.

This type of poetry is ancient, for the adventures of the traveling man are timeless. In fact, an adaptation of the plot crops up in Boccaccio's *Decameron*.[70] The fact that Duke William wrote this fabliau does tell us some interesting things: the immoral story, far from being the work of "the people," is usually the product of an intelligent and highly civilized, perhaps overcivilized, mind such as that of Henry Miller, the Marquis de Sade, Boccaccio, Petronius. The division in medieval society is not between nobles and serfs or commoners—the servants in William's court undoubtedly relished poems like this—but between nobles and clerics, as William's biography clearly shows. Surely the mention of loving a monk or a priest in William's poem is gratuitous at best, and surely there is no valid reason for mentioning St. Leonard in this context, even if he is often associated with prisoners. The fact that such poems did not take root in southern France also tells us about a difference in mores. As Bezzola suggests, the Poitevin people seem to have been more refined than their Norman, Breton, and Angevin neighbors.

Here, for example, is a poem in which elements of sex are included, but William has dropped the realistic plot as an ordering device, and has employed a sustained metaphor. When we remember that the word "troubadour" comes from *tropus* or "metaphor," we can further appreciate the development:[71]

1. Friends, I'll write a poem that will do:
   But it'll be full of fun
   And not much sense.
   A grab-bag all about love
   And joy and youth.

2. A man's a fool if he doesn't get it
   Or deep down inside won't try
   To learn.
   It's very hard to escape from love
   Once you find you like it.

3. I've got two pretty good fillies in my corral:
   They're ready for any combat—

They're tough.
But I can't keep 'em both together:
Don't get along.

4. If I could tame 'em the way I want,
 I wouldn't have to change
 This set-up,
 For I'd be the best-mounted man
 In all this world.

5. One's the fastest filly up in the hills,
 And she's been fierce and wild
 A long, long time.
 In fact, she's been so fierce and wild,
 Can't stick her in my pen.

6. The other was born here—Confolens way—
 And I never saw a better mare,
 I swear!
 But she won't change her wild, wild ways
 For silver or gold.

7. I gave her to her master a feeding colt;
 But I kept myself a share
 In the bargain too:
 If he'll keep her one whole year,
 I will a hundred or more.

8. Knights, your advice in this affair!
 I was never so troubled by
 Any business before.
 Which of these nags should I keep:
 Miss Agnes? Miss Arsen?

9. I've got the castle at Gimel under thumb,
 And over at Nieul I strut
 For all the folks to see.
 Both castles are sworn and pledged by oath:
 They belong to *me!*

The work is extraordinary for the way in which the metaphor is sustained without undue strain. One could compare the technique with E. E. Cummings' "She being Brand/—new," where the contours and workings of an automobile are analogous with the female shape and act of sex.[72] But after all, the obsession of the modern American man with his automobile is comparable to that of a knight or chevalier with his horse; in fact, the Provensal word *cavalier* descends directly from the Celto-Latin word *caballus*, "horse."

Another extraordinary element is the masculinity of the poem. This attitude of a bold connoisseur of love is strikingly similar to that maintained by Ovid in most of his love poetry. One clearly sees William singing this poem to his soldier-friends, the companions or buddies mentioned in the opening line. The frequent exhortations to the audience to "Listen!" or lend advice always assure us that the Provensal poem is part of a living experience, what modern artists call a "happening." Yet surely neither Ermengarde nor Philippa would have tolerated this song in her presence. Eventually what was needed to make secular verse more acceptable to a broader audience was a control of the sensual elements. This poem, delightful as it may sound to the modern emancipated ear, simply could not enjoy a very wide circulation in a society where a great many people were committed to the contemplative life. Obviously William did not care whether he was popular or not; a man who owned Poitou and Aquitaine did not have to "care a cock," as Provensal idiom has it.

But compare the structure of the following poem, where elements of praise for the lady add a tenderness to the work that is far more conducive for creating a romantic atmosphere and, consequently, a seduction:[73]

1. I'm going to write a brandnew song
   Before the wind and rain start blowing.
   My lady tries and tests me
   To see the way I love her.
   Yet despite the trials that beset me,
   I'd never break loose from her chain.

2. No, I put myself in her bondage,
   Let her write me into her charter.
   And don't think that I'm a drunkard
   If I love my good lady thus,
   For without her I couldn't live.
   I'm so hungry for her love.

3. O, she's whiter than any ivory statue.
   How could I worship any other?
   But if I don't get reinforcements soon
   To help me win my lady's love,
   By the head of St. George, I'll die!—
   Unless we kiss in bower or bed.

4. Pretty lady, what good does it do you
   To cloister up your love?
   Do you want to end up a nun?
   Listen: I love you so much
   I'm afraid that grief will jab me
   If your wrongs don't become the rights I beg.

5. What good will it do if I'm a monk
   And don't come begging round your door?
   Lady, the whole world's joy could be ours,
   If we'd just love each other.
   Over there at my friend Daurostre's
   I'm sending this song to be welcomed and sung.

6. Because of her I shake and tremble,
   Since I love her with the finest love.
   I don't think there's been a woman like her
   In the whole grand line of Lord Adam.

This poem marks the entrance of romance into modern western literature. By "romance" I do not mean Storm and Stress, Childe Harold in the Alps, or any Rousseauesque infatuation with nature. The troubadours use nature only as a formal, stylized introduction to the love poem; they do not write poems about nature per se. I define romance simply as the application to human beings of the language of praise that is usually addressed to divinities; the divine epic is eventually cast in an imaginative world intermediary between realism and religion, the never-never shadowland of King Arthur or Daphnis and Chloe. In English literature, perhaps the finest example occurs in John Keats's "Eve of St. Agnes," where the romantic vision of youth, beauty, and happiness-ever-after is surrounded by the cold, brutal world of the revelers downstairs and the aged, half-frozen beadsman in the drafty chapel; where the entire vocabulary of praise applied to the Madonna (mercy, grace, charm) is transferred to

Madeline, and where gentle fairies and guardian angels mingle in such a natural way that good St. Agnes becomes a benefactor for love affairs. It is significant that Keats chose the Middle Ages for his time scheme. What separates medieval romance from nineteenth-century romanticism are several centuries of technique and a further refinement and alienation of the aesthetic sensibility.

Still, there is no reason to regret the lack of Keats's romanticism in this poem. The trouble (if this is the proper word) is that William is almost always realistic; his manliness in the actual world around him can be heard through his imaginative persona, so that when the speaker of this poem tries to adopt the lowly position of the bonded knight in the second stanza, we still hear the lordly duke talking. And when we envision his "good lady" in ideal terms (the very same epithet is used to address Mary in Latin hymns: *bona domina*), we are startled by an expression such as "hungry for her love," which is clearly material. The third stanza is perfect as a casting of the earthly woman in the figure of a virginal statue, with "worship" itself mentioned, but we then go down, down, down to the bower and bed which close it. In between, we have mention of love as war (shades of Ovid's "Every lover's a soldier, and Cupid has his own camp"),[74] and the ludicrous notion that William's companions could storm the lady and help the lover. The curse on poor St. George's head is tossed in perhaps not so gratuitously after all, for the chivalrous saint belongs to the romantic dragon world of Christianity too.

The last two stanzas plus tornada (which is here simply a half-stanza) never rise very far above the social level. In fact, mention of the nun (reminiscence of Philippa? or forethought?) and the monk (Robert d'Arbrissel?) merely pulls the religious world down to a bathetic level. Furthermore, the tornada does more than just express the lyric ego ("My lady is better than any other who ever lived"); one has to remember that to the medieval intellect the greatest lady the world had ever known was Mary. Therefore, when a man says that a woman whom he wishes to seduce exceeds all others, and that his adulterous love is the "finest love," we can appreciate the wrath that William of Malmesbury vents against these verses.

Yet the modern ear, deadened by the trite repetition of these worn-out motifs in some popular songs, may not fully catch the religious overtone, may in fact mistake William's daring rhetoric for dull cliché. Nineteenth-century scholars saw no Mary here, no parody of charity. Besides missing the fact that all the Provensal words descend from Vulgar Latin and have double meanings in the twin secular-religious spheres, these scholars also failed to see the humor. Once observed, this wit may appear a bit diabolical; yet the purpose, the idealization of love, is noble, and the end of the poem, with Adam conceived as the founder of a medieval dynasty, is delightful.

The role that Duke William played in the vindication of love and, more broadly, in the idealization of secular affairs, is noteworthy. In the following poem, where the first sample of the spring opening occurs in Romance literature, one can see a reason for this little portrait of nature:[75]

1. In the sweetness of the springtime
   Forests flower, and the birds
   Sing—each in his native tongue—
   The verse of his new chant.
   Therefore, a man stands well
   When he has what he most desires.

2. From there where all is good and fair
   I see no messenger nor seal,
   And so my body can't sleep or laugh,
   And I dare not drag myself forward
   Till I'm sure about the end
   (If it's just the way I ask).

3. Our love affair moves on
   Like a flowering hawthorn branch
   Standing above a trembling tree:
   At night, only rain and frost;
   But the next day's sunshine gleams
   Through green branches and leaves.

4. I still remember that morning
   When we pledged an end to our war,
   And she gave me that great gift—
   Her loving, and her ring:
   O God, let me live some more
   To grope beneath her cloak!

5. I don't need any strange Latin
   That might part me from my Good Neighbor,

For I know how words will travel
In a quick talk that expands.
Let other gabbers brag about their love:
We've got the meat and the knife.

The vernal motif that opens the poem descends from the pastoral
interludes of the classical epic, ultimately from Homer, and was
employed, often in a highly abbreviated form, by the lyric poets
of antiquity.[76] One of the most memorable uses occurs in Ovid's
Art of Love, where spring is linked to a statement of the passage
of time and the urgency of desire:[77]

> While you can, now while living the spring of your years,
> Play! for the years are going like passing water,
> And the wave that slips over will never come back,
> And the hour that is passing will never return.

The most developed use of the spring opening occurs in the
haunting *Vigil of Venus*, that poem which stands metrically and
syntactically between two worlds.[78]

The Christians perpetuated spring poetry largely because
of the unforgettable passages in the very human-sounding Song
of Songs (2:10–12):

> My beloved speaks and says to me: "Arise, my love, my
>   fair one, and come away;
> for lo, the winter is past, the rain is over and gone.
> The flowers appear on the earth, the time of singing has come,
>   and the voice of the turtledove is heard in our land.

Throughout the early phases of Christian hymnology the Easter
hymn with its spring setting was a predominant art form. We
have samples from Prudentius and Ambrose, and especially from
Venantius Fortunatus, who provided the original source for the
Easter sequence *Salve, festa dies*. The rhetoric was drawn primarily from Vergil's pastoral poems and his *Aeneid* on the one
hand, and from the books of Genesis, Psalms, and Song of Songs
on the other.[79] During the Carolingian Revival notable nature
poetry was written by Sedulius Scottus, Alcuin, and others. In
the *Cambridge Songs*, some of which are datable one hundred

years before William, two of the amatory poems contain the spring motif: *Iam, dulcis amica, venito* (Now, my sweet love, come) and *Levis exsurgit Zephirus* (Lightly rises Zephyr).[80] Both of these poems show a Biblical influence blended with the classical in a new Christian-romantic framework, and although some scholars claim that these two poems are entirely religious allegories, the fair critic will at least admit the possibility of ambiguity.[81] Despite Hebraic and Christian allegorization, the Song of Songs can still be read as a humanistic love dialogue.

Why did the spring motif after William become a fixture and finally an obsession? Undoubtedly a medieval love poet in trying to defend human love against the often ascetic trend of Christian charity tries to create the most perfect ambience he can find. Therefore, he paints his own lyric garden of paradise after the model of Vergil's Elysium or the Christian Garden of Eden. He thus, in a sense, cheats in offering his chop-logic defense of love, which proceeds this way:

It is spring.
Birds are mating (as is natural).
Plants are reproducing (as is natural).
Man should—

Along with this assumption goes a corollary: birds are singing, as is their nature; ergo, I'm singing too; then by extension, every lover should sing. Although many people today may accept this argument, it has no real philosophical ground to sustain it. Bishop Peter of Poitiers would dismiss it as sugar-coated nonsense. Man is like the birds and the flowers and the bees? Not at all. Man is rational; man is capable of surmounting his environment and subduing the desires of the flesh. But, as William stated so succinctly: "It's very hard to escape from love / Once you find you like it."[82] Historically, he said the same thing to Peter upon his excommunication, and probably he meant to direct these words to his monastery-bound wives, Philippa and Ermengarde.

The second stanza shows the suffering lover as Christian martyr in an Ovidian situation. Further, the lover as letter-writer emphasizes the importance of the Roman "Master of Love," Ovid; in another poem William calls himself *maiestre certa*, "certain master."[83] Ovid was studied religiously in the schools; this we know from the rhetorical handbooks of John of Garland, Matthew of Vendôme, Geoffrey of Vinsauf, and Gervais of

Melkley.[84] His *Heroides*, a collection of melodramatic love letters written from famous heroines to their lovers, probably did exert an influence on the troubadour lyric, since a Provensal poem was written by a man to be sung before others, much in the same way a letter is composed and in those days was publicly read. Furthermore, the songs traveled around from castle to castle, and ultimately from realm to realm like letters.[85]

Ovid is also probably responsible for the war imagery in the fourth stanza, but the knightly posture of the duke makes it doubly fitting; similarly, the hand beneath the cloak can come from numerous passages of the Roman poet, or even from the Song of Songs (2:6). Yet one has to admit that these elements, which can be traced to both sacred and profane sources, emerge whole and newly unified in this poem as a creative entity. Fortunately, no one has yet found a clear-cut source for the hawthorn image in the third strophe, although some have tried. This metaphor, which forms the center of the poem, influenced Dante so strongly that he adapted it in his *Inferno* (2.127 ff.).

William must have had fun writing the last stanza. Since we can imagine the delight with which he used the name Malbergion for his mistress, the Viscountess of Châtelleraut, we are free to see as much mischief as possible in his mimicking Christian talk about loving one's neighbor in the secret name Good Neighbor. By comparison, it is interesting to read Baudri's *Life of the Blessed Robert d'Arbrissel* for a description of the Christian Elysium at Fontevrault, where William's wife fled: "To everyone silence at certain times was prescribed. They were commanded to answer mildly and not to curse; and all were cemented together in brotherly love (*amore fraterno conglutinabantur*). There was among them no bitterness, no envy, no discord."[86]

Also, is not the "strange Latin" the mumbo-jumbo of church ritual as it sounded to the uninitiated, as opposed to the natural or native "tongue" of the birds in the first strophe? Actually, in the Provensal William uses the word *lati* (from Latin *Latinum*) in both places, thus inviting a comparison. Yet he drops the religious overtone quickly, ending on the most realistic symbolism possible: the phallic knife and waiting meat. Herein lies William's genius: his stern, masculine temper never allows him to indulge in sentimentality, effeminacy, masochism—the vices of many of his successors. He is always the duke, the man in control.

The following poem shows the acme of romanticized idealism as it appears in William's work:[87]

1. Full of joy I abandon myself to love
   That joy from which I get the greatest ease,
   And since I always want to return to joy,
   Surely I should, if I can, seek out the best,
   For the best one honors me—no boast—
   The best that man can either see or hear.

2. I, you know, am never one to boast
   Or fashion for myself elaborate praises,
   But no other joy ever flowered like this:
   This one flourishes over all the rest
   And gleams far away from all the others,
   The way the sun brightens gloomy days.

3. No, never could anybody imagine
   How it is, not by will or desire,
   Not by his fancy or thought;
   For this joy you can find no equal;
   And who'd like to give it its merited praise
   Would have to spend more than a year.

4. All other joys bow down to it,
   And all other riches obey
   Milord—for her beautiful bearing
   And her beautiful, charming looks.
   A man would have to be more than a hundred
   Who could seize the joy of her love.

5. Ah, her joy can heal the sick,
   And her wrath can kill the hale;
   She can drive the wise to folly
   And turn the fair to foul;
   She can corrupt the civilized
   And civilize the depraved.

6. Since man can never find a prettier,
   Nor eyes see better, nor mouths tell tale,
   I'm resolved: I'd better hold her fast;
   She can requicken the heart within me
   And make my flesh come back anew:
   With her I can never grow old.

7. If Milord wants to give me love,
   I'm ready to take, with gratitude,
   And hide it and pay it court,
   And talk and act in its pleasure,
   And hold its value ever dear,
   And keep advancing its praise.

8. I dare not send her a messenger
   (I'm afraid it might make her mad),
   Not even myself: I'm afraid I'll fail.
   I dare not try to portray my love.
   But she should pick out what's best for me,
   Since she knows from her alone I'll heal.

This poem divides into three parts. The first three strophes are really little more than an extended discursus on the subject of "joy." This rapture then turns in the fourth stanza into an extravagant praise of the poet's lady. The last stanza is a kind of return to normalcy after the rhapsodic flight. William's word *joi* in the first three stanzas descends with some North French influence from Latin *gaudium*, the favorite word of hymnologists to describe the emotional impact of religious belief or awakening.[88] It occurs again and again in Easter hymns and in poems written in praise of the Virgin Mary. As a result, when William writes in praise of his own lady, he seizes upon the sacred word and travesties it with the same kind of exultant repetition that one finds more often in the Latin *Carmina Burana*.[89] It is also significant that William should use the sun as his basic image in the second strophe to express the superiority of his lady, since this traditional symbol of God becomes a vehicle for suggesting a hidden metaphysic. Aside from the fact that all three strophes are blatantly egotistical (despite the disclaimer in stanza two), William goes even further when he says that his love "flourishes over the rest" and has "no equal"; he is deliberately invading the realm of the sacred and escaping with some pilfered idealism.

The parody value of the poetry is heightened in stanza four when the poet calls his woman "Milord" (in Provensal *mi dons* from Vulgar Latin *mius dom'nus*). Why does the woman become masculine in troubadour poetry? Is it because only the male values were respected and deemed worthy of imitation in the secular world? Is it a concession to the notion developed in Plato's *Symposium* that only men were really capable of being friends (*companho*) with men? Is it a witty turn on William's part to make his woman his equal literally, even in sex? Is it because the woman is linked with the Ovidian, late-medieval love-god Amor, based on Cupid, whose name in Latin was masculine? Probably no single explanation can account for this startling shift, but knowing William's clever inventiveness, and the slavish imitation of so many of his followers, it is possible that his own funny turn of phrase accounts for the entire tradition. Certainly the lady does behave like a lord—both a miraculous Lord who can perform the magical deeds listed in the fifth and sixth stanzas, including the bestowal of rebirth, and also the earthly lord or duke of the seventh and eighth stanzas who moves in a world of courts. The lady in the last stanza seems more like a doctor than a miracle-healer, but that is part of the return to realism in which the poem moves after its fanciful caper.

Viewed as a whole, the work is a brilliant expression of mysticism applied to material objects. The grandeur of the flight and the gradual, natural return to earth at the end are organically controlled without being artificially regulated after the pattern of fixed musical modes or architectural panels. In fact, the last stanza, with the lady represented as a doctor and with mention of the letter, is clearly Ovidian. Yet the composition as a whole is original, is inventive, is a product of *trobar*. With this poem, romanticism is firmly established in the Christian world.

William also left two poems which venture into the mystical. One of these, translated below, bears the generic name of riddle poem. In Provensal this word is *devinalh*, derived from the Latin verb *divinare*, "to divine, to guess." The "divine" part of the root is important, for what else does one guess but mysteries? The words "mysticism" and "mystery," which both descend from the Greek *mysterion* (secret, hidden), are closely related, although the word "mystery" is more easily attached to the romantic ethos than to the religious. In this poem, the romantic clearly accounts for the statements of paradox with which the work begins, and the illness mentioned in the fourth stanza is obviously once again the famous *passio hereos* or "erotic passion" described by Avicenna and traceable to Plato, Ovid, and Sappho, who gave the original descriptions of its symptoms.[90] Similarly, the air of bewilderment with which the poem opens is obviously a case of Platonic love madness:[91]

1. I'll write a poem about pure nothing:
   Not about me or any other men;
   Not about love, and not about youth,
   Or anything else.
   Because I just composed it asleep
   On horseback.

2. I don't know at what hour I was born;
   I'm not exactly gay; I'm not fierce.
   I'm not very friendly, yet I'm not aloof,
   And I can't act otherwise,
   Because I was bewitched one night
   Atop a high hill.

3. I don't know if I'm asleep
   Or awake—unless someone tells me.
   My heart just barely escapes
   From its deepfelt griefs.
   And I don't count it worth a smile,
   Name of St. Martial!

4. I'm sick; I quake for dying;
   I only understand what I can hear;
   I need a doctor—for fantasies—
   But don't know which;
   Good he'll be if he can cure me;
   But bad if I get worse.

5. I've got a girl friend; don't know who:
   I've never seen her—faith help me!
   She never did what I wanted, or didn't;
   And it doesn't bother me,
   For I never let a Norman or Frank
   Set foot in my house.

6. I never saw her, but love her a lot.
   She never did me any good, or harm.
   When I don't see her, I'm happy;
   And I just don't care a cock,
   Because I know another one prettier, nicer,
   And worth a lot more.

7. I've made my poem, I don't know of what;
   And I'll send it over to someone
   Who'll send it for me through another
   Over there toward Anjou,
   So that someone can send from his locked box
   The counterkey.

Even if one guesses that love is the answer to the riddle, the poem is still somewhat elusive. Who are the two women in the fifth and sixth stanzas? Are they like Miss Agnes and Miss Arsen, the mares whom William must choose between? The first woman, whom William has never seen, seems to be an ideal lady of some sort, one who haunts and even torments by her aloofness. Yet before we conceive of her as some Dark Lady of Witchcraft or some Manichean angel-devil, she is utterly and thoroughly dismissed in the finest Ovidian tradition for "another one prettier, nicer, / And worth a lot more." It would seem that the second woman is one who cooperates, and therefore the poem is grounded in materialism at the end, closing on the note of that riddlelike, possibly sexual image of the counterkey. This tendency to grasp out for the real is typical of William's creative bent. In Jaufre Rudel's work we will encounter these very same problems, but stated in a different temper.

One of the greatest poems that William wrote is his Farewell Song, which is, in effect, both a hymn and a dirge. The *aaaB* rhyme scheme is especially effective in giving the work a serious, formal tone:[92]

1. Now that I've singing's bent
   I'll strike a tune for a lament
   Never to be love's obedient
   In Limoges or in Poitou.

2. Now into exile I will go.
   In peril, in frightful woe,
   I leave my son to face war's throe
   And the wrongs my neighbors do.

3. O, leaving the lordship of Poitou
   Is such a bitter thing to do!
   Watch my lands, Foulques d'Anjou—
   And your little cousin too.

4. If Foulques refuses to lift a hand,
   Like the King, grace of my land,
   Evils will come from those bands
   Of Gascons and men of Anjou.

5. Unless my son is wise, shows worth,
   Once I've left this native earth
   Tossing him over will bring them mirth
   Because he's weak and new.

6. Mercy I beg of you, dear friend.
   If ever I wronged you, make amends.
   To Jesus enthroned, I pray: defend!—
   In Provensal, in Latin too.

7. O, I was a man of prowess and wit,
   But now I renounce each single bit;
   I'll go to Him Who sin remits
   Where men can end renewed.

8. Yes, I was a jaunty lord, and gay,
   But another lord points another way.
   Now these shoulders, burdened, sway
   As my end looms in view.

9. Now I abandon chivalry, pride,
   Everything I was never denied.
   What pleases Him I'll abide:
   May He hold me ages through!

10. At my funeral, friends, I pray:
    Gather around, shout your praise,
    For I've known many happy days
    Far and near, and in Poitou.

11. But now I surrender my joy, my pleasure:
    My vair and gris, my sable treasure.

The historical details surrounding the poem are naturally impossible to establish firmly. Those who assert that William wrote
it in about 1101 before going off on crusade ignore the fact that
Foulques of Anjou was not on very friendly terms with William

at that time, and the future Duke William X was a mere baby. The poem is not really a crusade song at all, as Diez long ago established, and surely he and Jeanroy are correct when they suggest a time between 1112 and 1117 (the year of the lifting of Girard's excommunication); at that time the younger William was eighteen, still young enough to be a novice at ruling a vast realm, and his father was 46, old and mature enough to have adopted a philosophical attitude toward life.[93]

The poem itself dramatically illustrates the surrender of the medieval lord to his Lord. We see the spheres of correspondence locking together, despite the Duke's passionate will to cling to life, to joy (once again that word!), and finally to the very tangible furs—*vair* and *gris* and *sembeli*. The work manages to blend the gaiety of William's earthly existence, which is the one consistent factor in his personality, with seriousness when that quality is called for. It is a poem that should have been read with much more understanding by those nineteenth-century philologists who could not relate William to the Church. For even when we look back over William's life, past the obvious scandals and the scurrilous anecdotes assembled by the pro-English, anti-French William of Malmesbury or the Church-oriented Ordericus Vitalis, we sense William's opposition to Church politics and ecclesiastical personalities, rather than to mysticism or to idealism themselves. In fact, William's funeral was conducted in regal splendor with great respect by the prelates of Montierneuf, who regarded him as the noble son of their founder, in whose reign the monastery was given papal consecration:[94]

> . . . for him all the drums are sounded. . . . And the sepulcher should be prepared with great honor, with four wax tapers burning during the second service, with two lamps which ought to burn with two wax tapers until after the recitation of the funeral Mass. This Mass should be celebrated solemnly by two brothers clad in capes, and by two boys dressed for the responses. This done, the group should return to the chief altar, singing *Libera me*, with three of the usual verses, that is, *Dies ille tremens, Creator omnium*, with the Psalm *Miserere*, with prayers and collections.

It is significant to note that the good fathers did not include William's own poem as part of his funeral service, probably feeling, quite rightly, that it is too concerned with furs and frolic, the stuff of life.

Duke William's voice was an outcry against the vulgar spiritualism of his day, the urge to destroy the flesh in an orgy of self-flagellation or a fast of self-denial; he was similarly opposed to the hypocrites who tried to conceal their real selves under cloaks of sanctity. William IX of Aquitaine was the whole medieval man—long before the so-called Renaissance came into being. He composed ribald story poems, tender romantic verses, and a hymn celebrating his own death centuries before Villon and Boccaccio. He is the first troubadour, and, in many respects, the greatest.

2

MARCABRUN

In Scorn of Love

The law of action and reaction helps to explain the rise of the poet Marcabrun, who flourished from 1130 to 1150. If ever a voice was needed to cry out against the new love being sung by William of Aquitaine, Marcabrun was ingeniously equipped for the task. The later biographers in the vidas caricatured him in these unequivocal terms as an attacker of love:[1]

B.

Marcabrun the baby was deposited at the door of a rich man, and no one knew either who he was or where he was from. And Sir Aldrics of Vilar gave him care. Later he stayed so long with a troubadour who had the name of Cercamon that he began to compose. And at that time he had the name Pamperdut [Lost Bread, or perhaps Lost Breeches]. But after this he got the name Marcabrun [Dark Spot]. And at that time people did not call what men sang a song [canson] but a verse [vers]. And Marcabrun was much called for and heard throughout the world, and feared because of his tongue; and was so evil-talking that finally the castellans of Guyenne did him in, about whom he had said many a very wicked thing.

A.

Marcabrun was from Gascony, the son of a poor woman who had the name Marcabruna, as he himself says in his song:

Marcabrun, son of Lady Bruna,
Was conceived under such a moon
That he knows how Love crumbles—
Listen!—
He never loved any woman,
And no woman ever loved him.

He was one of the first troubadours that men remember. He wrote verses and satires [sirventes] about wretchedness, and spoke ill about women and about love.

No doubt there is a great deal of authority for this time-honored judgment of the poet. For example, the poem quoted above presents Marcabrun as a misogynist in as clear-cut a manner as one could wish:[2]

63

1. I'll tell you without any doubt
   The way this verse begins:
   The words have the semblance of truth—
   Listen!—
   He who wavers from Goodness
   Has the semblance of a lout.

2. Youth topples, cracks, and shatters.
   And Love enacts the part
   Of a censor collecting taxes—
   Listen!—
   Each man brings in his share,
   And never after's excused.

3. Love, like a spark, keeps the fire
   Smoldering under a coat of soot;
   Then burns the bushes, then the hay—
   Listen!—
   And he doesn't know where to run,
   The man devoured by its flame.

4. I'll tell you how Love gestures:
   Here he peeps, there he squints;
   Here he smooches, there winces—
   Listen!—
   He'll walk a straight enough line
   Once I become one of his.

   . . . .

10. Don't you think I understand
    Whether Love's cross-eyed or blind?
    He planes his words, then polishes—
    Listen!—
    His sting is gentler than a bee's,
    But harder it is to be cured.

11. If a man reigns under a woman's wits
    It's right that ill should befall him,
    For so Solomon tells us—
    Listen!—
    An evil fate will get you
    If you don't watch out!

12. Marcabrun, son of Lady Bruna,
    Was conceived under such a moon
    That he knows how Love crumbles—
    Listen!—
    He never loved any woman,
    And no woman ever loved him.

Yet the difference between Marcabrun and a conventional moralist is obvious. He is witty in a way that medieval sermons on the
subject of lust never are. Tertullian and Augustine can match
him for intensity in their vilifications of "fornication," and Augustine especially can compete in the matter of forceful, vivid
imagery (the frying pan of lust, the dark forest of desire), yet
neither possesses Marcabrun's sometimes malicious but always
effective humor.[3]

Marcabrun did things to the Provensal language that lexi-
cographers and Romance philologists are still trying to puzzle
out. His "trobar" was wildly inventive. Yet after we recover
from the dazzling impact of the surface, we begin to see clearly
recognizable adaptations from standard classical and Christian
sources. For example, the love god Amor of the tenth stanza
seems to have been inspired by Ovid's mischievous Cupid. The
words of wisdom cited in the eleventh strophe are taken from
the Bible, as the poet himself reminds us. Marcabrun is fond of
quoting from the book of Proverbs; he mentions David and
Solomon directly, as well as Ovid, as we shall see. Although the
"flame of love" in the third stanza is an age-old trope, Marcabrun
manages to create an aura of originality because of his vigorous
mode of expression and his addition of homely figures which
suggest events of everyday life, such as tax-collecting or a
raging fire; he thus particularizes the general tropes, charging
them with new life.[4] Perhaps the essence of his style lies in the
way that he forces the abstractions of allegorical expression
(Goodness, *Proeza;* Youth; Love) into violent action; this movement of ideas into act is what frees his poetry from the rigid
sphere of easily assimilated, fixed meanings, and forces the reader
to *think.* One does not nod his head over a poem of Marcabrun,
as he well may over some of the long-winded sermons preached in
the churches.

In criticizing romantic love and upholding Christian charity,
Marcabrun did not create an entirely new allegorical system, nor
simply take recourse to the sententious forms offered him as

models in Proverbs. He adapted for his own ends the very structure which such men as William of Aquitaine, who preceded him by a generation or so, were building. Therefore, if William sang of the joy of physical love and the pleasures of youth, Marcabrun sang of the Christian exultation that antedated secular joy, and of the perennial newness, the *vita nova*, of which Paul spoke. In other words, he unmasked the new impostors by restoring the original sacred values to their terminology, as can be observed in the following work:[5]

> 1. Through the chilly gusts that guide
>   The winter that is full of frenzy
>   Not one bird chirrups or cries
>   Beneath a leaf or through the green,
>   For summerlong in cosy ease
>   They blend together their certain joy.
>
> 2. I hear no chant, no echo,
>   I see no branch in flower;
>   No, instead I only catch
>   A very curious outcry
>   From Joy, who plainly weeps
>   In Vileness' grasp.
>
> 3. Goodness is all abandoned
>   And the worst, who are now riding high,
>   For a long time have forced the husbands
>   To admit their own dishonor
>   Through those crouchers with filed tongues,
>   Uprooters of sincere [*fina*] trust.
>
> 4. From among the ladies has fled
>   Shame, and he runs not here;
>   The most have greased up their tails
>   And handed the age into error;
>   Ah, but their dastardly seeding
>   Will cast wicked fruit on the bloom!
>
> 5. Gallantry's been all banished
>   While Whoredom's honor still grows,
>   For the married men have grabbed it,
>   Turning themselves into swains.

Hearing one brag is as wonderful
As watching a dog knead dough.

6. As long as Marcabrun has life,
One of that barbaric tribe
Will get no affection from him,
For they're all just evil givers,
Forgers of a wicked creed,
Through France and through Guyenne.

7. Lord Alfonso, who holds the peace—
Virtue inclines toward him!

Here the poet adapts the spring opening of romantic poetry
for a moral work, using the word *drudaria*, which I have translated "gallantry," to describe a secular life well lived. This
Romance word seems to stem from Old Germanic *drut* (beloved)
and is akin to English *troth* and modern German [*ver*]*traut;* it
was used by William in the love situation, but its meaning seems
to be as often "friend" or "buddy" as "lover."[6] Marcabrun picks
up the word, which has been used to cover a multitude of adulterous sins, and employs it in a colloquial, old-fashioned way;
probably the modern English word "courting" has a similarly
staid, respectable meaning. Marcabrun is reminiscing about a
time when friendships were not cover-ups for illicit love affairs.
Thus, although he moves freely in this new romantic world, the
poet works frantically to dispel the mists surrounding these
pseudo-mystical rites. In the sixth stanza he speaks with the
ferocious zeal of a crusader against the "barbaric tribes" and
the "forgers of a wicked creed" (*Mesclador d'avol doctrina*).
He thereby points up the swollen pretensions of the new society
and also its antipathy toward the genuine *doctrinas* of the Church,
which emphasized the sacrament of marriage, bitterly attacked
adultery, and treated the sexual act realistically, but, of course,
unromantically. Gascon or not, Marcabrun was obviously deeply
disturbed by the far-reaching scandals of the Ile de France and
Aquitaine. The outrageous affairs of Bertrade and Malbergion are
typical situations which the poet is assailing.
It is amazing to note how Marcabrun can win over a
reader who has just given his sympathy to William of Aquitaine.
One wonders: how is it possible to honor these antithetical views?
The answer is that Marcabrun's morality is offered with a differ-

ence: he employs concrete detail, rather than endless abstract haranguing. As the tornada of the poem brilliantly indicates, he places a firm emphasis upon the things of this world seen through a kind of Christianity that moves and functions in everyday life, that exposes sham and ridicule in an instructive way and yet also manages to delight. This added condiment, wit, peppers the traditional system, lending it much-needed zest. We begin to *feel* why a religious song such as the pilgrim tune *O Roma nobilis, orbis et domina* can be sung to the melody of a love song addressed to a young man, *O admirabile Veneris idolum.*[7] The difference is not one of quantity or intensity of expression, but of quality. A man can exalt Lord Alfonso VII of Castile with the same kind of joy and bravado that another man uses to exalt his lady.

Marcabrun's craving for movement is perhaps best conveyed in his poem *L'iverns vai*, where two short refrains create two long sense pauses. The cry *Ai!* sounds like the sudden crash of a drum or the clash of cymbals; the *Hoc!* should be read more softly, more suggestively. Although this poem accords beautifully with the free movement of jazz, a form is maintained throughout with almost classical perfection. The structure of the stanzas can be readily compared to various hymns in which short cries like *Eia!* punctuate the longer lines:[8]

> From Adam's vices
> Our damnation
> Had its start:
> A pact was made
> 'Twixt God and man
> By Christ our Lord—
> *Eia!*
> So let the Church's faithful
> Rejoice!

When we recall that jazz had its roots in Negro spirituals, where religious matter eventually gave way to secular laments and songs on the plight of the self, we can understand why an ecstatic poem like the following sounds familiar to the modern ear:[9]

> 1. Winter goes, and the time is pleasant,
>   And the woods again are growing green,

And flowers peep along the hawthorn,
As birds go bounding with their joy—
Ay!
Now all men are gay with love;
Each one's drawn to his mate—
Yeah!
According to his heart's desire.

2. Cold is quaking, drizzle rustles
Against the gentle season's coming;
Through the groves and thickets
I hear the contests of those songs—
Ay!
And put myself to the trobar task,
For I'll tell you how Love wanders,
Yeah!
And, maybe, how he rolls back too.

3. Low Loving spreads, confounding
Control with gluttonous appetite,
Searching for that sweet dish of meat [*conina*],
Ever warmed by those nasty fires—
Ay!
Once a man slips in there—
For real or just for a try—
Yeah!
Got to leave his skin behind in the pot!

4. Good Love [*Bon' Amors*] packs a panacea
To heal his loyal followers;
But Low Loving spanks his disciples
And sends 'em straight to Hell—
Ay!
As long as the geld lasts here,
The poor fool thinks he's loved,
Yeah!
But once the geld's gone, botch-up [*buzina*]!

5. Low Loving lays a marvelous trap,
Luring the dupe into his lime
From the top down to his toes:

All messed up! Shall I? No?
Ay!
Want a blonde, brunette, or black?
And will I do it? Or won't I?
Yeah!
This way a fool gets a skinny rump.

6. A lady who loves her farmhand
Just doesn't know Refined Love [amor fina].
No, she's got the bitch's instinct
Like the greyhound for the cur.
Ay!
Out come those savage, mongrel rich
Who won't give you parties or pay—
Yeah!
So swears Marcabrun!

7. The farmhand sneaks into the kitchen
To warm up some fire among the twigs
And lap up some of the fresh bouquet
From the cask of Milady Goodfount—
Ay!
I know how he stays and loafs there,
Separating the grain from the chaff—
Yeah!
Impeasantizing his master.

8. Who has Good Love as neighbor
And lives within his bondage
Sees Honor and Worth inclining
And Value—not any danger—
Ay!
Does so much with honest words,
He need never fear the wrath—
Yeah!
Of that lecher-livin' Sir Aigline.*

9. I'll never pledge my troth
With Lord Eblés' pack of poets,
For too often there good sense

* Sense obscure: MS *Del trut dullurut (deliurat?) n'Aiglina*

Falters, contrary to reason—
Ay!
I said, I say, and always will:
High and Low Love have different cries—
Yeah!
And whoever blames Good Love's an ass.

The dichotomy here seems fairly clear-cut. Marcabrun uses two different words to express his basic antinomies: *Amors* is what I call in the translation "High Love"; *Amars* is "Low Loving." It is clear from the context that Low Love is sexual, a thing to be spurned in Marcabrun's system. We can therefore apply Augustine's term "cupidity." But are we also free to call Marcabrun's *Amors* Christian charity, the opposing Augustinian virtue? *Amors* in Provensal descends from Latin *amor*, a highly ambiguous word that covered both divine and secular love, despite Christian attempts to substitute the terms "charity," "lust," and "love of God" for the single word. There is not much ambiguity about *Amars*, which is merely the gerund of the verb: "loving." This substantive, which has no traditional history, is obviously colloquial. The question posed here is: must the refined love (*amor fina*) of the sixth stanza be the holy love of God? Might it not be a more perfected kind of human love, say between the noble lady and a knight, or even between the lady and her husband?

There is no doubt that Marcabrun attacks adultery involving mixtures of classes. He likens Low Loving to falling into a pot; we may remember that both the English word "stews" and the Romance *bordello*, from *brodo* or "broth," refer to a house of prostitution in culinary imagery. By the fourth stanza, Marcabrun's position is somewhat clarified, for he says that Good Love offers a panacea; in hymnology, Christ is often referred to as a curer or healer, just as the lady-lover in the secular sphere frequently plays the same role.[10] When we read further that Low Loving sends its disciples to Hell, we infer that High Love must send its followers to Heaven, and we feel somewhat assured that Marcabrun is extolling the praise of brotherly love, the gallant feeling of the good old days. Marcabrun is always practical, socially oriented in his approach. He paints the lady who loves beneath her degree in stanza six in a realistic light: the medieval moralist shows no gracious sympathy toward the Lady Chatterley of his day. Here we see how the Church and the court poet can work together. We are reminded of the fine relations between William and Bishop Peter of Poitiers, as long as the Duke obeyed the laws of morality; we also think of the subsequent scathing attacks of Ordericus Vitalis and William of Malmesbury against the Duke when his conduct became scandalous. These vignettes, the seriocomic incidents in the chronicles of the day, come very close in tone to the work of Marcabrun. Since the chronicles were usually written by ecclesiastics, Marcabrun once again aligns himself with the Church.

In the eighth stanza, the rewards for Good Lovers are Honor, Worth, Value, typically Christian virtues, although the words also have entirely secular connotations. In fact, the two spheres of reference complement themselves so naturally that the work is shrouded with ambiguity. Only the very last stanza with the reference to Lord Ebles, probably the famous Ebles II the Singer of Ventadorn, suggests that Marcabrun is attacking the new secular-love tradition for its false reasoning. Furthermore, since throughout Marcabrun defends marriage and morality, his position is easily reconciled with that of the Church. But although the attitude of the poem is conservative, the rhythm and the sound effects are daring, radical. Marcabrun's poetic capacities sometimes seem to interfere with his rational presentation, yet this defect can ultimately become an aesthetic virtue.

The quality of the vagabond moralist is best seen in one of Marcabrun's most famous productions, his crusade song:[11]

1. *Pax in nomine Domini!*
   Marcabrun made the words and the song:
   Hear what he says.
   The most gracious Lord of Heaven,
   Out of his sweetness has fashioned
   For our use here a washing-tub,
   Unlike any other (except the one
   Overseas in the vale of Josephat).
   But to this one I summon you.

2. And it's rightful that we should bathe
   Our bodies from night till morn—
   I assure you.
   Everyone has his chance to scrub,

And until he's healthy and hale,
He ought to go straight to the tub,
For there's our true therapy.
And if we pass first to death,
We'll fall to lowly lodging.

3. But Small-Souledness and Lack-of-Faith
Part Youth from his good companion.
Ach, what grief!
That most men prefer to go where
The winnings belong to Hell!
If we don't run quick to that big wash-tub
Before our mouths and eyes are closed,
Not a one's so puffed with pride
That he won't face death's stronger match.

4. For the Lord who knows all that is
And all that will be, and all that was
Has promised us
Honor in the name of the Emperor.
And the beauty to come—do you know?—
For those who will go to the tub:
More than the star of morning joy,
If only they'll avenge the wrongs
To God, here and in Damascus.

5. In the line of Cain's descendants,
From that first villainous man,
Come many heirs
Who won't bear their honor to God.
We'll see now who's His loyal friend.
For by virtue of the washing-tub
We'll all own Jesus equally.
And let's throw back the loot
That accrues from luck and fortune.

6. And all those horny wineheads [corna-vi],
Dinner-snatchers [Coita-disnar] and brand-blowers
[bufa-tizo],
Highway-crouchers [Crup-en-cami]
Can lurk behind in the lazy house [folpidor]:

God wants the brave and the fair
To step up to his washing-tub;
And those will keep his mansions safe
And find the adversary strong
And, 'gainst their shame, I chase them out!

7. In Spain, over here, Marquis Ramon
And those from the Temple of Solomon
Suffer the weight
And the pain of the Paynim pride.
And so Youth gets a vile report.
And the cry for this washing-tub
Rolls over the richest overlords
Who're feeble, failing, bereft of nerve,
For they don't value Joy nor Fun.

8. The Franks are all degenerates
If they say no to the task of God
That I commend.
Ah, Antioch! Virtue and Valor
Are mourned in Guyenne and Poitou!
God our Lord, to Your washing-tub
Bring the Count's soul in peace;
And here guard Poitiers and Niort,
O Lord Who issued from the tomb!

The notion of the battle against the infidels as a bath is ingenious, for it concretizes the action, spelling out the beneficial end to be gained by engaging in the hazardous war. Guido Errante has cited several plausible Biblical sources for the figure,[12] but no exact one is needed, since what could be a more natural way of stressing the values of spiritual purgation than by using an object meant for physical cleansing? Yet one feels that an important subsidiary reason for writing the poem lies in stanzas six to eight, with their commentary on the manners of the day and their direct reproaches against the Franks and the Aquitanians. The Christian satirist can be moral and yet have his fun too, poking the lazy and the lecherous, while all the time holding himself on the side of righteousness. Juvenal never had it quite so comfortable.

Curiously to some, the Christian moralist adopts the entire

chivalric code without any questions. Many modern readers expect the scholar-poet to show more mercy and humility, to place less emphasis on *vir*-tus in the old Roman sense of "being manly." This apparent paradox does not really exist for the medieval writer. Like the author of the *Song of Roland,* who mows down the wicked Moors in rapid-fire sequence, Marcabrun espouses a vigorous, masculine kind of Christianity that emphasizes the things of this world. We may search for what we consider the more appropriate passive virtues, and we may try to imagine (with difficulty) Christ in the same context exhorting the Jews to war against the Romans, but the paradox of war and Christian love seems to trouble our minds more than it did those of the day. A war against the infidels was obviously justified.

Furthermore, if the notion of a Christian warrior jars the sensibility, this figure has a strong basis in such historical personages as Charlemagne, and the iambic dimeter marching beat of early Christian hymnology certainly could be easily adapted to sending soldiers onward into war. If we have trouble aligning the fiery words of Urban II with the sermon of Christ on the Mount, we must remember that Urban faced different problems in a different position. To survive, the Church had to contend with the problems of the world; the crusaders, after all, did preserve European culture—especially those who fought in Spain. If William of Aquitaine was masculine in the domain of love, Marcabrun is equally masculine in the realm of being good. His virtue has a rough, hardy nature; the cross is meant to be borne by those who swear by it; Christianity is not for the weak and the lazy. The martyrdom which Marcabrun preaches is not a passive rolling around on a wheel or immersion in a cauldron of lead; his washing-tub spills over as much with blood as with soap suds. In keeping with the general vigor, Christ emerges brilliantly at the end. One sees the issuance from the tomb as a dynamic, creative act. In this sense, although we may typically associate Christ with peace and passivity, we feel his power in the same way we do in a Gerard Manley Hopkins poem like "The Windhover."

If, in the final analysis, we see Marcabrun as the spokesman for all that William of Aquitaine opposed, we do not accord the Gascon his full merit. Actually, Marcabrun was more than adept at creating a full sense of the dialectic of love. Granted that Ugo Catola sings one side in their famous debate poem (*tenso*),

still the poem as a whole reflects the age-old arguments for and
against human love that were authoritatively stated by Ovid in
his *Art of Love* and *Remedy of Love*:[13]

1. UGO CATOLA:
   Come, friend Marcabrun, let's sing
   A song of love, for I strongly hope
   That while we make our song in parts
   The chant may ring for long.

2. MARCABRUN:
   Hugh Catola, all right, let's go,
   But let me complain of false girl friends
   For since the serpent lowered the branch,
   Were never so many female cheats.

3. Marcabrun, I don't like the way
   You speak of Love so negatively,
   And so I'll start debating with you,
   For I was born and bred by Love.

4. Catola, can't you listen to reason?
   Don't you know how Love fleeced Samson?
   You think—like those other scamps—
   That everything you say is true.

5. Marcabrun, where's the authority
   On Samson the strong and that wife
   Who says she robbed him of his love
   At the time she did him in?

6. Catola, because she gave a viler man
   Her love, and took it from a better,
   That day she threw away her merit,
   Betraying her man to a stranger.

7. Marcabrun, since you declare
   That Love's all mixed with treachery,
   Then almsgiving's also a crime,
   And plant tops lie beside their roots.

8. Catola, the Love of which you speak
   Furtively shifts the dice;

After the throw—take heed!—
So say Solomon and David.

9. Marcabrun, friendship's failing,
   Because it finds Youth wholely hostile;
   And I feel wrath and terror
   Because of those horrible howls.

10. Catola, Ovid shows here
    And traces the action's course
    How he never says no to brown or blonde;
    No, he's drawn to the most perverse.

11. Marcabrun, I'm sure that Love
    Never followed you, violent man!
    And never was anything counted less
    By a brainless, witless jongleur.

12. Catola, Love never once lifted
    His foot without scampering right away,
    And let him shrink even further now,
    And keep on going until he's through.

13. Marcabrun, when I'm sad and tired
    And my good girl friend greets me
    With a kiss, and whisk! go my clothes—
    I walk away whole and hale and cured.

14. Catola, out of love for the winepress
    A fool's gold leaps over the threshold
    And mockingly thumbs toward the road
    Where he can walk with other men of scorn.

The passage referred to in the tenth stanza is probably Ovid's
Amores 2.4.39–44:

A fair blonde will take me, a golden-haired girl,
Yet Love goes well with a dusky color.
Do black ringlets dangle over a snowy neck?
Leda's hair attracted for its blackness.
Or does it gleam? Aurora had lovely golden hair.
My love can adapt itself to any myth.

Yet despite the strong Ovidian influence, one finds a closer usage of the book of Proverbs. There, for example, occurs the antithesis of wisdom and folly that mirrors Marcabrun's polarities of reason and lack of sense:

> 14:1 Wisdom builds her house,
> but folly with her own hands tears it down.

Furthermore, Solomon clearly aligns folly with the adulterous love of women:

> 5:3–4 For the lips of a loose woman drip honey,
> and her speech is smoother than oil;
> but in the end she is bitter as wormwood,
> sharp as a two-edged sword.
>
> 6:32 He who commits adultery has no sense;
> he who does it destroys himself.
>
> 3:35 The wise will inherit honor,
> but fools get disgrace.

Solomon also describes evil persons in ways that are strikingly similar to Marcabrun's rhetoric; for example, Marcabrun constantly denigrates the so-called "crouchers-in-the-road" (*crup-en-cami*), who are similar to the wicked men who "lie in wait for their own blood, [and] set an ambush for their own lives" (1:18). The description of a sinner in Proverbs 6:12–14 strikingly recalls Marcabrun's description of Love:

> A worthless person, a wicked man,
> goes about with crooked speech,
> winks with his eyes, scrapes with his feet,
> points with his finger,
> with perverted heart devises evil,
> continually sowing discord.

Conversely, the notion of the good man as a straight man is echoed in 8:8 f.:

> All the words of my mouth are righteous;
> there is nothing twisted or crooked in them.

They are all straight to him who understands
and right to those who find knowledge.

The action of harlotry is embodied in an extended parable in
Proverbs 7:18–23, where a woman representing folly seduces a
young man from his good sister, Wisdom, by saying:

"Come, let us take our fill of love till morning;
   let us delight ourselves with love.
For my husband is not at home;
   he has gone on a long journey;
he took a bag of money with him;
   at full moon he will come home."
With much seductive speech she persuades him;
   with her smooth talk she compels him.
All at once he follows her,
   as an ox goes to the slaughter,
or as a stag is caught fast
   till an arrow pierces its entrails;
as a bird rushes into a snare;
   he does not know that it will cost him his life.

Despite these indisputable sources, the book of Proverbs
never shows the kind of dynamic wit that Marcabrun constantly
employs. The Bible supplies the words, but Marcabrun supplies
the music. The charm of the tenso lies in the blending of the
two points of view. One must go beyond the Bible to uncover a
source which shows a similar blending of dialectic, say to Vergil's
pastoral poetry, where the wandering Meliboeus pauses to talk
with Tityrus, reclining under the shade of a beech tree, in
Eclogue 1; or Damoetas and Menalcas talk about their love
affairs in the beauty of the forest in *Eclogue* 3; or the death
of Daphnis is mourned in *Eclogue* 5; or, in the famous *Eclogue*
10, Vergil attempts to arouse his friend Gallus out of his love
sickness, but Gallus refuses, saying, "Love conquers all; and
me, let me yield to love" (69).[14] These friendly nooks in groves
and forests obviously contributed to the formation of the nature
opening of the medieval love lyric. During the Carolingian
Renaissance, for example, there was a fresh outburst of pastoral
poetry, especially by Alcuin, who composed a debate poem
between Winter and Spring, songs for the cuckoo and the

nightingale, and partook of the tradition so completely that he even called himself by the Greco-Roman shepherd name Menalcas.[15] These poems thrive on dialectic although the correspondences remain intact.

The fact that Marcabrun wrote pastorals, then, should not come as any surprise. The two most famous examples of this genre are actually somewhat different from each other. The longer of the two describes the encounter of an apparently noble figure with a lowborn shepherdess in the open countryside. The direct confrontation of a man with a woman is an innovation of the medieval pastoral, since classical poems of this type deal almost exclusively with male characters, and the love affairs mentioned are often homosexual. The fact that the protagonist in Marcabrun's poems seems more like a cleric or scholar than a dashing knight underscores the intellectual quality of the genre. Pastoral poems are never written by shepherds; they are the products of wealthy aristocrats or the poets in their employ who feel some kind of yearning for the simple, rugged life. In Marcabrun's longer *pastoreta* this desire for simplicity is stated explicitly, and wisdom, as it is expressed in the poem, is ironically transferred to the little farm-girl:[16]

1. The other day along a hedgerow
   I found a lower-class shepherdess
   Who was rich with joy and sense,
   Seeming the daughter of a farmer,
   Wearing a hood and cape and gown,
   And a blouse of very rough stuff,
   With shoes and stockings of wool.

2. I approached her across the meadow:
   "Little girl," said I, "pretty thing,
   I'm worried the wind may sting you."
   —"Lord," said the little farm-girl,
   "Thanks be to God and my nanny too,
   Little care I if the wind should blow
   Because I'm light-hearted and hale."

3. "Little girl," said I, "charming thing,
   I've torn myself away from the road
   To lend you some companionship,

For a little farm-girl like you
Shouldn't go around pasturing beasts
Without some equal fellowship
In country like this, all by yourself."

4. "Sir," said she, "whatever I am,
At least I know folly from sense.
This equal fellowship of yours,
Milord," said the little farm-girl,
"You can put where it rightly belongs,
For whoever thinks she's got it
In her grip's got only a pose."

5. "Little girl with noble manners,
That man must have been a knight
Who engendered you in your mother,
And she was a courtly farm-girl.
The more I look, the prettier you are,
And the joy of you makes me glitter.
If only you'd be a bit humane!"

6. "Sir, my line and my heritage
I see reverting directly back
To the sickle and to the plow,
Milord," said the little farm-girl,
"But some men pretend to be knights
Who by right should be toiling away
In fields for six days a week."

7. "Little girl," said I, "a kindly fairy
Cast a spell when you were born,
One of radiant enchantment
Far beyond any other farm-girl's;
And this charm would even double now
If I could see you just one time
Below me, with me on top!"

8. "Sire, you've praised me so much
You've made me completely annoyed.
Since you've raised my value so,
Milord," said the little farm-girl.
"Now you'll draw this reward

As my goodbye: 'Gape, fool, gape!
And stand there staring till mid of day!' "

9. "Little girl, a savage heart and fierce
A man can tame with a little handling.
I'm well aware, at this time,
That with a little farm-girl like you
A man can have some fine company
In good, warm-hearted friendship,
As long as one doesn't dupe the other!"

10. "Sir, a man screwed-up and mad
Will swear, pledge, put up stakes;
And so you'd bring me homage, eh?
Milord," said the little farm-girl.
"But I, for a piddling entrance fee
Don't want to change my name
From a virgin into a slut."

11. "Little girl, every creature
Reverts directly to his nature;
You and I, my little farm-girl,
Ought to join our kindred spirits
In the bower down by the meadow;
There you'll feel much safer
When we do the sweet, sweet thing!"

12. "Sire, yes! but according to rightness:
A fool pursues his own folly,
A noble man a noble outcome,
And a farmhand with his farm-girl;
Good sense is ruptured in that place
Where a man doesn't look for measure—
So say the ancient folk."

13. "Little girl, I never saw a figure
More mischievous than yours,
And I never met a heart more vile."

14. "Lord, the owl sends you this prophecy:
One man gapes at a painting
While the other prays for his manna.

✳   ✳   ✳

15. Never should he gape at the painting,
   The man who expects his manna."

The poem sounds very much like one of the prose dialogues between people of various classes to be found in Andreas Capellanus' treatise on love, but there is a significant difference: there the mixing of social stations is sanctioned—at least until the final chapter; but here the breaking of the classical-medieval aphorism *similis simili appetit* ("like seeks after like") is clearly frowned on.[17] The first stanza declares that the shepherdess, although poor in station, is rich in sense, and her taunting words at the end carry the day. We might look at the ending, for it is somewhat riddlelike: a man who gapes at a painting is compared unfavorably with a man who prays for his manna. When we look back at the body of the poem, we find that the would-be seducer (not necessarily Marcabrun himself) has clearly violated laws of decent behavior: he has taken recourse to outright exaggeration or lie (suggesting that a pretty, low-born girl must have had a high-born father), to fanciful romanticism (talk about fairies and enchantment), to direct lascivious language in stanza 7, and to a violation of the natural hierarchical order in stanza 11; this last indiscretion is stated in a way that neither the Church with its insistence on hierarchies of all kinds nor the Frankish-Germanic society around him would have openly sanctioned. He has, in fact, behaved like a man acting with passionate lack of control (gaping) toward a beautiful object (painting), which he tries to reduce to a material form to be grabbed.

The shepherdess suggests instead that the man should have behaved like one praying for his manna or spiritual reward from Heaven: we assume that she has elevated her love to this high plateau. In other words, instead of brashness and rhetorical trickery, he should have used some form of humble, heartfelt praise. Such a gesture, she implies earlier, would show measure, control. Her words are very suggestive, not only to the male protagonist, but for the whole development of Provensal poetry. A man must walk between the extremes of immersion in the sensual (where William sometimes falls) and possibly, on the other side, projection into the too esoteric (where Jaufre Rudel threatens to recede). Although Leo Spitzer has stressed ideas of equality in the poem, the real moral (and one exists) is that one cannot mix what was not meant to be mixed; Christian love

of one's neighbor meant brotherhood in Christ, not "equal" companionship down by the hedgerow.[18] Once again, Marcabrun takes the side of the Church in the total form of his composition.
  The other pastoral is Marcabrun's most famous poem:[19]

1. By the fountain in the orchard
   Where grass is green along the sand,
   Under the shade of a planted tree,
   Comforted by whitish blossoms
   And the usual spring refrains,
   I found alone, without companion,
   Her who did not want me there.

2. She was a lady whose body was beautiful,
   The daughter of a castle's lord;
   And when I thought the songs of birds
   Gave her joy, and the green grove too,
   And the sweet new season of the spring,
   And I asked her to attend my talk,
   Suddenly her manner changed.

3. Her eyes then wept beside the spring,
   And sighs were choking from deep within:
   "Jesus," said she, "King of the world,
   It's You who cause this heavy grief,
   It's Your fault that I'm sorely pressed,
   For the finest man in all this world
   Is serving You, and this You like."

4. "Away with You has gone my friend,
   Who's handsome, gentle, noble, rich;
   And here I'm left with great distress,
   Constant desire and weeping too.
   Ach! Curses on that King Louis!
   Who made that summons, those sermons too
   That helped this grief to gain my heart."

5. When I had heard her thus make moan
   I went to her by the fountain clear:
   "Beautiful," I said, "all these tears
   Just destroy your complexion and face.

You shouldn't want to despair so much,
For He who makes the woodland bloom
Can give you share of joy enough."

6. "Lord," said she, "I know full well
That God may have mercy on my soul
In that other age for aye and aye,
As He will toward other sinners—
But *here* He's snatching that very thing
That gives me joy; what more care I,
Except for that man too far away?"

This poem reflects one of the highest points of the medieval sensibility, the awareness of the urgency of the flesh and the loneliness of the human condition, set against a backdrop of crusades and the demands of a higher order. Marcabrun the actor here seems to be taking his favorite part, emphasizing the world of superior, capitalized virtues. But of course he is merely a glib-tongued seducer who refers to a certain god in a speech urging obedience to human instincts (his god in this context is really Natura); yet the woman interprets him in a traditional way, although she too in her isolation is as far removed from theological values as the scholar-wanderer.[20] There is no reason to allegorize this poem—to say that the woman is Despair or Loneliness and that the man is Lust and that the two are incompatible in a universe where a *super*natural God prevails, in spite of His dissident worshipers. This type of interpretation is as unnecessary here as it is when applied to the strikingly similar *Levis exsurgit Zephirus* of the *Cambridge Songs*.[21] There is no need to add anything to this poem; the spheres are explicitly stated, and the reader is left with an unresolved tension. Since Marcabrun leaves the work open, he allows us a choice of attitudes; with his characteristic shrewdness, almost as if he knew which voice would appeal to most of his hearers, he gives the lovely lady the last, most memorable word. Yet her word by no means sums up the poem, for the God, though rejected, is there. And so is Marcabrun, a frustrated persona whose failure to effect his scheme ironically points up the poet's favorite doctrine: that lust is self-defeating. Morality is thus maintained, but in a warm, dramatic form that speaks even across the chasm of the ages.

Marcabrun carried sermons into the court. We can see that although he fearlessly spoke out for morality, marriage, and the concerns of the Church, he nevertheless spoke in a colloquial manner, with dynamic rhythms and ecstatic phrasing. He was a preacher for the street corner, not for the cathedral; he belonged in the local fairs and markets and banquet halls, not in the monasteries or the schoolrooms. Yet if the Bible is his favorite text, he also knows his *Song of Roland*, and he mourns for the good old days when men and women were content in the simple joys of marriage. Standing at a time when the old virtues—the *vir*tus of the battlefield and the goodness of the Church—were being redefined, he fought the new movement with its own weapons, throwing singing birds and glozing flatterers and babble about a mystique of love back at the poets. Fortunately for the course of European literature, he did not succeed. In fact, his own success with the craft of writing helped to guarantee the perpetuity of poetry, for Marcabrun propagated the arguments, the attitudes, and the grammar of the things he was attacking in the very fabric of his attacks. We miss his presence in later troubadour poetry, because the later moralists seldom work themselves up to his high pitch of fanaticism or show that humorous tendency toward a kind of detachment through overcommitment that the Gascon manifested. Morality did not die with Marcabrun; but after his passing, it was never again quite so funny.

3

JAUFRE RUDEL

The Ecstasy of the Flight,
The Agony of the Fall

Jaufre Rudel has in many ways become the victim of his own romantic achievement, for in the fabric of his poetry, other poets have found the inspiration for weaving designs of their own. Petrarch, for example, spoke of:[1]

> Jaufre Rudel, who used the sail and the oar
> To seek his death.

In the nineteenth century the Provensal poet was especially popular with those romantics who were trying to fan the glowing embers of medieval romance into a huge blaze. Perhaps the greatest tribute to Jaufre's supposed *Liebestod* came from Edmond Rostand, whose play *The Far-Off Princess* cast the imaginary lady of Rudel's dreams into a dramatic vehicle for the chief enchantress of the day, Sarah Bernhardt.[2] The nameless lady of Rudel's poems even acquired the honeyed name Mélissinde, and thus what was originally an airy, ethereal poetic flight descended into the arena of hard, kinetic facts.

Part of the blame rests with Rudel's Provensal biographer, who composed one of the most interesting vidas ever written about a troubadour. Like those tales told about Peire Vidal's disguising himself as a wolf and Cabestanh's heart being served by a jealous husband, Rudel's narrative shows a remarkable feeling for dramatic myth. The fact that not a word therein contains the least shred of historic proof is unimportant, for the tale exudes the kind of sentiment that can easily sway the imagination:[3]

> Jaufre Rudel of Blaye was a very noble man, and was the Prince of Blaye. And he fell in love with the Countess of Tripoli, without seeing her, because of the good things that he had heard from the pilgrims who came from Antioch. And he made for her many verses with good sounds but poor words. And through his desire to see her, he took up the cross and set out to sea. And he took sick on the ship and was carried half-dead to Tripoli to a lodging [*alberc*]. And this was made known to the Countess, and she came to him, to his bed, and took him into her arms. And he knew that she was the Countess, and suddenly he recovered his hearing and his breathing. And he praised God that He had sustained his life until he could see her. And then he died in her arms. And she gave him the great honor of

burying him in the dwelling of the Temple. And then on
that very day, she became a nun because of the sorrow that
she felt for his death.

Long ago Gaston Paris showed how the later Provensal vida
writers abstracted interesting bits from the poems and wove
their fantastic tales around the lives of the already dead, but
half-legendary troubadours.[4]

It is easy, for example, to relate this vida to the greatest
achievement of Jaufre:[5]

1. In May when the days are long
   I like the sound of birds far away,
   And when I depart from their songs
   I remember my love who's far away.
   Head hanging I go, grief-torn.
   No song, no flowering hawthorn
   Do I admire more than winter ice.

2. And lord I'll rightly call the one
   Who'll help me see my love so far!
   But now instead of good I've won
   Two evils: he and I so far!
   Ah, I'd take to the pilgrim's way
   And stand with a staff, arrayed
   In a cloak, reflected by her eyes!

3. For the love of God, what bliss
   To seek out her hostel far away,
   Where, if she wants, I'll insist
   On lodging by her, now far away.
   Then talk will be truly dear
   When this far-off lover, near,
   Hears speech that brings me solace's prize.

4. Half joyed, half pained would I depart
   From sight of my love so far away;
   But now! when can I even start?
   Our lands are so very far away!
   O, I'd just get lost in the maze
   Of those many lanes and highways. . . .
   But—in God the matter lies!

5. Never will I know happiness
   In love, without my love who's far.
   She's the most graceful, very best,
   In any place, either near or far.
   For her, so fine beyond comparison,
   Even in the realm of the Saracens
   I'd gladly suffer the captive's cries!

6. God Who made all that comes and goes
   And created this far-off love:
   Over me strength and courage dispose
   So that I really see my far-off love
   Abiding in such a dwelling-place
   That her room, that her garden space
   Will always assume palatial size!

7. You're right if you say I lust or
   Burn for my far-off love.
   All other joys lose their luster
   Compared to that from my far-off love.
   But what I want is now denied
   Just as my godfather prophesied:
   I'd love but not feel love's reprise.

8. So what I want is now denied.
   Curse that godfather who prophesied
   I'd love but not feel love's reprise!

The biographer created his sketch simply by imagining an
end to Jaufre's wish; the poet finally gets a chance to see his
lady, but then falls from his state of grace. Because of the
mention of the Saracens and the pilgrimage, the far-off lady is
assumed to be living in the Holy Land. The place where she
lives seems to be a palace, says Jaufre; therefore the author of
the vida makes it one, and by extension the lady, who is superior
to all other women, becomes a princess. Despite the fact that
no land whatsoever is mentioned, and the woman's supremacy
is treated more mystically than socially, the author of the life
story also overlooks elements which are contradictory. For
example, the troublesome godfather of the seventh and eighth
strophes should be accounted for. In this literal, realistic sense,
however, he could simply be a flesh-and-bones godfather, and

therefore ignored. The story is made tragic because the poem's tone is humorless and grave. As a result, the poet dies in the hostel mentioned in the third strophe after completing the perilous voyage mentioned in the fourth. Then, possibly because the vida writer felt the importance of the God summoned in Jaufre's third and sixth stanzas, he makes the lady immediately become a nun.

Peculiarly enough, this reading of the poem comes very close to the literal level of allegorical interpretations employed by twentieth-century critics who want to endow the lady with an abstract meaning such as the Holy Land or the Blessed Virgin.[6] Yet these allegorizers encounter trouble from the fact that if the far-off princess is Mary, there is no real reason for the tragic nature of the composition. The Virgin and her grace are present everywhere for one who believes in her: "She can be compared to the speed of a young hind, because her mercy rushes more swiftly than it is called for, and she even anticipates the plights of the miserable."[7] The modern allegorizer, insisting on his fixed equations, has to shift back and forth awkwardly from the literal to the allegorical; he is stuck with the rather feeble portrait of a man who wants to take a journey to the Holy Land, but is somehow unable to work up the courage because of an evil relative. As a matter of fact, this hard and fast kind of transformation of poetic symbols into abstract concepts is typical of the procedure of St. Bernard and Richard of St. Victor writing about the Song of Songs; but that body of lyrics is redolent with faith, hope, and love requited; the "little foxes" who might ruin the human situation are faced openly. Medieval treatises which transform the literal into the conceptual encounter no opposition in the text. In Jaufre, however, as the nineteenth-century romantics did see, mysticism is present as an overriding spirit, although its overtone cannot be labeled standard allegorical Christianity. The work is too elusive.

Because of this elusiveness, Jaufre's poem has been subjected to an examination in terms of Catharist heresy, especially after the publication of Denis de Rougemont's *Love in the Western World*.[8] Despite the bold nature of De Rougemont's assumptions —that the love described in medieval lyrics was really propaganda for this heretical mystery cult—the Frenchman coyly took refuge in the fact that most Catharist documents have been destroyed: it is always easy to prove a theory which, because of the paucity of documents, cannot be disproved.[9] The problem of explicating the principles of Catharism is an especially difficult one because the religion was subterranean in nature and unprolific in literary production; furthermore, it was painfully and thoroughly stamped out by the zealous Albigensian Crusaders. However, thanks to the work of Arno Borst and others, one can piece together a great deal about the belief.[10] Catharism flourished in western Europe from the 1100's to the 1200's. Originating in Asia upon a fractured base of Gnosticism, Manicheanism, and the teachings of Marcion, it was kindled anew in the 900's in Bulgaria under the direction of the preacher Pop Bogomil. One large group of Cathars migrated into northern Italy, then on into southern France, where they attracted numerous followers. Here they were safely tucked away from the popes in Rome, the counts in Poitiers, and the kings in Paris.

Catharism, like its South French offshoot Albigensianism, was a grass-roots religion, appealing largely to the *pagani*, the unsophisticated country folk who to this very day have kept the Roman rites of Maia and maypoles alive. Catharism's appeal to intellectuals and to aristocrats was at first minimal, largely because of the ascetic nature of the belief. It did attract some wealthy support in the Toulousain, however, where anti-Roman and anti-North-French feelings ran equally high. But the great age of the heresy was the thirteenth century, and its political effects will be discussed in the chapter dealing with Peire Cardenal, who was of that later period.

For a statement of the basic beliefs of the religion, the Cistercian writer Alain de Lille (Alanus de Insulis; c. 1128– c. 1202) is useful, for his tract *On the Catholic Faith Against the Heretics of His Time* attacked Catharism along with Judaism, Mohammedanism, and Waldensianism. It is extremely suggestive to note that Catharism was not the sole enemy of the Church; the time, in fact, was rife with beliefs exfoliating in every direction. Hence, we should never really expect to explain any one artistic work in any one dogmatic way, for the various forces at play in the age were intertwined. Alanus summarizes the basic Catharist belief as follows:

> The heretics of our time say that there are two principles of things, the principle of light and the principle of darkness. . . . [And thus] the creator of the world was the principle of darkness, and thus the author of the world was evil, who began his creation from the shadows.[11] If sin

dwells in the flesh and is from the flesh, and the flesh cannot exist without sin, then the flesh is evil and thus is not from God.[12]

This dualistic conception, with consequent treatment of the material world as evil, is the heart of Catharist belief; it pits Satan against Christ and God, and denies the presence of Christ as a mortal on earth. The heretics further rejected the necessity of an intermediary between man and God, denied the validity of the sacraments and most Church ritual, condemned marriage as well as any act of lust, and conceived of the afterlife in terms of spiritual rather than bodily salvation.[13]

The Cathars—their name comes from the Greek word *katharos*, meaning "pure one"—dismissed almost all of the Old Testament and especially the Mosaic laws as the work of the Devil. Their own rites, which are fortunately preserved in a fragment called the "Provensal Ritual," stressed the act of *consolamentum*, which is described by Alain as follows: "For these same heretics say that every sin, no matter what it is, can be remitted by the imposition of hands, especially if one of those whom they call 'perfect ones' (*perfectos*) lays on his."[14] These perfect ones were the highest members of the Cathar Church, the most rigorous self-flagellators and tormentors of their bodies. The majority of the members, like the lay division of any belief, were not so severe: "They call those 'the consoled ones' (*consolatos*) who have recently joined their heresy, and are not yet confirmed in it."[15]

The excellent summary of Alain, who is after all contemporary with both movements (incidentally, he in no way connects the hundreds of troubadours and jongleurs with this "diabolical" movement), is supported by the "Cathar Ritual in Provensal," which adds the further information that members of the sect were called "good men" (*bos homes*).[16] This term and "the perfect ones" might together be related to the "pure love" of the troubadours if that pure love were not directed toward a woman. The Provensal document is infinitely more valuable than Alain's rebuttal or the piecework of modern scholars because it offers us a dramatic presentation of the Catharist movement. It shows that, instead of dealing with some dark, secret, druidlike movement, we are confronting plain, simple, even naive people who welcomed a fire-and-brimstone kind of religion in the same way the hillfolk of any age delight in simple dualism, with its fiery exhortations against those eternal devils, wine, women, and song.

The troubadour tradition, with its emphasis on women and the enjoyment of life, is as far removed from the Cathar world as the court of Duke William in Poitiers is from the rude country churches of the Toulousain. Here, for example, is the Cathar elder talking about the forces of life: "If anyone loves the world, the love for the Father is not in him. For all that is in the world, the lust of the flesh and lust of the eyes and the pride of life, is not of the Father but is of the world."[17] He is quoting the First Epistle of John (verses 15–17), a kind of rhetoric that recurs in the *contemptus mundi* literature of the Catholic Church (the Cathar makes frequent Biblical citations).[18] This rhetoric is not at all typical of the troubadours—not even a troubadour like Marcabrun, who had his morality and the world too.

Now if we try to relate Jaufre Rudel to this system, we can see that certain points are easily correlated. For example, one could graph the major elements as follows, with the lower line representing a realistic interpretation:

principle of good (Christ)	Cathar	Satan
far-off love	exiled poet	evil godfather

Furthermore, since the Cathars believed that all angels were masculine and even changed the name of Mary to Marinus, we could switch the gender of the ideal and thus explain the term "Milord" used for a woman and the male secret names of many troubadour ladies.[19] On the other hand, because the Cathars took such a degrading attitude toward women, one that goes far beyond that of the early Church Fathers, we will have trouble explaining those parts of Rudel's work that specifically mention female virtues, with female adjectives, no less. A great deal of this correlation works out very well because the dualistic foundation of the religion accounts for the underlying dualism of the poem; the wicked godfather can be called Satan. Still, there are two things which are wrong: first, the tone of the poem is tragic, and the tone of all Catharist writings is as triumphant as those of the Christian mystics; second, this masculinized Mary living in a palatial mansion (most Catharist images of Paradise are homely and simple, like the first people who took up the faith) is not consistently pictured as a goddess or a divine force, as we shall see in some of the other Rudel poems; here, for example, the emphasis is constantly upon *seeing* the woman, being physically in her presence in a way that no Cathar would conceive of as a form of salvation.

Note too that in the sixth stanza Jaufre explicitly says that *God* made all things, whereas the Cathar believes that Satan made all physical things, and that God created only the soul; in fact, the Cathars had great trouble getting a good soul into an evil body in terms of mythology, let alone logic. Similarly, the opposition in this poem is between whatever Rudel believes on the one hand, and what the Jews and the Saracens believe on the other. Going back to Alain de Lille, we can see that the Jews and the Saracens fall into a general catalogue with the Cathars, all of them outsiders, removed from traditional Christian belief. Further, the Cathars did not go on pilgrimages. This "duty" was reserved for the leisured orthodox and privileged rich. Finally, the problem that crops up with any system arises here: the gap between ideals and reality. Rudel's poem works clearly on a realistic level, so clearly, as I have mentioned, that the nineteenth century tended to view it almost totally as a flesh-and-blood romantic drama.

But let us look at another of the six extant Rudel composi-tions to see the scope in his writing. I have selected here the one I believe to be the furthest removed from the rarefied at-mosphere contained in the previous work:[20]

1. When the waters of the fountain
   Sparkle as they're wont to do,
   And out the dogrose blossom peeps
   And the nightingale upon the bough
   Turns and shapes and planes anew
   His song of love, and tunes it too,
   It's right that I should shape my own.

2. O love of a far-away land,
   For you my whole heart is paining me;
   And I can't find any medicine
   Unless I hear your special call
   With its lure of sweet, sweet love
   In a bower or under some covers
   Alone with my desired companion.

3. Since every day I miss my ease,
   No wonder if I'm full of flame,
   For never did nobler Christian girl
   Live—nor ever shall God will it—
   Nor any Jewess, nor Saracen.
   He'll be well repaid with some manna
   Who gets a little piece of her love.

4. My heart knows no end to yearning
   For that thing that I love the most,
   And I fear that this will may cheat me
   If lust should try to snatch her,
   For it's more prickly than a thorn,
   This grief that heals itself with joy:
   Never should anyone blame me for it!

5. Without any letter of parchment
   I forward this verse that we sing
   In a plain old Romance tongue
   To Sir Hugo Brun through Sonny [Filhol],
   And I'm glad that the folks of Poitou
   And those of Berry and Guyenne
   Rejoice for him, as does Brittany.

Here, suddenly, the mist vanishes. Here is a simple love song in which the tropes of Jaufre's contemporaries appear; one remembers how the writer of the vida accuses Jaufre of using "poor words" set to pretty tunes. The sickness in the second strophe is the malaise already encountered in Duke William's work, along with the similar bower and bed.[21] The manna in the third strophe is a play upon Marcabrun's heavenly food.[22] As the poet himself apostrophizes, this song was composed in a "plain old Romance tongue" (*plana lengua romana*), almost as if he himself were tired of the twelfth-century critics who plagued him with complaints of obscurity. In fact, the playful description of the fire in the third strophe is about as close as Jaufre ever comes to true humor. Compared to Duke William and the "moral" Marcabrun, he is somewhat poker-faced. However, even in an uncomplicated song such as this, he mentions his far-off love. The Provensal phrase *amors de terra lonhdana* is ambiguous, meaning either "love of a far-off land" (objective) or "love from a far-off land" (adjectival). In either case, must one conclude that the far-off land is the Holy Land? Note that the frame of reference established at the close of the poem is quite immediate, embracing Poitou, Berry, and Brittany. Only the mention of Jewish and Arabic girls, who are used for contrasts of the broadest kind, suggests a wider frame of reference. Yet one will not quibble to restrict the range to France here, since actually the scope of Jaufre's poetry extends beyond Arabia and the Holy Land into heaven.

The Christian side of Rudel's rhetoric is as inescapable as his phrase "God who made all that comes and goes." A critic trying to prove a Catharist thesis would not only have to account for every image in terms of the heresy, but would also have to prove that a kiss in Rudel is not a romantic kiss or a kiss from Christ: "O that you would kiss me with the kisses of your mouth!"[23] He would have to prove that the "consolation" or "solace" mentioned in troubadour poems derives from that rite of laying on the hands, rather than from a real embrace or, in theological-philosophical terms, from a Boethian consolation of philosophy or St. Bernard's imprecation to "Learn through this word from me to hope for a double help from above in spiritual exercise: a sudden seizing away and consolation."[24] In short, such a critic would have to do the impossible: deny the easy correlation of Christian symbolism with troubadour rhetoric, and at the same time prove that a religion preaching the abnegation of the flesh and the denigration of women fathered a poetic tradition celebrating the joys of the flesh and containing the praise of womanly beauty.

This earthly side of the rhetoric can be seen very clearly in one of Jaufre's most famous poems:[25]

1. I have a lot of singing-masters
   Around me, and female ones too:
   Fields and flowers, trees and bowers,
   Songs and lays and cries of birds,
   Thanks to the sweet and gentle season,
   Yet I stand with just a bit of joy
   For there's no pleasure that can cheer me
   Except the solace of a mighty love.

2. Let the shepherds have their pipes
   And the children their little rhymes,

But I'll take that special kind of love
That makes me rejoice for joy!
For I know it's good in every way
Toward a friend who's ill beset.
And so too often I feel I'm lost
For I don't have what my heart awaits.

3. Far is the castle, far the tower,
Where she lies—her husband too—
And if by some clever counselors
I'm not advanced in counsel wise—
For other advice does little good
Since my fine yearning springs from heart—
Then I'll have nothing left but death—
Unless I get some joy right soon.

4. All her neighbors I hail as lords
In that realm where this joy was bred,
And I think it would be a great honor
To be one there, for the lowest serf
Can call himself a loyal courtier;
Toward the love enclosed in my heart
I have good feeling, good thoughts too,
And I know she's aware of these.

5. My heart [cors] is there so completely
That it has neither top nor root;
And my spirit's there with her too,
Sleeping beneath her covers;
But this love of mine bounds back ill,
For I love her much: she doesn't care.
Soon I'll see if my suffering brings
Me some share of good enjoyment.

6. My will sets out upon the course
In night and in the light of day,
Over there for some hope of help;
But later it comes back and tells me:
" 'Friend,' says she, 'the jealous ones
Have raised up such a commotion
That it would be hard to slip away
So that we could enjoy each other some.' "

7. And so my discomfort grows and grows,
   For I don't possess her in a place of ease;
   Yet tears and sighs don't cause such grief
   That one little kiss (and nothing more!)
   Couldn't restore the heart hale and safe.
   Good is my love; much good it's worth,
   And for this evil I know a cure
   Without the probe of a wise old doctor.

Although there is a separation of body and soul in the fifth stanza, one could hardly label the terms Catharistic. This is the love mania mentioned centuries earlier by Plato, hymned by classical poets, and now revived in medieval song.[26] The poem moves in the easy, familiar atmosphere of castle beds and jealous husbands and budding orchards. Only the most single-minded allegorizer would want to convert the kiss in the last strophe into a Cathar ritual. Yet despite the social nature of the rhetoric, even the fourth stanza about lords and servants has the overtone that dominates most of Jaufre's other poems.

As Leo Spitzer showed in his seminal monograph on the poet, the mystical side of Jaufre cannot be denied.[27] It occurs most strikingly in one of those riddle poems which Duke William originated and Jaufre continued:[28]

1. He can't sing who can't make tunes;
   He can't write verse who can't work words,
   And he doesn't fathom the ways of rhyme
   If he can't encompass the sense itself.
   But my song starts like this:
   The more you hear it, the more it'll mean:
   Ah, ah!

2. Nobody should wonder about me
   If I love a thing that will never see me,
   For my heart never found any other joy
   Except in that one I've never seen,
   And for no joy does it laugh so much,
   And I don't know what good will come,
   Ah, ah!

3. Blows of joy strike me, they kill—
   And the prick of love starts stripping off
   My flesh, so my body's soon all bones;
   Never was I so gravely stricken,
   And for no other blow have I languished so,
   For it's no comfort, nor fitting either—
   Ah, ah!

4. Never did I sink sweetly to sleep
   But that my spirit wasn't quickly there;
   Never did my heart feel such wrath here
   But it soon found itself again back there;
   And when I wake up in the morning,
   All my good knowledge [sabers] deserts me,
   Ah, ah!

5. I know I never found joy in her
   And never will she be rejoicing for me,
   Nor ever consider me her friend;
   Nor will she make me a pact to herself;
   She never told me truth, nor lies,
   And I don't know if she'll ever do it:
   Ah, ah!

6. Good is the verse—I never once failed—
   And everything here stands in its place,
   And he who wants to learn from me
   Should guard against jostling, breaking it,
   For this way they'll get it in Quercy,
   Sir Bertran and the Toulousain Count:
   Ah, ah!

7. Good is the verse—and there they'll do
   Something about which a man can sing,
   Ah, ah!

Here we have what might be called a specimen of secular mysticism, expounding the joys of the invisible. In fact, the contrast of this with "In May when the days are long" is unavoidable. In that work, the emphasis lies upon attending the lady, upon standing before her; here, the lady seems to evaporate totally.

This spirit of competing contradictions operating in a world of imponderables is best expressed in the Middle Ages in a series of riddle dialogues, one of the finest of which is the *Disputation of Pippin with Albinus (Alcuin)*.[29] The exchange of the young son of Charlemagne and his teacher runs as follows:

2. Pippin: What is a word?
   Albinus: A betrayer of the spirit.

3. P: Who produces words?
   A: The tongue.

4. P: What is the tongue?
   A: A scourge of the air.

5. P: What is air?
   A: The guardian of life.

6. P: What is life?
   A: Joy for the blessed, sadness for the wretched, the expectation of death.

7. P: What is death?
   A: An inevitable event, an uncertain pilgrimage, tears for the living, the establishment of one's will, the thief of man.

8. P: What is man?
   A: The servant of death, a transient traveler, a guest of space.

9. P: What is man like?
   A: An apple.

10. P: How is he situated?
    A: Like a lantern in the wind.

11. P: Where is he placed?
    A: Within six walls.

12. P: What are they?
    A: Up, down, before, behind, right, left.

Perhaps the seminal exchange is: 85. P: What is faith? A: The certainty of an unknown and miraculous thing.

This literature of the enigma expresses both the mystery of

a world without the stabilizing presence of God (Augustine's "I became to myself a great question", *Conf.* 4.4) and the natural world seen through the dark glass of Christian Neoplatonic mysticism, with its insistence upon the contemptibility of physical phenomena. Certainly this system supplies a structure that comes closest to accounting for Jaufre's rhetoric:

Beauty or Love	soul seeking perfection	Adam
far-off love	earthbound poet	godfather

Jaufre is surely as close to St. Bernard in mode and spirit as in time and place when the wise man of Clairvaux said of the Christian soul in his commentary on the Song of Songs:[30]

> We are driven on, beset by our temptations and our trials; we rush forward, visited by our inner consolations and inspirations, as if we were breathing in sweet-smelling unguents. And so what seems harsh and severe I hold back for myself, as if I were strong, healthy, and perfect, and I say only, "Draw me forward. . . ." O bridegroom, snatch me away, work upon me, try me, drag me after you; because I am ready for the scourge, and am strong to sustain it.

Yet there is naturally a gap between the two writers, the same breach that exists between religious and secular thought. The primary difference is that Christ or Mary always responds to the Christian servant of love kneeling in adoration; the dark lady of Jaufre's poetry remains cold, distant, aloof. Yet it would be a mistake to align her with Manicheanism or Catharism, for the heretic's Christ responds to his faithful worshiper:[31]

> For the people of God departed long ago from God their Lord; and departed from His counsel and from the will of that Holy Father, because of the deception and the undermining of the evil spirits. And for this reason . . . the Holy Father would like to bestow mercy upon His people and receive them in peace and in His concord, through the intervention of His son, Jesus Christ.

But the alienation of a Christian from a far-off source of perfection was also stated in poignant, dramatic terms by St. Bernard:[32]

Alas, poor me! living far off [*longe*] and calling out from
far away [*de longe;* like Rudel's *de lonh*]; behold, the remem-
brance of it provokes me to tears.

And similarly he expressed the hope of fruition:[33]

We expect from far-off [*porro*] the fruit of our love, which
He Himself, whom we love, promised us, saying: "good
measure, pressed down, shaken together, running over, will
be put into your lap."

The ends, then, ultimately determine the differences between
lyric poetry and philosophy or theology. St. Bernard leads us
to a divine comedy; Jaufre, to a personal tragedy. The writer
of Rudel's vida was sensitive at least in this respect.

In the last analysis, if one is trying to graph Jaufre's poetry,
he must fail. The range is simply too wide. At times the overtone is clearly metaphysical; at other times, it is realistic. Even
standard Christian allegorizers have something of a point because
in one of Jaufre's poems where he mentions the Second Crusade,
the Holy Land or the Virgin Mary seems to merge with his
lady, Good Reward:[34]

1. When the nightingale upon the branch
   Pleads for and takes his gift of love
   And joyously swells out his song of joy
   And looks and looks again at his mate,
   And brooks are clear and fields are fair
   Because of the new vigor reigning,
   A great joy comes to claim my heart.

2. I'm desirous of having a friendship
   For I know there's no jewel greater,
   And I yearn and pray that she'll be good
   If she makes me a gift of her love,
   For she has a body plump [*gras*], gentle, fine,
   Without a thing to mar it,
   And good loving with fine, good savor [*saber*].

3. About this love I'm anxious,
   Wakeful and then asleep in dreams,

For there I have my miraculous joy
By which I rejoice and give joy too;
But all of her beauty doesn't help a bit,
For no friend's here to teach me
How to get that fine, good savor.

4. About this love I'm so worried
That when I start rushing toward her,
It seems to me suddenly I'm turned around
And she is fleeing the other way;
And my horse jogs along so slowly
Scarcely could I ever grasp it,
If Love doesn't make her stay for me.

5. Love, most willingly now I leave you
For away I go to seek my better,
And my outcome's already so good
That now my heart's all full of joy,
Thanks to my lady Good Reward
Who wants me, calls me, makes me hers,
And has turned me back to good hope.

6. And he who remains here in luxury
And doesn't seek God in Bethlehem,
I don't know how he'll ever be brave
Or how he'll come to good healing;
For I know and I believe with right
That he whom Jesus teaches
Can keep his schooling secure.

The change in the fifth strophe from the paradoxical love of a
woman to the espousal of the crusade and the Good Reward is
clearly Christian and shows the two spheres joining neatly.
However, the fact that they have to come together to join
also attests to their separation. Here the name Good Reward
sounds more like an epithet of the Virgin than the secret name
of a lady. We know from a poem written by Marcabrun that
Jaufre Rudel did go overseas, did in fact answer the call to the
crusade sent out by the Gascon moralist:[35]

The verse and sound I'd like to send
To Lord Jaufre Rudel overseas,

And I want the Franks to hear it
To make their spirits glad,
For the good Lord will grant them
Either wicked deeds or merits.

It is interesting to note this connection between these two poets,
who were temperamentally and tonally so unlike: the bonds are
French politics, morality, and the love of God.

When we compare the rhetoric of Jaufre Rudel and St.
Bernard, however, we always return to the question of the self.
The Provensal poet, except when gripped with the fervent
desire to go on crusade, is basically mournful and pessimistic.
Despite this earthbound condition, Jaufre constantly keeps
striving for higher ideals. These ecstatic flights, more clearly
pronounced in him than in any other troubadour, show him as
a forerunner of Dante.[36] Jaufre's poetry suggests the framework
of *The Divine Comedy*. Unlike Dante, however, the Provensal
poet left only a few scattered works, brilliant fragments from
an elusive mosaic. And although Jaufre's work suggests orthodox
Christianity, as well as Neoplatonism and Albigensianism, ultimately he escapes all of the ideological tabs that we would like
to pin upon him. Yet is it not precisely this elusiveness, this con-
tinuing sense of mystery, that constitutes his greatness?

4

BERNART
DE VENTADORN
The Master Singer

In every movement of poetry, one figure usually emerges to embody the finest qualities of the group. Such a man was Bernart de Ventadorn (c. 1140–c. 1180). Although he was obviously heralded in his own day, Bernart has reached the pinnacle of acclaim only within the twentieth century. In the France of the twelfth century, so Dante informs us, Guiraut de Bornelh was usually reckoned the master singer; Dante himself chose Arnaut Daniel as his favorite.[1] Yet to the taste of most modern critics, Guiraut is dull and labored, representing the age only in the sense that he repeats with a kind of dreary consistency all of the basic tropes. Arnaut Daniel, exciting as he was to Ezra Pound and to those other poets who could read him, remains a kind of literary curio, a virtuoso lonely in his eccentricities, with a slight suggestion of pompous sham to color his magnificent forays into the far frontiers of sound.

Bernart wins the laurel of master singer because the poet of Ventadorn walked a mean. He never indulged in the intentionally obscurantist techniques (*trobar clus*) of his contemporaries; nor did he run through the forms and modes of composition, by his day well established, as if they were so many exercises to be neatly circumscribed and laid away in a chest (*trobar leu* or *pla*)[2]. Bernart is lively; he has one of the best senses of humor in medieval literature. Furthermore, he is diversified: his stanzas constantly surprise with their sudden, sometimes illogical shifts of tone that keep the reader's wits on edge. He has the same kind of brittle, inexhaustible melodic quality that crackles in Mozart's sonatas.

In fact Bernart's poetic line seems at times to flow so clearly, so effortlessly, that he has been nicknamed "the Racine of the troubadours." Yet that phrase somehow rings false, for although Bernart's grammar is lucid, and his stanzas are organized coherently, his thought follows the rather helter-skelter pattern of the somewhat crazed, moon-bewitched lover. His verses abound with paradoxes and apparent contradictions. At one point, he berates his lady for not granting him everything that he asked for; and the next moment he admits that he has never revealed his love for her. This mania, long ago pointed out by Plato, is typical of the love poetry of any age, and it is one of the most endearing facets of Bernart's work.[3]

Of the man himself, we really know only what we can piece together from the *cansos*, and that is very little. Two biographies circulate for him, and for years these little *vidas* were accepted as authorities for his life. The more famous of the two runs as follows:[4]

> Bernart de Ventadorn came from the Limousin, from the castle of Ventadorn [modern Ventadour]. He was a man of lowly birth, the son of a servant who tended the furnaces, who heated the oven for cooking the bread for the castle of Ventadorn.
>
> And he became a handsome, well-mannered man, and he knew how to compose and sing well, and he was gracious and learned. And the Viscount of Ventadorn, his lord, became very fond of him and his composition and his songs, and did him great honor. And the Viscount of Ventadorn had a wife who was beautiful and gay and young and noble; and she became fond of Lord Bernart and of his songs, and fell in love with him, and he with her, so that he wrote verses and songs for her, about the love that he had for her, and about the great worth of his lady.
>
> Their love lasted a long time before the Viscount, husband of the lady, or the other people realized it. And when the Viscount became aware, he had Bernart removed from him, and he had his wife locked up and guarded. Then he made the lady say goodbye to Lord Bernart, and he made her tell him to go away and stay far from that country.
>
> And he parted, going off to the Duchess of Normandy [Eleanor of Aquitaine], who was young and of great worth, and knew a lot about nobility and honor, and looked with favor on things said in her praise. And she was extremely fond of the verses and songs of Lord Bernart, and so she received him and honored him and feted him and gave him many pleasures. For a long time he remained in the court of the Duchess, and fell in love with her, and the lady loved him too, and Lord Bernart wrote many good songs about it.
>
> But King Henry [II] of England took her for wife, and led her away from Normandy over to England. And Lord Bernart stayed on this side, sad and dismayed.
>
> And then he parted from Normandy and went off to the good Count Raymond [V] of Toulouse, and stayed with him in his court until the Count died. And when the Count was dead, Lord Bernart abandoned the world and composing and singing and the comfort of the age, and he took

himself then to the monastic order at Dalon, and there he
made his end.

And all that I have told you about him was told to me
by the Viscount Ebles of Ventadorn, who is the son of the
Viscountess whom Lord Bernart loved so much.

In some of the manuscripts there is the further rather dubious
information that this vida was written by Uc of Saint Circ.

Unfortunately for those who feel that biography is necessary for interpreting the work of a poet, almost all of the facts
contained herein can be deduced or extracted from statements
in Bernart's work. For example, some of his poems mention his
residence in Ventadorn, and others are addressed to a beautiful
woman who lived in the vicinity of that once lovely, now abandoned castle; these are established facts. Yet it is extremely
doubtful that Bernart's parentage was as humble as is indicated
here, because this same information can be found in a scurrilous
satire written by Peire d'Alvernhe, in which the author confesses
at the end that he has been slandering his victims for the sake
of laughs:[5]

And the third is Bernart de Ventadorn,
A hand's breadth less than Guiraut de Bornelh;
His father made an excellent serf,
Bearing his handbow cut from brush,
And his mother warmed up the ovens
And gathered together the twigs.

Even if Bernart did rise from humble origins, his acknowledged
talent enabled him to live among the privileged.

Another group of Bernart's poems mentions the English
King Henry II, and the beautiful Queen's presence can also be
deduced.[6] As a result, the writer of the vida immediately en-
visioned a love affair between Bernart and Eleanor. Since this
imaginary affair had to have an ending, the marriage of Henry
to Eleanor, who had previously married the French King
Louis VII, was used as a convenient finale; yet actually Eleanor
did not become Duchess of Normandy until her marriage to
Henry in 1152. Still, there is good reason to believe that Bernart

knew Eleanor, either after her divorce from Louis VII or before
1173, when, separated from Henry, the great lady is believed to
have conducted a brilliant court in her native Poitiers, perhaps
visited by her clever daughter Marie of Champagne.[7] Bernart
also knew Henry, whom he mentions not unpleasantly in his
poems. In fact, Henry's ascent to the British throne in 1154
from the countship of Anjou and dukedom of Normandy provides us with one of the most important dates in pinpointing
Bernart's poetic activity. The poem beginning "Whenever I see
amid the plain," translated below, leads us to believe that Bernart
lived in England under Henry's benefaction. But the love affair
with Eleanor, embraced by many scholars for sentimental reasons, is, like the affair at Ventadorn, simply conjectural.

Another song mentions the city of Narbonne, where Ermengarde held court, and some poems seem to refer to Raymond V
of Toulouse in warm tones, but nothing concrete can be adduced
about the relationship of Bernart to these historical figures.[8] It
is not even known, for example, which Ebles of Ventadorn was
the first patron of the poet, for Ebles II and Ebles III were both
intimately connected with artistic affairs, and each had a wife
who might well have been friendly with the poet.[9] The only
thing that we can safely say is that Bernart was reared in the
castle of Ventadorn, whence his name, and that this palace and
its cultural activity rivaled Poitiers and the influence of William
IX of Aquitaine in the formation of early Provensal secular
song: Ebles II was nicknamed Ebles the Singer, and the poetic
activity at Ventadorn is referred to by other writers.[10] It is also
safe to assume that Eleanor and other wealthy patrons supported
the poet for a time when he began his peregrinations upon leaving his native place. However, one must not necessarily posit
banishment as the cause for departure. Instead of being forced
to move by a discovered love affair, could the poet not have
begun his journeys out of mere wanderlust or a desire to achieve
a reputation in the world at large, an ambition that still attracts
young poets to Paris, London, San Francisco, and New York?

The most intriguing part of the biography is the mention
of Bernart's final departure from the world to the Cistercian
abbey of Dalon, near Dordogne and his place of birth. Since
nothing in the poetry suggests such a view, except perhaps his
clerical-sounding denunciation of love in his debate poem with
Peire (d'Alvernhe?), this information might not have been

expanded by the biographer.[11] Certainly such an end would not be inconsistent for a poet whose sense of the absurd, even in his most compelling love lyrics, was always threatening to pierce his control of dramatic realism.

To define Bernart's position in the development of the Provensal lyric is not difficult, for he simply assimilated the basic attitudes of his three great predecessors. He has some of the naked frankness of William of Aquitaine, but also shows control and reserve. He shares Jaufre Rudel's sense of the mystical and ethereal, yet he always returns to the ground after his larklike flights. He frequently exhibits some of the misogynism of Marcabrun, even in the midst of a tender love lyric, but he never becomes cantankerous, and his moralizing, whenever it does appear, almost always has something of the comically ineffectual about it.

It is also easy to see Publius Ovidius Naso in Bernart, for the two of them loom behemothlike in the development of world lyric poetry.[12] The Roman poet, living in an age without a universal church with fixed dogma and articles of faith, nevertheless approached love with the encyclopedic attitude of a Thomas Aquinas. Somehow he managed to include all of the basic tropes of death in love, martyrdom, and the attainment of virtue, which are part of the fabric of the Christian religion and which appear again and again in Bernart. Ovid also had a keen sense of wit, so keen that it almost prevents the mist of romance from forming over his pages. The difference between the Roman and the poet of the Limousin is that Ovid, pagan and proud, accepts the material, the sensual, as a given good, whereas Bernart must wrestle somewhat with his conscience and can accept the gift of sex only as the last reward after a great deal of torment and suffering. Still, granted the broad gap between pagan Rome and Christian southern France, it is amazing to see the similarities. For just as Ovid raised his Corinna to the level of a "friend" in his poems (no mean feat, if one considers the attitude toward women shown by the intellectuals in Plato's *Symposium*), Bernart, following Duke William, went a step further in making his girl-friend masculine ("milordess"). If Ovid defended love against the vulgar, material Roman capitalists, Bernart and his fellows seem to have faced down the Church.

So much for comparisons. When we look at a typical poem of Bernart's, we are greatly impressed by the way that it sings:[13]

CAN LA FREJ'AURA VENTA

1. When biting breezes blow
   Out of your demesne,
   It seems to me I feel
   A wind from Paradise
   Because of my love for the noble one
   Toward whom I bow my head,
   To whom I pledge my will
   And direct my emotions;
   From all other ladies I part:
   So much she pleases me.

2. Even if she only gave me
   Her beautiful eyes and noble face,
   And never granted further pleas,
   Still she'd have conquered me.
   Why should I lie about it?
   (For in no way am I sure.)
   Hard it would be to show repentance
   After that time she told me
   That a good man gathers his strength
   While a bad one crouches scared.

3. The ladies, it seems to me,
   Are making a big mistake
   Because in no way at all
   Do they love their sincere lovers.
   I know that I shouldn't accuse them,
   Should say what they want to hear,
   But it pains me when a cheater gets
   Some loving out of sleight of hand,
   Or even more or just the same
   As a fine, true, noble lover.

4. Lady, what are you trying to do
   To me who love you so?
   For you see how I'm suffering
   And how I'm dying of desire.
   Ah! noble woman, debonair,
   Give me a pleasant look,

One to lighten up this heart,
For I'm racked with many woes
And I shouldn't have to pay the price
Just because I can't break free.

5. If it wasn't for evil people
And savage smooth-tongued spies,
My love would be guaranteed to me,
But instead I'm tugged back.
She is human to me in her comfort
When time and place are right,
And I know that underhandedly
I'll get a lot, lot more,
For the blessed man sleeps in peace,
And the unlucky one in pain.

6. I'm a man who never scorns
The good that God creates for him:
For in that selfsame week
When I parted from her side,
She told me in clear, plain terms
That my singing pleases her much.
I wish every Christian soul
Could have such joy
That I had then and have:
It's the *only* thing to brag of.

7. And if she guarantees me this,
Another time I'll believe her;
If not, never will I believe
Another Christian lady.

This poem exhibits as completely as any the range of sensibility in the Provensal lyric. In the first eight verses the woman looms as a goddess, equated through the simile with the Virgin (but not identical to Mary, since only similarity is implied). The poet's reaction to her is one of adoration. Then, in the second strophe, the lady is treated as a more earthly creature who is capable of bestowing a material good upon her liegeman; her physical features are mentioned, and the abstraction of nobility is rendered incarnate. Yet even here in the sphere of the court, such terminology as "repentance" is primarily religious, just as, conversely, the prayer of the opening stanza appears as a "plea" in the second stanza. These two spheres are so interlocked in the Provensal poem, and indeed in the Provensal language itself, that they are inseparable. The man kneeling before Our Lady in a church and pledging fidelity is raised just slightly above the troubadour bowing his head before his own special lady and assuring her of his fealty. Because Provensal descends from Latin, where words had acquired new metaphysical meanings in addition to their original Roman denotations, ambiguity is very much evident. The Provensal word *precs*, for example, means both a prayer uttered to a divinity and an entreaty proffered to a noble person. Words like "grace," "mercy," "adore" have both religious and romantic connotations, just as they do in English; sometimes these two meanings are impossible to separate.

By the third stanza one comes upon still another sphere of reference: the woman as devilish denier. At first Bernart simply lumps his own lady into a large group, thereby stripping her of her particular identity. Instead of being the noble one (of stanza one), she is now simply one among many ladies. This is a severe jolt for lyric poetry, because poets traditionally claim that their own mistresses stand out from the mass, are singularly distinct from the many. In fact, aside from the inherent antifeminism that runs as a subcurrent through the poem, one notes that Bernart, not his lady, gradually emerges as the idealized figure: he is the noble sufferer, clinging to his ideals, willing to undergo the tortures of his unwilling Milordess. Only when one realizes that the poem is constructed around sex do the attitudes and postures become genuinely funny.

The invective aimed at the uncooperative woman becomes directed in the fifth stanza to the rest of the world, especially the hangers-on, the spies who are not admitted to the inner sanctum of the lover, the jealous pretenders who are eager to seize upon the real name of the secret goddess. The tirade breaks off abruptly as Bernart assures himself of the goal before him: conquest of the lady in terms of human comfort (*umana . . . solatz*). Bernart is too refined to refer to the sexual act directly, but an expression like "underhandedly" (*a sotzma*) comes through vividly, as does the picture of the triumphant, even smug, hero-lover sleeping in well-rewarded peace. Meanwhile, the unfortunate of the world, who are those who are not star-blessed, have to undergo a hell-like torment. One thinks of Marcabrun's contrast of High Love and mere animal Loving, and sees how Bernart has shaped the system entirely toward secular ends.

Having pictured his successful conclusion in almost gloating terms, Bernart closes with a burst of praise and a boast. The braggart quality of Provensal verse, the *vanto*, sounds like an adaptation of the epic device. The love game is seen by the troubadours on the one hand as a deadly serious game involving good guys and villains, and on the other hand as pure jest. In the sixth stanza, Bernart not only insists upon joining his lady to God, but even goes so far as to claim that this love is the sole source of satisfaction. Modern readers tend to take such statements too lightly, to ignore the travesty of values current at the time. Yet Bernart is boasting about an adulterous love affair in "clear, plain terms," and this kind of conduct is sacrilegious.

The tornada is sheer whimsy, showing Provensal humor at its best. Almost as if the sixth stanza were too strong, Bernart comes back to say that he will pledge his faith to his lady if she grants him his fun, but he will deny her Christianity if she denies him his reward: in other words, he makes the whole validity of the Christian faith hang upon his success in seduction! Despite the potential seriousness of these travesties, the modern reader, accustomed to hearing human love praised to the skies, is not really shocked. The humor throughout the poem is a constantly warming feature. Still, can we really appreciate the courage of the medieval poet if we do not somehow acknowledge this sometimes playful, sometimes rather malicious manipulation of terms?

Although Provensal poetry has been criticized for being too abstract and unreal, we might very well note that Bernart does not lose touch with the object of his adoration. The woman is very much a part of this poem. Similarly, these songs have been attacked for travestying the tolerant position of the Church with regard to marriage. However, the official position of the Church toward love and marriage cannot encompass the romantic attitude, and hence it is useless to make such a comparison at all. If one is forced to make some comment about Bernart's attitude toward sex, he can certainly say that the poet surrounds it with a world of idealized abstraction, yet never surrenders himself unwittingly to a false world of illusion. The poem ends on a realistic note of awaiting a tangible reward from a very tangible lady; it is not unlike the Song of Songs in this respect.

To run through Bernart's poetry pointing up the interplay of sacred and profane values (the constant shifting of the woman from angelic divinity dispensing grace to a superior earthly lord-lady bestowing favors to a Satanic denier of the "natural" functions of life) would be an extremely tiresome, repetitive process. Instead, I have selected what I consider to be a representative group of some of the most famous poems, and have translated these in such a way as to underscore this dynamic quality of the verse. Too many tomes have been written about the dullness of Provensal verse. It is, in the long run, perhaps best to let the poems speak for themselves.

TANT AI MO COR PLE DE JOYA[14]

1. I have a heart so filled with joy
     Everything changes its nature:
   Flowers white, crimson, and gold
     Seems the frost,
   For with the wind and the rain
     My fortune keeps on growing;
   Ah yes, my worth keeps mounting,
     My song's improving too.
   I have a heart so full of love
     And joy and sweetness,
   That the ice appears to me a flower,
     And the snow lies green.

2. I can go out without my clothes,
     Naked in my shirt,
   For fine, true love will keep me safe
     From wintry blasts.
   But a man's a fool to lose measure
     And not to toe the line,
   And so I've taken special care
     Ever since I fixed on
   The most pretty love who ever lived,
     From whom I expect great honor.
   For in place of the wealth of her
     I'd not take Pisa.

3. She can cut me off from her friendship,
   But I rest secure in my faith
That at least I've carried away
   The beautiful image of her.
And I have for my own devices
   Such a store of happiness
That until the day when I see her,
   I'll feel no anxiousness.
My heart lies close to Love and
   My spirit runs there too,
Though my body's anchored here, alas!
   Far from her, in France.

4. Still I have steady hope from her
   (Which does me little good),
For she holds me as if in a balance
   Like a ship upon the waves,
And I don't know where to hide myself
   From woes besetting my senses.
All night long I toss and I turn
   Heaving upon my mattress:
I suffer greater torment in love
   Than that arch-lover Tristan,
Who underwent so many pains
   To gain Isolde the Blonde.

5. O God! Why am I not a swallow
   Winging through the air,
Coming through the depths of night
   There inside her chamber?
My good, joy-bearing lady,
   Your lover here's expiring.
I'm afraid my heart may melt
   If things go on like this.
Lady, because of your love
   I join my hands and adore:
Beautiful body with healthy hues,
   You make me suffer great woe.

6. There isn't any affair of the world
   That can occupy me more

Than the mere mentioning of her;
   Then my heart leaps high
And light suffuses my face, and
   Whatever you hear me say of it,
It will always appear to you
   That I really want to laugh.
I love that woman with such good love
   That many a time I cry,
And to me my sighs contain
   A better savor.

7. Messenger, go on the run:
   Tell to my pretty one
The pain, O yes the grief
   I bear—and torment.

LO TEMS VAI E VEN E VIRE[15]

1. The seasons come and turn and go
   Through days and months and years,
And I, alas! have nothing to say,
   For my desire is always one.
It's always one; it never changes:
   I want the woman I've always wanted,
The one who never gave me joy.

2. Because she never ceases mocking,
   I'm rewarded grief and loss,
For she made me sit at such a game
   That I've been the loser, two to one;
Yet this kind of love soon is lost
   When only one side maintains it,
Unless somehow a pact is reached.

3. I should stand my own accuser
   Indicting myself with every right,
For never was man of woman born
   Who served so long, yet all in vain.
And if she doesn't punish me for it,
   My folly will keep on doubling still,
For a fool never fears till he's taken.

4. Never again shall I be a singer
   Nor part of that school of Lord Eblés,
   For all my songs aren't worth a jot,
   Nor my voltas, nor my melodies.
   And not a single thing I do
   Or say would seem to work me well:
   No, I see no improvement there.

5. Even though I make show of joy,
   My heart is filled with wrath.
   Who ever displayed such penitence
   Before he even committed a crime?
   The more I beg her, the harder she is,
   But if she doesn't soon relent,
   We'll come to a parting of the ways.

6. And yet it's good that she should bend me
   And make me subject to her will,
   For even if she dallies wrongly,
   Soon, I'm sure, she'll pity me.
   For so declares the Holy Scripture:
   A cause that has a happy outcome
   Makes the day worth a hundred more.

7. Never would I part from my life
   As long as I am safe and sound,
   For after the bran has blown away,
   The straw keeps fluttering a long, long time.
   And even if she isn't hot yet,
   Never would I take her name in vain
   If, from now on, she mends her ways.

8. Ah, my good, my coveted lover,
   Body well-shaped, delicate, smooth,
   Lively features all rosy-hued,
   Which God created with His very hands,
   All this time I've desired you,
   And nothing else has pleased me.
   No other love do I want one bit.

9. Sweet and well-instructed creature,
   May He who formed you grant to me
   The happiness I long for.

CHANTARS NO POT GAIRE VALER[16]

1. A song cannot in any way have value
   If the singing doesn't spring from heart,
   And the singing cannot well from breast
   Unless its source is fine, true love.
   And so my verse looms high,
   For I have joy from love, devoting there
   My mouth and eyes, my heart and mind.

2. Dear God, I pray: never grant the might
   To ward away this rage for love.
   And if I knew I'd never have a thing,
   And every day would bring worse ill,
   Still I'd have my good heart at least;
   For I have much more enjoyment:
   Yes, good heart, and the strength to strive.

3. Foolish folk in their ignorance curse
   The work of love; yet no loss!
   For love is not about to crumble,
   Unless it's that "vulgar" kind;
   For that's not love; it's acting
   With the name, it's sheer pretense;
   There nothing's loved except what's grabbed.

4. And if I wanted to tell the truth,
   I know from whom comes all this deceit:
   From ladies who love for mere possessions,
   Who are nothing but common whores.
   I should be a liar—yes, false,
   But instead I speak the truth shamefaced,
   And I'm worried that I can't tell lies.

5. In mutual pleasure and in common will
   Resides the love of two fine lovers.
   And nothing good will ever come
   If the desire is not an equal thing.
   And he's a natural-born idiot
   Who reproaches love for what it wants
   And asks for a thing that's not quite right.

6. I know I've rightly placed my hope
   Whenever she shows me a cheerful face,
   The one I desire, want most to see,
   That noble, sweet, true, faithful one
   By whom a king would be saved;
   The lovely, gracious, perfectly shaped
   Who raised me from nothing into wealth.

7. I've nothing dearer, fear no one more,
   And there's no task that's burdensome to me
   If it should please my lady-master.
   That day will seem like Christmastime
   When she gives me one sure look
   With those beautiful, those spiritual eyes—
   So slow, that day will last a century.

8. The verse is polished; it's natural too,
   And good for the man who gets it all,
   And better for him who expects his fun.

9. Bernart de Ventadorn has made the plan;
   He spoke and made it; he expects his fun.

LO GENS TEMS DE PASCOR[17]

1. The sweet season of rebirth
   With its freshening green
   Draws for us flower and leaflet
   With many a different hue;
   And therefore every lover
   Is gay and full of song—
   But me, I cry and clamor
   Without a taste of joy.

2. To all I lament, good men,
   About Milordess and Love,
   For I placed my faith in them—
   Those ever treacherous two—
   And they've turned my life to grief;
   And the good and all the honor
   I have rendered to the fairest
   Counts for nothing, gives no aid.

3. Pain and grief and damage
   I've had, and I have a lot;
   And yet I've borne it all.
   And I don't even think they're harsh,
   For you've never seen any other lover
   Offer better without deceit:
   No, I don't go around changing
   The way those women do.

4. Since we both were children,
   I have loved her, courted her well,
   And my joy goes ever doubling
   Through each day of every year.
   And if she doesn't offer me
   A welcome-look and her love,
   Then when she's aging, let her beg
   Me to offer my desire then!

5. Woe's me! What good is living
   If I can't see day by day
   My fine, true, natural joy
   In her bed, stretched under a window,
   Body pure white head to toe
   Like the snow at Christmastide,
   So that we two lying together
   Can measure each other's sides?!

6. Never was loyal lover seen
   Who enjoyed a worse reward;
   For I love her with sincere love,
   And she says: "What do I care?"
   In fact, she says that's why
   She shows me her deadly rage,
   And if she hates me for this cause,
   Then *she's* guilty of a mortal sin.

7. Surely there'll some day be a time,
   My lady beautiful and good,
   When you can pass me secretly
   The sweet reward of a little kiss:
   Give it only on the grounds

That I am taken with desire.
One good is worth two others
If the others are gained by force.

8. When I behold your features,
Those gorgeous eyes full of love,
I can't help wondering to myself
How you can answer me so vilely.
And I consider it high treason
When a person seems honest and pure
And turns out puffed with pride
In places where he is strong.

9. Pretty Face, if my above-all
Didn't stem from you alone,
I'd long ago have left my songs
Through the ill of the evil ones.

LANCAN VEI PER MEI LA LANDA[18]

1. Whenever I see amid the plain
The leaves are drifting down from trees
Before the cold's expansion,
And the gentle time's in hiding,
It's good for my song to be heard,
For I've held back more than two years
And it's right to make amends.

2. It's hard for me to serve that woman
Who shows me only her haughty side,
For if my heart dares make a plea,
She won't reply with a single word.
Truly this fool desire is killing me:
I follow the lovely form of Love,
Not seeing Love won't attend me.

3. She's mastered cheating, trickery,
So that always I think she loves me.
Ah, sweetly she deceives me,
As her pretty face confounds me!
Lady, you're gaining absolutely nothing:

In fact, I'm sure it's toward your loss
That you treat your man so badly.

4. God, Who nurtures all the world,
Put it in her heart to take me,
For I don't want to eat any food
And of nothing good I have plenty.
Toward the beautiful one, I'm humble,
And I render her rightful homage:
She can keep me, she can sell me.

5. Evil she is if she doesn't call me
To come where she undresses alone
So that I can wait at her bidding
Beside the bed, along the edge,
Where I can pull off her close-fitting shoes
Down on my knees, my head bent down:
If only she'll offer me her foot.

6. This verse has been filled to the brim
Without a single word that will tumble,
Beyond the land of the Normans,
Here across the wild, deep sea.
[Apparently England.]
And though I'm kept far from Milordess,
She draws me toward her like a magnet:
God, keep that beauty ever safe!

7. If the English king and the Norman duke
Will it, I'll see her soon
Before the winter overtakes us.

8. For the king I remain an English-Norman,
And if there were no Lady Magnet,
I'd stay here till after Christmas.

AMORS, E QUE.US ES VEJAIRE?[19]

1. Love, how does it seem to you?
Ever find a bigger fool than I?
Think that I'll always be a lover,
Yet never find a drop of grace?

Order me do whatever you will.
It's done; it's right for me.
But you! where O where's the good
In always working me some wrong?

2. I love the woman of fairest air
In all the world, none better;
But she doesn't care a jot,
And I don't know how it's happened.
Just when I think I'm breaking free,
I can't! Love's got me fast.
I'm betrayed because of my good faith.
Love! Surely I can accuse you of that!

3. And so I'll have to wrestle with Love
Since I can't seem to break away.
He's let me know I'm in a hold
Where I'll never have any hope of joy.
Far better perhaps to hang myself,
For having had the heart and nerve,
And yet I haven't got the strength
To ward away the work of Love.

4. Yet Love knows how to descend
Wherever he most wants to go,
And he knows how to grant good rewards
For his torments and his pain.
But so poorly can he buy and sell me
That he's no longer any good for me,
Unless milady should deign to see me
And listen to my words.

5. What a bother! O, what trouble
Every day begging for some grace,
But the love that's pent up inside me
I can't cover, I can't hide.
Woe's me! No sleep nor even pause,
And I can't even stand in one place,
And I know I can't keep on going
If the pain doesn't soon abate.

6. I know the reason, the cause,
   And can prove it to Milord:
   No man could, nor ever dared
   Enter the lists against Lord Love,
   For "Love conquers all"*
   And forces me to adore her;
   And he could do the same to her
   In just one little moment.

7. Lady, no one can say a single word
   About the good heart and pure desire
   I have when I consider them,
   For I never loved anything so much.
   Already a year ago my sighs
   Would have murdered me, my lady,
   If it wasn't for that gorgeous sight
   That started my desires doubling.

8. Lady, you only scoff and laugh
   Whenever I ask you for anything,
   But if you learned to love enough,
   You'd certainly talk a different line.

9. Nimblefoot (Alegret), learn to sing my song;
   And you, my trusty Iron-Heart (Ferran),
   Carry it for me to my Tristan,†
   Who knows well how to scoff and laugh.

CAN L'ERBA FRESCH'E.LH FOLHA PAR[20]

1. When grasses fresh and leaflets sprout
   And the flower blossoms on the bough,
   And the nightingale high-pitched and clear
   Lifts his voice and moves his song,
   I've joy from him and joy from the flower,
   And joy from me and more from Milord;
   From everywhere I'm circled round with joy,
   And this is a joy that overcomes the rest.

---

* Quotation from Vergil not so emphasized in the text, but it was almost a medieval cliché.

† Apparently the lady's name, masculinized to accord with "Milord."

2. Alas! and yet I'm dying of worry!
   So often I stand in grievous thought
    That thieves could carry me away
    And I'd never know what happened.
By god, Love, you've found me your prey,
With too few friends and no other lord.
Why didn't you upset Milordess once
Before I was stricken with this desire?

3. I wonder how I can carry on
   Without showing her my yearning.
    For when I see her, just a glance,
    Those eyes of hers so beauty-filled,
Scarcely can I stop from running toward her.
Yes, that I'd do, were it not for fear,
For never was body better painted or cut,
And yet so cruelly slow for the task of love.

4. I love Milordess and hold her dear,
   I respect her and I give her praise,
    So much that I dared not speak to her,
    Not beg a thing, not even demand.
And yet she knows my ill and my grief;
And when she wants, she can yield me honor,
And when she wants, I'm content with less
So that she will never suffer blasphemy.

5. If I knew how to bewitch people,
   My enemies I'd turn into babes,
    So that they could never trap us
    Or say a word to turn to damns.
And then I know I'd see my pretty one,
Those lovely eyes, her lively hue—
I'd kiss that mouth in every way
So that the marks would last a month!

6. Yes, I'd like to find her alone,
   Asleep or just pretending,
    So that I could steal one sweet kiss
    (I'm not worth enough to openly beg).
By God, lady, we accomplish little in love!

Time's going by; we're losing the very best part.
We'd better talk with some secret signs:
If nerve won't help, then maybe cunning will!

7. It's right a man should blame a lady
   Who keeps putting her good friend off:
   A long sermon on the subject of love
   Is just a big bore, and a cheap trick too,
For a man can love and make a pretense,
And sweetly lie with no witness around.
My good lady, if only you'd grant me your love,
Never would I be troubled again by lies.

8. Messenger, run, and please don't prize me less
   If I'm afraid to rush there to Milordess.

5

THE COUNTESS OF DIA, OFTEN CALLED BEATRITZ

"The Sappho of the Rhone"

We are predisposed to like the Countess of Dia because of her position in history. She is not the only female troubadour, for we have bits of the work of Azalais of Porcairagues, Maria of Ventadorn, Lombarda, and the Countess Garsenda of Provence, among others.[1] But she is clearly one of the few poetesses between Sappho and, say, Emily Dickinson who sang in measures that are comparable with the best work of the men of her day.

Actually very little is known about the Countess, except, as her name indicates, that she was of noble standing and had some connection with the charming town that is now called Die, lying about 67 kilometers southeast of Valence in the valley of the Drôme, a tributary of the Rhone. In the manuscripts her poems are headed only by her title, not by the name Beatritz. In fact, it has even been suggested that the rubric heading "Comtesa de Dia" was meant to be taken in a general sense: "a certain countess from Dia."[2]

Her vida says simply: "The Countess of Dia was the wife of Lord William of Peitieus, a beautiful and good woman. And she fell in love with Lord Raimbaut of Orange and wrote of him many good songs."[3] The information about William of Peitieus is more troublesome than illuminating; the place name seems to refer to Mount Peytieux (Peiteu) near Die, where a castle stands in ruins. The traditional identification, asserted by a popular French reference work in an unqualified manner, runs as follows: Beatrice, Countess of Die, was the daughter of Guigue VI, Dauphin of Viennois; she married William I, Count of Valentinois (1158–1189) in the vicinity of Valence; it goes on to mention the love affair with Raimbaut III of Orange in authoritative terms.[4] This traditional identification of the Countess' ancestry is boldly taken, for the Beatritz rather sketchily identified was not the Countess of Dia, and even her son Aimar would not have held the countship; furthermore, the amatory details, here as elsewhere in the biographies, are suspect.

One would like to identify this Countess with Raimbaut, since the city of Orange lies close to Die, and both poets flourished in the latter half of the twelfth century. Furthermore, the somewhat dark, brooding portrait that we get of Raimbaut, an arrogant exponent of poetic obscurantism (*trobar clus*) who wasted most of his patrimony in gambling and riotous living, accords perfectly with the handsome, noble, unresponsive lover to whom the Countess addresses her work. However, Walter T. Pattison, who has published an excellent edition of the works of Raimbaut III, suggests a linking of the *trobairitz* with a descendant of Raimbaut's brother William, Raimbaut IV of Orange.[5] If this younger Raimbaut was the Countess' lover (and he himself was a man with strong artistic interests), then the poetess would have lived closer to the end of the twelfth century than to the middle. Yet, after suggesting five different identifications for William of Poitiers (Peitieus), Pattison concludes that the love affair is probably fictional. He reconstructs the linking of the Countess with Raimbaut as follows: A famous debate poem attributed in the manuscripts to Raimbaut contains a dialogue between a Friend and a Lady; since the Countess was the most famous troubadouress, the biographers seized upon her as the female voice. Nowhere in Raimbaut's work is a Beatritz or a Countess of Dia mentioned. Pattison insists upon the possibility that Raimbaut III wrote the entire poem, since feigned tensos crop up in the work of Guiraut de Bornelh, Raimbaut de Vaqueiras, and the Monk of Montaudon, among others.

The poem itself shows how tenuous any identifications must be, for the dialogue takes place in the anonymous half-light of romance:[6]

1. Friend, I stand in great distress
   Because of you, and in great pain;
   And I think you don't care one bit
   About the ills that I'm enduring;
   And so, why set yourself as my lover
   Since to me you bequeath all the woe?
   Why can't we share it equally?

2. Lady, love goes about his job
   As he chains two friends together
   So the ills they have and the lightness too
   Are felt by each—in his fashion.
   And I think—and I'm no gabber—
   That all this deepdown, heartstruck woe
   I have in full on my side too.

3. Friend, if you had just one fourth
   Of this aching that afflicts me now,
   I'm sure you'd see my burden of pain;
   But little you care about my grief,

Since you know I can't break free;
But to you it's all the same
Whether good or bad possess me.

4. Lady, because these glozing spies,
Who have robbed me of my sense and breath,
Are our most vicious warriors,
I'm stopping: not because desire dwindles.
No, I can't be near, for their vicious brays
Have hedged us in for a deadly game.
And we can't sport through frolicsome days.

5. Friend, I offer you no thanks
Because my damnation is not the bit
That checks those visits I yearn for so.
And if you set yourself as watchman
Against my slander without my request,
Then I'll have to think you're more "true-blue"
Than those loyal Knights of the Hospital.

6. Lady, my fear is most extreme
(I'll lose your gold, and you mere sand)
If through the talk of these scandalmongers
Our love will turn itself to naught.
And so I've got to stay on guard
More than you—by St. Martial I swear!—
For you're the thing that matters most.

7. Friend, I know you're changeable
In the way you handle your love,
And I think that as a chevalier
You're one of that shifting kind;
And I'm justified in blaming you,
For I'm sure other things are on your mind,
Since I'm no longer the thought that's there.

8. Lady, I'll never carry again
My falcon, never hunt with a hawk,
If, now that you've given me joy entire,
I started chasing another girl.
No, I'm not that kind of shyster:

It's envy makes those two-faced talk.
They make up tales and paint me vile.

9. Friend, should I accept your word
So that I can hold you forever true?

10. Lady, from now on you'll have me true,
For I'll never think of another.

The poem is interesting for the way in which the lady pursues her point to the end, brushing away the man's rationaliza-
tions and extracting a pledge of loyalty. The fact that intimate
possession is clearly implied as an end in the affair shows the
realistic side of the work. If we had only the man's dialogue, we
would have just another insistence upon the fine, true, noble
love of the poet. Instead, the woman's voice cuts through the
poetic artifice, chiding the man for his cowardice and duplicity,
forcing him eventually to utter the words that she wishes to
hear. Here we have no pallid heroine of romance.

The opening line of this poem is very much like the opening line of the Countess' *Estat ai en greu cossirier*. Furthermore,
the moods of the two poems are similar, and the frank insistence
of the woman upon the sensual side of love is apparent in both:[7]

1. I've suffered great distress
From a knight whom I once owned.
Now, for all time, be it known:
I loved him—yes, to excess.
His jilting I've regretted,
Yet his love I never really returned.
Now for my sin [*error*] I can only burn:
Dressed, or in my bed.

2. O, if I had that knight to caress
Naked all night in my arms,
He'd be ravished by the charm
Of using, for cushion, my breast.
His love I more deeply prize
Than Floris did Blancheflor's.
Take that love, my core,
My sense, my life, my eyes!

3. Lovely lover, gracious, kind,

When will I overcome your fight?
O, if I could lie with you one night!
Feel those loving lips on mine!
  Listen, one thing sets me afire:
Here in my husband's place I want *you*,
If you'll just keep your promise true:
  Give me everything I desire.

It is easy to see how a Provensal vida writer could match the woman of Raimbaut's dialogue with the Countess. What this lyric adds to the store of Provensal literature is a direct, fiery kind of poetry that is surprisingly lacking in most of the songs written by men. One would expect, after reading the masculine poetry, that the ladies were far too refined to mention sleeping naked in beds or devouring their lovers. One might also expect that the adulterous situation would force the woman into a quiet, submissive role; one might even doubt that a woman would have written anything at all. Yet here we have quite the contrary; in fact, the Countess openly mentions her husband in rather unpleasant terms in the third stanza. We may well wonder how the husband of the poetess felt about this admission. Or are we being too literal-minded? The poem is, after all, a poetic monologue with a persona. We have to make that distinction between poet and fictional character that crops up again with Chaucer as pilgrim and Dante as universal traveler. Perhaps the Count was amused by the way his wife portrayed a love-starved woman; perhaps the love mentioned here is as illusory as that of Floris and Blancheflor, those archetypal figures of romance.

Yet we should not feel that this fictional quality damages the poetry in any way. Too many critics have spoken almost matter-of-factly of the Countess' sincerity.[8] Aside from the current low repute of the "doctrine of sincerity" in evaluating literary works, we must acknowledge that dramatic realism is not actual frankness. Is Hamlet sincere? We should read the Countess' poems with the same kind of detachment that we use in reading Robert Browning's monologues. In fact, the notion of sincerity, with its emphasis upon the poetess' personal life, provides a barrier to her work. Since an examination of historical records unearths nothing about the *trobairitz*, we should forget what her age did not want us to know and admire what she has actually left us.

The poem is strikingly dramatic, rivaling William of Aquitaine at his most intense moments. Here, we feel, is a woman who could have faced the lordly duke down. Instead of the swooning lady out of Sir Walter Scott's romances, we have a woman who resembles the Wife of Bath in her unblushing attitude toward sex. Furthermore, although the basic situation of a jilting lover, a jealous husband, and a love-distraught writer are fixtures in the Ovidian scheme, we feel the substance of the medieval world around us. We get more than what one gets from an Ovidian poem, where the laughter often drives away the spell, and the theme is sometimes lost for the sake of ingenious embellishment. This poetry is tight, concise, and directed toward a given point: the pledge extracted from the man. The additional note of seriousness shows us that we are firmly entrenched in the Middle Ages, where pledges of fealty and oaths of fidelity were not taken lightly.

The poem crackles with an inner fire that is often lacking in the works of the Countess' contemporaries. In this sense, and not out of mere historical accident, it is not inappropriate to call the troubadouress "the Sappho of the Rhone," for the Greek poetess had a similar gift for making the intangible lucid and the oft-felt come alive.[9] The fact that Sappho wrote her love poems to women matters very little, since the loved ones in both cases are never described in great detail. The lyric works best with the reader's own imagination about the beloved, and even when one is forced to transpose the sex, the poem, if it has any real life, communicates.

Another canso written by the Countess reminds one of Sappho's bitter outcries against her rivals:[10]

1. Happiness grants me fine, true joy
   And so I sing, more gaily than before,
   With never a thought about despair
   Or any other worrisome care,
   For I know false flatterers and liars
   Are all around me, conspiring.
   Does evil talk make me afraid?
   No, I'm just twice as gay.

2. I don't put my faith in the chatter
   Of any wicked-minded flatterer,

For no honor ever comes to a man
Who takes that two-faced stand!
No, their semblance is the same
As a cloud of wintry rain
That steals the sun's bright ray.
Vile-hearted people, take them away.

3. Jealous ones, keep up your talk.
   I haven't slowed to a walk.
   Joy and youth are still my rage:
   Go on and suffer! Envy! Age!

The female voice, reveling in its harangues against flattering
spies, sounds more effective than the male. Suddenly the same
situation that is sung in poem after poem comes alive, and we
see the endless intrigues of the court, with private names for
lovers and secret meetings in bowers and bedrooms. What is
not provided—historical fact—is unimportant. The situation was
the same on Lesbos as in Ovid's Rome. The lovers are blessed
and pure; the rest, who are jealous and seek to destroy this
sanctitude (especially a husband), are condemned to the hell
of old age, the nightmare end for all those who are concerned
with the pleasures of the senses. Instead of saying that the Countess sounds like Sappho, we should say simply that she is a genuine
creator, one who could form dramatic situations out of stock
material.

The Countess of Dia was every bit as adept at handling a
longer poem as she was at writing shorter songs. Out of the
four works which are attributed to her alone, the following is
the most complex:[11]

1. Now I must sing of what I have no will,
   For greatly am I tried by him I love,
   The one I love above all other things;
   He sees no worth in mercy or in manners;
   My beauty's nothing, like my conduct and my sense,
   For he deceives and cheats me as if I
   Were nothing more than just a homely wretch.

2. And yet I've comfort, for I've done no wrong
   To you, my friend, not for any gain;

I love you more than Seguin did Valence,
And how I'd like to conquer you in love,
My dearest friend, for you're by far the greatest;
And yet you're proud in actions and in words;
But still to others you're a kindly man.

3. O, I wonder: why all this arrogance
Toward me, friend? Reason why I grieve.
It isn't right for another love to seize you
For anything she may say or offer you;
And just recall the start of our affair:
O, God forbid that ever I should bear
The blame for having hastened our farewell.

4. That wondrous virtue that within you dwells
And your rich worth upset me totally,
For I know there's not a woman near or far
Wanting love who doesn't veer toward you;
Ah yes, my friend, you have the finest taste,
And out of all, I know you'll choose the best:
And just remember too our secret pledge.

5. My merit should help me, my lineage too,
My beauty, and even more, my loyal heart;
And so I'm sending over to your abode
This little song to serve as my messenger;
And please reply, my sweet and handsome lover,
Why you're so harsh, so very cruel to me.
Tell me: is it arrogance or wicked will?

6. But at least let this message tell you this:
Many a man has paid for too much pride.

There is no doubt about the plaintive quality of the song, the
medieval counterpart of the twentieth-century "torch song."
What sounds like weakness in a male troubadour, when voiced
by a woman, becomes natural. Then, in the tornada comes a
real turn: the man is warned against the cardinal sin of pride.
We have Eve admonishing Adam, and the effect is delightful.

It is a pity that the Countess of Dia did not leave us many
more samples of her work, for the charm and delicate strength

of the few pieces we do have are incontestable. Even those critics who have most bitterly complained about the monotony of Provensal verse have found in her an outstanding talent, a distinctive voice. She is not unique, for her tropes are those of her male counterparts. Yet how glad we are to feel a live female personality at a time when the women in songs were evaporating into the mist that surrounds second-rate composition or were drifting off into an Italianate heaven. This Beatrice, if that was actually her name, had her feet on the ground.

6

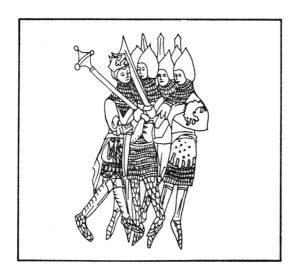

BERTRAN DE BORN
War, Wit, and Morality

Bertran de Born (c. 1140–c. 1214) was last seen wandering head-less in the reaches of Dante's Hell:[1]

Truly I saw (and it seems that I see it still)
A trunk was going there, without a head,
Like the other members of that wretched herd;
And he held the torn-off skull by its hairs,
And swung it in his hands like a lantern,
And the head surveyed us and said: "Woe is me!"
Yes, he was using his head as his own lantern,
For he was two in one: the two were he.
How this can happen, He Who governs knows.
When he had reached the bottom of the bridge,
He raised his arm high; up rose the head
So its words could reach us with greater ease;
The words were: "Now gaze upon this bitter pain,
You who, breathing, go looking at the dead.
See if there's any grief so great as this.
And so that you may have some news of me,
Know that I am Bertran de Born, the one who
Offered the Young King those evil comforts.
I made the sons rebel against their father:
Achitophel did nothing more for Absalom
And David with his wicked instigations.
Because I split apart those persons joined together,
Divided I carry my own brains, alas!
Parted from their source here in this torso.
And thus you see in me the counterpace [contrapasso].

This is the classical picture that has come down to us: Bertran as sower of discord. It is backed in turn by the *razos* or explications that accompany many of his songs in the chansonniers. If ever there was a troubadour caught in the flow of history, Bertran is he. Despite the wealth of references to people and to events of his day, however, Bertran's name is surprisingly absent from all of the major chronicles. Only Geoffrey of Vigeois (Gaufredus Vosiensis) mentions him directly, in his chronicle written largely in 1183.[2] Even the archives of the castle of Alta-fort (Hautefort) contain next to nothing in the way of facts about the singer. The nearby abbey of Dalon, which figured so importantly in the affairs of the time as a refuge, yields almost all of the documents about Bertran: pieces showing that he was the head of a family that included two sons in 1159, was married a second time to a certain Philippa in 1192, was extremely active in affairs of ceremony in 1196, and was deceased by 1215.[3] Yet these scraps and pieces of assorted information do not begin to create the unique and whole personality that emerges from the poems.

Nevertheless, in order to approach Bertran's work with some sort of order, one must be at least sketchily acquainted with the leading personages of his day.[4] The unifying figure of the last half of the twelfth century is Eleanor, the granddaughter of the first troubadour, William IX of Aquitaine. This perennially fascinating woman succeeded her father William X as ruler of the dukedom of Aquitaine in 1137; about one month after her father's untimely death, she married the man who suddenly ascended the French throne with the title of Louis VII. These double moves of inheritance and marriage might have been expected to bring the trouble-torn land of France the peace it desired. But unfortunately Eleanor produced no male heirs for the King. Furthermore, as she demonstrated throughout her life, the great patroness of arts and letters constantly asserted her own rights and privileges, at least insofar as the men around her would let her. William of Newburgh quotes the Queen as saying of Louis that she thought that she had married a king, but learned that she'd married a monk.[5] For a time the couple struggled to hold the marriage together, but the bond began to split during their journey to the Holy Land on the Second Crusade. Having seen the opulence of Constantinople and Antioch, Eleanor could never again be content in the cold, rainy land of the Franks with her mystically inclined husband. The marriage was dissolved by mutual consent on the grounds of consanguinity after a synod held at Beaugency in 1152, and Eleanor fled back to Poitiers, the sophisticated capital of her sunnier domain.[6]

The delicate situation following the divorce was rendered even more perilous by Eleanor's next move: a few months later she married a man who was capable of protecting her, Henry Plantagenet, Count of Anjou and Duke of Normandy.[7] Two years later this man ascended the English throne as Henry II. To the horror of Louis and those other Franks whose lands lay outside Eleanor's yawning southwestern realm and Henry's extensive northern holdings, a great part of the continent now lay in the hands of the English monarch! The stage was thus set for the dreary succession of wars that ensued between England and France for these possessions.

There is no point in recounting the numerous intrigues of the reign of Henry II. The dispute with Thomas à Becket, which spanned the 1160's, is not so important here as are the schismatic quarrels between Henry and his sons, which filled the period from 1173 to 1189. It is precisely these constant altercations for which Bertran is blamed by Dante, and Eleanor has been blamed by historians. From 1168 to 1173, while Henry was openly claiming the attentions of Fair Rosamond Clifford, Eleanor was supposedly establishing her world-famous court in Poitiers, attended by such noted writers as Wace, Benoît de Sainte-Maure, Chrétien de Troyes, and, if one accepts the account, probably by Bernart de Ventadorn and other troubadours.[8] There, too, she may have helped to promote the ill feelings of her progeny against their father.

Eleanor had given the English king four sons who survived the rigors of childhood. The oldest was the brilliant and beloved Henry, whom Bertran and the chroniclers fondly call the Young King. The next was Eleanor's favorite in later years, Richard the Lion-Hearted, whom Bertran jestingly calls *Oc e Non* ("Yes and No"), possibly the most famous princely figure of medieval times, himself a troubadour and a leader of crusaders, and, like Bertran, a bit of an unabashed troublemaker. The Welshman Giraldus Cambrensis says in his *Instruction of the Prince* that Richard was "furious in matters of war, delighting in entering no paths except those in which blood ran"; yet he quotes Ovid's famous statement in the *Remedy of Love* that "Evils are neighbors of goods," adding that Richard was also "fervent in his zeal for peace and justice."[9] The third eldest surviving son was Geoffrey of Brittany, who died suddenly of unknown causes in Paris in 1186 during the troubled period of revolt. The baby of the family was John, nicknamed Lackland because no possessions of note were left to give him. John was the favorite of his father after the Young King's death; he was also the final victor of the struggles, for after Richard's untimely death, he ruled England with tyrannical hand until 1216. Bertran was familiar with all of these men; his castle of Altafort lay in that section of the Limousin-Périgord where much of the family feuding took place, for in those days the kings of England were as often in France as in London.

Boiling down the complex actions into their simplest phases, one can say that the sons, with the exception of the pampered youngster John, rose up against their father because of his despotic behavior toward Eleanor and them, and also because of their invidious desires to better their own positions in the struggle for the throne. King Henry is described by Giraldus in bitter terms as a "seller and diffuser of justice," whose wretched treatment of Eleanor deserved punishment; in fact, Giraldus, who was partial to Becket, almost considers the fractious sons the God-sent ministers of divine retribution for the callous-hearted old man's unchecked lechery and greed.[10]

Real trouble erupted in 1173 with a revolt by the Young King that was squelched by Henry a year later with surprising ease, considering that the English king was opposed not only by his own offspring, but also by the King of France and by many English and Scottish barons.[11] Henry's forces stormed into Poitiers, capital of the expatriate Queen, and the British monarch took Eleanor back to England and a long period of semiconfinement, usually at Winchester or Salisbury, until Henry's death. Henry had triumphed, but the family strife went on. After the Young King's death in 1183, Richard, who had been active as lord of Aquitaine, continued the insurrection. He joined Philip Augustus of France in a secret pact against Henry, even persuading spoiled John to bite his father's hand.[12] John's defection hurt his father more than Henry's defeat at Le Mans. William of Newburgh describes how the pathetic old man died of heartbreak on July 6, 1189, at Chinon on the continent.[13] He was buried at Fontevrault, the monastery founded by Robert d'Arbrissel, the very place where Henry had wanted Eleanor to retire as a nun, and the same place where she in 1204 was laid to rest, supposedly in the garb of a sacred sister.[14]

By the time that Richard succeeded his father in 1189, only John had survived war and disease to offer competition. That sibling, already famous for conniving against his father, acted true to form; only Eleanor and public sentiment seem to have held him in check when Richard embarked in 1190 on the Third Crusade. History has kept alive the story of how Richard infuriated his fellow crusaders in the Holy Land and, on his return home, was shipwrecked and captured in the disguise of a scullery helper by Duke Leopold II of Austria in the vicinity of Vienna in 1192. His minstrel Blondel discovered his place of captivity. He was finally ransomed at great cost from Emperor Henry VI two years later at Mainz by Eleanor herself. Richard returned to rule for five more turbulent years and was constantly engaged in bickering among the lords of Aquitaine and with Philip Augustus. He died suddenly of a wound suffered during a meaningless attack on the little castle of Châlus.[15]

The almost ceaseless skirmishes between the Plantagenet father and sons are not encountered in Bertran's poems as often as Dante might lead one to suspect. The struggle between England and France is given a wider play, and Bertran is much more frequently concerned with the embroilments among such nobles as Aimar (Ademar) V of Limoges, Ebles III and IV of Ventadorn, Raymond V of Toulouse, Elias VI (Talairan or Talleyrand) of Périgord, William IV of Angoulême, and Alfonso II of Aragon and Barcelona. With the exceptions of Alfonso and some other Spaniards, these characters fall into a class that Bertran frequently calls The Barons, a fractious group of lesser lights who seem to have whiled away the daylight hours with endless clashes.

To understand his poetry, one should have some knowledge of Bertran's own background. The international wars which were then raging reached close to Bertran's home and the family of the troubadour seems to have moved from its native holdings in Born (probably the little town located about 12 kilometers north of modern Hautefort) to the easily defensible fortress of Altafort after the marriage of Bertran's brother Constantine to Agnes de Lastours (de Turribus).[16] It seems that Bertran, as the eldest son, was entitled to half of his brother's newly acquired holdings; there was still another son named Itier, and possibly a fourth. Constantine, who embarked on a series of tests of strength against his eldest brother, is described by Geoffrey of Vigeois as a notorious instigator, not only a scourge against Bertran, but also against the other nobles in the neighborhood.[17] The events narrated by Geoffrey for 1182 correspond with the details of one of Bertran's most famous poems, which is preceded by the following explication:[18]

> Bertran de Born, as I've told you in my other explications, had a brother who was called Constantine de Born, who was a good knight at arms, but was not a man who com-

bined valor and honor; instead, he constantly wished evil
upon Lord Bertran and good to all those who wished ill to
Bertran. And one time he seized the castle of Altafort that
belonged to the two in common. And Lord Bertran recovered it and chased him from all his power. And Constantine
went to the Viscount of Limoges, begging to be supported
against his brother; and the Viscount supported him. And
King Richard also supported him. And Lord Richard waged
war against Lord Aimar, the Viscount. And Lord Richard
and Lord Aimar waged war against Lord Bertran, and set
fire to his land and burned it. Bertran had won pledges from
the Viscount of the Limousin and the Count of Périgord,
who was named Talleyrand, from whom Richard had seized
the city of Périgueux, and Talleyrand did not do any damage because he was weak and powerless. And Lord Richard
had taken Gourdon from William of Gourdon, and he had
promised to make a pact with the Viscount and with Bertran de Born and the other barons of Périgord and the
Limousin and Quercy, all of whom Lord Richard had dis-
enfranchised; and for this reason Bertran took Richard
strongly to task. And with all of these reasons, Bertran
wrote this song:

1. I've made a sirventes* where not a word
   Will fail, and it didn't cost me an onion,
   And I've learned the art of living so
   That with brothers, first and second cousins,
      I'll share an egg or a copper-piece,
   And if later they try to grab my share,
      I'll toss them out of the tribe.

2. All my thoughts I keep in my safe,
   Although they've caused me trouble galore
   Between Sir Aimar and Sir Richard;
   A long time they've watched me distrustfully,
      But they're making such a ruckus
   That their babes, unless the King parts them,
      Will get it in the guts.

---

* A non-amatory poem, often satiric.

3. William of Gourdon, a muted clapper
   You've attached there inside your bell,
   And I like you—God help me, yes!
   But as a lunatic and a fool
      They count you, those two viscounts
   Who made the pact; yet they yearn
      To lock you in their buddyhood.

4. Every day I'm struggling, I'm brawling,
   I joust, I beat back, I contend;
   And they light my land and they burn it,
   And they turn my orchard to a pile of twigs,
      Blending my barley with my straw,
   And there's not one coward or diehard
      Who's not assailing my door.

5. Every day I resole, I regird,
   I recast those barons, I heat them up
   For I want to send them hot to war.
   Yet I'm a fool to even consider it
      Because their workmanship's worse
   Than the chains that bound St. Leonard;
      A man's a damned fool to bother!

6. Talleyrand can't leap, he can't trot,
   And he can't even move from Arenalh;
   He can't pitch a lance or a dart:
   No, he's living like a Lombard
      So stuffed up with inertia
   That when other folks splinter away,
      He just stretches out and yawns.

7. At Périgueux, up to the wallwork
   As far as a man can throw with mace,
   I'll come all armed on my Bayard,
   And if I find some paunchy Poitevins,
      They'll find out how this sword cuts,
   For I'll cover their heads with mud
      And mix their mail with brains.

8. Barons, God save you, God watch out,
      And help you, see you all wax hale;

And may He tell you to tell Lord Richard
What the peacock said to the daw.*

What strikes one immediately about this poem are not so much the violence and the bloodshed, but the wit. If we have a warmonger here, we have one who cries out as much in self-indulgent sympathetic pleas as in bold cries of "go to hell." Furthermore, the reasons advanced for the poet's irascibility are fairly clear, and they agree with what little we know historically about Bertran's situation: he was beleaguered both inside his castle by his unruly brother and outside by petty barons. Richard, who was obviously Duke of Aquitaine at this time and not King of England (though he was often called King later in an indiscriminate way) is thrown in for good measure as a final object of contempt and ridicule. Yet the picture that Bertran paints of himself, going alone to Périgueux on his old horse Bayard, is far more amusing than convincing. There is more concern here for other people's lack of masculinity than an assertion of the poet's own. There is more thought given to the waste of war than to the thrills and plunder of conquest. The net result is not so much one of direct confrontation as of vehement, complete spurning. What relieves the poem from the heaviness of Juvenalian satire is the good humor, the Sancho Panza-like voice of the poet-warrior, that runs throughout.

We must go to another poem to find that kind of typically bloodthirsty poetry that Ezra Pound characterized so convincingly but two-dimensionally in his "Sestina: Altaforte":[19]

1. The Count has moved and commanded me
   Through Arramon [Ramon] Luc of Esparron
   That I should write him a song
   In which a thousand shields are split
   And helmets, hauberks, coats of mail,
   And doublets pricked and tattered.

2. And I have cause to attend him
   Since he makes me recount his theme,
   And never should I tell him no
   When I see we're in agreement:

* He warned him not to transgress the bounds of nature through vanity.

But the men of Gascony will curse me
Because I hold myself back from their pledge.

3. At Toulouse, down by Montaigu way,
   The Count will plunge down his gonfalon
   In the Field of the Count [*prat comtal*] along the wall;
   And when he has his tent spread out
   And we're lodging all around about
   For three whole nights we'll lie unroofed.

4. And to our quarters then will come
   The men of might, the barons bold,
   And all the highest-honored friends
   Of all the world, the most renowned;
   Some for the gain, some for the fame,
   Some for the valor will heed the call.

5. And as soon as we're all assembled there,
   We'll spread out for tourney across the fields,
   And the Catalans and the Aragonese
   Will tumble often, a minute apart,
   For their saddles cannot sustain 'em:
   Our buddies [*drut*] will deal 'em such blows!

6. And soon there'll be nothing left
   Since they don't want to save a stick,
   Not a fold of Oriental silk,
   The samite left ripped into shreds:
   Ropes and tents, grapples and stakes,
   Awnings and wide pavilions in shards!

7. Alfonso, who's lost his Tarascon,
   And the lord of Montauberon,
   Roger and his son Bernard Athón,
   And Count Peter can help them too,
   And the Count of Foix with Count Bernard,
   And Sancho, brother of the beaten king!

8. Over there let them think of plunder,
   While here we'll attend their charge.

9. Forever I hope that the highest barons
   Among themselves rage for war!

Here we have a classical portrait of the man of arms, almost as if it were lifted from a North French *chanson de geste* and given voice; this is Roland inciting his men to battle. The persona is ruggedly masculine in a way that recalls Duke William; the subject matter is also what one might have expected the Poitevin lord to have written. Yet can we really say that the tone is vicious, depraved? Is it not totally in keeping with the genuine craft of a medieval lord, the protection of himself and his belongings? Furthermore, the skirmish described is more of a scrimmage than a raid; it probably took place around the year 1181, when Count Raymond V of Toulouse and the Aragonese had many quarrels.[20] One sees the banners and pennants of an athletic contest in the background, the meticulous preparation for the encounter, the careful drawing up of sides, the pitting of the pride of the Aquitanians against the Spaniards and men of the Toulousain. True, the contest will be rougher than a modern football game, for not only will goal posts be torn down, but even the surrounding tents and pavilions will be destroyed. Still, the concept of "war as game," "battle as joust," is obvious. The silks that one customarily associates with women and decadent men will be left hanging in tatters. It is definitely a man's world in a way that jars by comparison with the world of the love poem, where the woman tends to rule. Yet the love poem exists primarily in the poet's fancy, whereas Bernart's sirventes draws closely from the actual world outside the poem; here is reality. The modern reader may at first be shocked by the poet's casual acceptance of brutality, but after we consider this age of nuclear weapons and wholesale murders in concentration camps, the portrait may on second glance look merely like a disrupted pastoral.

There is still another poem which shows the author in his most violent mood. However, we are not certain that this poem was written by Bertran, since some of the manuscripts attribute it to Guilhem de Saint Gregori, Lanfranc Cigala, Guillem Augier, Blacasset, or Pons de Capduelh.[21] If Bertran did not write it (and there is every reason ranging from manuscript attribution to a comparison of texts to suggest that he did), then these other writers were excellent imitators of his strikingly individual style:[22]

1. How I like the gay time of spring
   That makes leaves and flowers grow,

And how I like the piercing ring
Of birds, as their songs go
Echoing among the woods.
I like it when I see the yield
Of tents and pavilions in fields,
And O, it makes me feel good
To see arrayed on battlefields
Horses and horsemen with shields.

2. And I like it when the scouts
Make people with property flee,
And I like it when I see the rout
Of a swarm of opposing armies;
And O, how my spirits adore
The sight of strong castles attacked
With barricades broken and hacked
And troops waiting on the shore
That's completely encircled by ditches
With strong-staked rows interstitched.

3. And likewise I like a lord
Who's the first man out in the fray,
On horse, armed, fearlessly forward,
Inspiring his men to obey
With his valiant deeds;
And when the battle's fierce
Everyone's prompt to pierce
And freely follow his lead,
For a soldier is soon forsaken
Unless he's given many blows, and taken.

4. Maces, swords, helmets—colorfully—
Shields, slicing and smashing,
We'll see at the start of the melee
With all those vassals clashing,
And horses running free
From their masters, hit, downtread.
Once the charge has been led,
Every man of nobility
Will hack at arms and heads.
Better than taken prisoner: be dead.

5. I tell you: no pleasure's so large
(Not eating or drinking or sleep)
As when I hear the cry: "Charge!"
Or out of the darkened deep
A horse's whinnying refrain,
Or the cry: "Help! Bring aid!"
As big and little in turn cascade
Into ditches across the plain,
And I see, by the corpses whose sides
Are splintered, flags unfurling wide.

6. Barons, put up as pawns
Those castles, cities, and villas well-stored
Before bringing each other war!

Here we have the kind of poem that earned the lord of
Altafort a place in Dante's *Inferno*. It is about as realistic a
literary portrait as we have anywhere of the brutality of war.
The opening scene of springtime bliss, of blossoming nature, is
suddenly shattered by the ironclad trespass of knights and horses.
The Provensal word for spring, *pascor*, which descends from
Late Latin *Pascha*, meaning Easter, seems to be doubly travestied.
The time of the lily and the season for Christian meekness are
trampled over as Franco-Germanic aristocrats turn to their favorite pastimes. Granted the apparent viciousness of the detail, one
is still faced with the problem that Goya's portraits of war
present: can one portray brutality without being necessarily
brutal himself? The speaker in the poem, with his constant
repetitions "I like it," "I like it," shows some of the almost
incredible naiveté that Chaucer uses in his comic self-portrait
as pilgrim.[23] And does the tornada not really serve the opposite
purpose from what most people think? Instead of inviting war,
as one expects a warmonger to do, does Bertran not in fact
actually discourage combat by painting it in all of its starkest
colors? The poem is an invitation to havoc, with stress laid on
the barons' precious holdings in town and country.

True, this sirventes does not show the whimsy of some of
Bertran's other work; the glorying tone runs rampant to the
climax. Many editors seem to read the tornada as a call to a
pre-battle pledge. Yet the notion of war as mere game certainly
vanishes, to be replaced by nightmarish visions of splintered

standards and hacked corpses and flags meaninglessly unfurling wide. In the season of the crucifixion one sees the age-old agony re-enacted on a secular level. Would the barons rush out for action after reading the work or would they be checked by the poet's threats? One cannot claim too much detachment for the poem; in fact, the way that the images are heaped upon each other might ultimately suggest that it is the work of an imitator; but if Bertran was the author and here shows the kind of blood-thirstiness for which Dante condemned him, the Provensal poet elsewhere shows the kind of rational distancing, even moral judgment, that Pound himself was trying to justify when he wrote: [24]

> How would you live, with neighbours set about you—
> Poictiers and Brive, untaken Rochecouart,
> Spread like the finger-tips of one frail hand;
> And you on that great mountain of a palm—
> Not a neat ledge, not Foix between its streams,
> But one huge back half-covered up with pine,
> Worked for and snatched from the string-purse of Born—
> The four round towers, four brothers—mostly fools:
> What could he do but play the desperate chess,
> And stir old grudges?*

One of the best examples of Bertran's willful manipulation of startling imagery, turning it piece by piece toward a measured end, occurs in the brilliant "Half-a-Sirventes": [25]

> 1. About two kings I'll write half-a-sirventes,
>   For shortly we'll see which one has more knights:
>   Brave Alfonso of the Castilian throne
>   Has come to look for hirelings, if I hear right.
>   Richard will let his gold and silver fight
>   By the bushel and peck; to him's no great fuss
>   To lavish and spend; who cares about trust?
>   Why, war's more to him than a quail to a kite!
>
> 2. If both these kings prove strong and hale,

* Ezra Pound, *Personae*. Copyright 1926 by Ezra Pound. Reprinted by permission of New Directions Publishing Corporation and Faber and Faber Ltd.

Soon we'll see strewn among our fields
Helmets, swords, shields, and mail,
And bodies, spear-split from belt to brain,
And stallions running unmounted, unreined,
And many a lance through thigh and chest,
With tears and joy, sorrow and happiness.
The loss'll be great; greater still the gain.

3. Trumpets and drums, banners and flags,
   Standards and stallions of every hue
   Soon we'll see as our great age drags
   The holdings from every usurious Jew.
   Down no highway will go no laden mule
   Trusting the day, no burgher unaskance,
   Nor any merchant heading out from France.
   No, he'll be rich who grabs as he chooses.

4. If the king comes, I'll put my faith in God:
   Either I'll live or lie hacked on the sod.

5. And if I live, great will be my bliss;
   And if I die, thank God for what I'll miss!

There is no doubt that this poem differs markedly in tone
from the previous one. The phrase "half-a-sirventes" sets the
mood from the start as one of satiric detachment. At the end
delivery by Richard is found lacking, and death would be par-
tially a salvation in a world gone mad.[26] There is no question
that the tone adopted here toward universal chaos and human
devastation is one of utter contempt. The self rises over the
pandemonium to hiss its disgust. Throughout, the attitude is one
of superiority on the part of the poet: for example, the two
important historical figures deserve only half the size of an
ordinary poem; "brave" Alfonso VIII of Castile has to go around
scouting for mercenaries, since he attracts no ready volunteers;
Richard also has to purchase his men; neither man exhibits or
elicits loyalty, the primary virtue of the military leader. The
second stanza creates a typical Bornesque landscape of carnage,
and if joy and happiness and gain are mentioned, so are tears,
sorrow, and loss. The heroic cannot overweigh the human.

The third stanza portrays an anti-society in which every
man hates his brother and the moneylenders are victimized in

order to subsidize the butchery. There is no real sympathy expressed for either Jewish usurers or rapacious Christians; everyone is simply a vulgar, money-grabbing opportunist. The metaphor of the first stanza, the hawk attacking the helpless quail, thus broods over the entire poem. The tornada occurs almost as a logical outcry: in such a world, there is no possibility of happiness; the fields of spring blossom with corpses, and man's only recourse is to a world outside of time, a world of divine values. Without being the least bit sententious or preachy, the poem is still very moral. Yet the morality throughout is basically secular. The *virtus* will satisfy both the Church and the court because of the concept of the *vir*, the man, behind it. Valor is upheld when courage is truly noble, but so is a code of ethics that modifies the laws of the brawling baron and his buddies. In the absence of a perfect earthly lord, one can only look upward. There was no reason for Dante to put Bertran in Hell; if we read his poems correctly, we realize that the Provensal poet was there already.

Furthermore, Dante the aesthetician was a different man from Dante the author of the *Divine Comedy* looking for scapegoats to people his underworld. In the *De vulgari eloquentia* 2.2 the Italian distinguishes among three separate fields of poetry, based on Aristotle's divisions of man's nature, with three different ends: amatory verse stems from the animal function, seeks what is pleasurable (*delectabile*), love, and expresses itself in the burning of desire; moral verse arises from the rational function, seeks what is noble (*honestum*), virtue, and shows itself in the direction of the will; the lowest function, the vegetative (*vegetabile*), seeks only what is *utile* (useful), as do plants, and its end is health or, more properly in the human sphere of conduct, excellence in arms. In assigning writers to the three functions, Dante mentions Guiraut de Bornelh as a poet of virtue, Arnaut Daniel and Cino da Pistoia as love poets, and Bertran as an outstanding poet of arms. In other words, Dante specifically cites and even compliments Bertran by including him as the primary spokesman of his own arena, the lyric poet of war; Dante adds that he can find no Italian who fulfilled the same role. Furthermore, the Aristotelian categories in which Bertran is placed clearly indicate that the poet is performing a salubrious function: maintenance of the self. Dante himself seems to be as torn as Ezra Pound and other critics who have considered the problem of the "two Bertrans." Dante wanted to condemn Bertran for his strong leaning

toward violence, his almost puerile fascination with competition
and striving (although at times Bertran seems to be more like an
overzealous athletic director than a confirmed hawk). But Dante
could not ignore the strength of Bertran's verse, the glory of
the masculine virtues which the poet of Altafort propounded
and which Dante himself, lost in leaderless Italy, could not help
but admire. Bertran seems to make his critics as schizophrenic as
himself, for Christian morality and warmaking are not easily
reconciled. Yet it is precisely this tortured persona, filled with
ambivalence, that constitutes Bertran's greatness.

The more positive, praiseworthy side of the poet is evident
in the following poem:[27]

1. Ah, how I like to see great power pass
   As young men gather in the estates of old
   And everyone, with babies by the mass,
   Bequeaths hope for a leader brave and bold.
   Then I think that the age will soon renew
   Better than any flower or bird's refrain,
   For knowing that certain lords and ladies are through,
   We allow the young to take up hope again.

2. You can tell a lady's old by her balding hair;
   She's old, I say, when she hasn't any knight,
   Or if she takes her lovers by the pair,
   Or if she takes a lover full of spite;
   Old she is if she loves in her estate,
   Or if she uses magic as a crutch.
   I call her old when jongleurs irritate
   And certainly she's old if she talks too much!

3. A lady's young when she values noble rank
   And likes good deeds whenever good's been done;
   I call her young if her heart is fine and frank
   And she casts no evil eye on valor won.
   She's young if she keeps her body well looked after,
   Young if she knows exactly how to behave;
   I call her young if gossip brings her laughter,
   And if she can keep herself with her lover safe.

4. A man is young if he'll risk his hard-won hoard,

He's young if he's ever suffered need or want.
I call him young if he spreads an expensive board
Or if his gifts approach the extravagant.
He's young when he burns all his chests and treasure
And wars and jousts and hunts and rambles.
He's young if he knows every woman's pleasure,
And young he is if he yearns to gamble.

5. A man is old when he's scared to take a dare
And stores away his bacon, wine, and wheat.
I call him old if he offers eggs and Gruyère
On days when he and his friends are allowed meat.
He's old when he shivers under both cape and cloak,
Old, if he rides on a horse he hasn't tamed;
Old, if a day of peace doesn't seem a joke,
Or if he runs away from a gory game.

6. Arnold, jongleur, take my song "Young-Old"
To Richard, let him watch it, see it's sung:
Let him not care a damn for gold that's old,
But only prize his treasures when they're young!

The unforgettable voice here is hardly that of a warmonger,
even though the opening line suggests a preference for transience
rather than stability. The work shows the virile side of Bertran's
personality at its most insistent, with his refusal to accept the
status quo, his demands for destruction in order to ensure creativity. Here is the muscular Christian aristocrat, far more
realistically portrayed than is the sage Oliver or noble Roland
or fearless Charlemagne of epic. In addition to espousing the
traditional values of the nobility, Bertran stands for love, poetry,
and sports; in fact, the song might well serve as a preliminary
model for the Renaissance prince or courtier. Certainly the
antithesis of Youth and Age has a wider reference than a mere
contrast of the youthful soldier and the impotent old man. Youth
here must be defined in a broader sense as that quality of liveliness to which lyric poets have always addressed themselves. The
opposite, Old Age, includes traditional morality, bourgeois values,
rejection of art, and, in this case almost by definition, the Church.
If we are prepared to call Bertran immoral or, less severely, material, we must still admit that the values which he defended

are those which preserved western Europe from the onslaughts of the Arabs and the Huns. They are also those which we today associate with "high culture"; in fact, even the much-praised French cuisine is here given its due. Bertran is in many ways far more civilized than François Villon; he has the later poet's vigor, without the accompanying crudity of manners. The aristocrat, when being frank, sounds sensible; his lustiness combines taste with reason in the secular sphere.

To show Bertran's complete role in his society, we must examine another poem which reveals a deeper dimension in the poet's craft:[28]

1. Gladly would I write a sirventes
   If anyone would like to hear one sung,
   For valor's dead, with honor and with good,
   And if I tried to avenge their murderers,
   Unless the end of the world would come,
   Waters couldn't drown them all
   Nor worldly fires cremate enough.

2. And yet it isn't foolish or wrong
   For a man to hear my poem's theme
   Since God lets out rent and income
   For good sense, which is there to guide,
   Fit for a man and his possessions;
   But without some measure nothing stands:
   A man who likes to swerve extreme
   Can't raise his deeds on high.

3. Realms there are, but royalty—no!
   Counties, yes; of counts bereft;
   Marches there are—but no marquis;
   Castles are rich, demesnes bulk broad,
   And yet the châtelains do not appear,
   Though the hoardings are huger than before;
   Lots of feasts (yet with little fare)
   Because of those shabby, greedy rich.

4. Beautiful bodies in garb deluxe
   A man can always find and see;
   But tell me, where's Ogier the Dane?

Berart and Baudouin don't appear.
Some men are good at slicking their hair,
Polishing teeth, and growing beards,
But nobody knows how to love any more,
Hold court, handle the women, and give.

5. What sissy folk! Where are the men
Of tourneys, who used to raise the siege
On castles, and for weeks and months
Could handle their courts with kindly rule?
And the rich gifts they used to give!
And the bonuses always on hand
For a warrior or a good jongleur!
I don't see *one* now, I dare say!

6. If Philip the King, King of the French,
Has wanted to make Richard a gift
Of Gisors, the lofty keep and the land,
Richard should certainly thank him lots;
But if Philip had a heart like mine,
Richard wouldn't move those heels
Without a showdown—to Richard's loss.
But since he says no, put the horseshoes on!

7. Papiols, get yourself all heated up:
Go tell Richard I think he's a lion,
And Philip the King's a little lamb
Who likes to feel himself fleeced.

As we catch the echo of those sibilant, stentorian perorations of Marcabrun, we suddenly become aware of Bertran's status as "secular" moralist. What Marcabrun shouted, from the square outside the cathedral, Bertran screams on the field of combat. Marcabrun rails at the world for its lack of faith, Bertran for its lack of guts; both despise the preponderant lack of taste around them. Whereas Marcabrun is sentimental for the Solomons and Davids, the prophets, the men of deep spiritual faith, Bertran yearns for the good old days of moral heroes; Ogier the Dane, Berart of Mondidier, and Baudouin (Baldwin) of Sebourg are semilegendary figures out of Carolingian epic material, but to Bertran and to the medieval Frenchman they are also actual personages. In his ethical outlook as stated in the second stanza, Bertran seems to harken back to Horace's "golden middleness," Aristotle's mean, and Apollo's "nothing in excess"; but these phrases were as much clichés in his own day as they are today. To both Marcabrun and to Bertran control over women is essential. To Marcabrun, this woman-handling (*domneiar*) is a basic tenet of morality, for the moralist can never forget the treason of Eve. To Bertran women are threats only insofar as they may control the basic tenor of society, making the men effeminate and effete. To both poets, the humbly born Marcabrun and the aristocratic lord of Altafort, the decay of hospitality, the corruption of generosity in a tangible sense, is one of the worst of all mortal sins, for society cannot exist without a proper host, and even noble but needy poets like Bertran demand patronage.

Bertran's poem is conceived in the tradition of prophetic indictments, and is as close to Jeremiah and the Biblical sages as to Marcabrun. Yet the work is stamped indelibly Bornesque because of the way that the comments about society in general come to a focus in the last stanza, pinpointing Richard and Philip Augustus as objects of ridicule. Philip is flayed because his allowing Richard to take Gisors dramatically illustrates the general weakness of society. This traditional meeting place of Normans with their Frankish overlords was ceded by Philip to Richard in 1189 after the death of Henry II.[29] Yet the actual historical details are vague and immaterial; Bertran's writing abounds with topical references, yet manages to rise out of the particular and, in the way suggested by Aristotle, soars toward the universal. The humorous ending does not obscure the fact that the work is also a serious commentary on societies which were verging upon decadence.

No consideration of Bertran's achievement could omit his love poetry, for although he is not primarily an amatory poet, he has left us at least two love songs which are outstanding because of their concrete details. One is:[30]

> 1. I apologize, lady; I deserve no ill
> For what the glozing spies have said of me;
> And mercy I beg: may no man confuse
> The fineness of your loyal, noble form,
> Humble yet frank, refined and pleasure-bearing,
> Nor say, lady, I spoke of it with lies.

2. At first throw let me lose my sparrow-hawk;
   Let common falcons pounce on for the kill
   And swipe him off, and let me see him plucked
   If ever my longing for you did not surpass
   My yearning to possess another woman
   Who'll give her love and keep me for repose.

3. Now I shall take an even stronger risk
   (I couldn't pray against greater unpleasantness):
   If ever I fail you—even in my thoughts—
   When we're alone in chamber or in bower,
   Then may my potency flag with other companions
   In such a way that they can't help me out.

4. And if I sit down to tables to gamble,
   I hope I never catch a single coin
   Nor, with all the chips taken, even begin;
   And always may my throws come out snake-eyed
   If ever another lady I woo or seek
   Except you whom I love, desire, hold dear.

5. Let me be lord of a castle split in shares,
   And let me live in the tower with three peers,
   And let us all hate each other's guts,
   And may I always need a good crossbowman,
   A doctor and serf, watchmen and porters too,
   If ever I've heart to love another lady.

6. May milady desert me for another knight
   And let me not have any idea where I am:
   May the wind fail when I'm far out at sea;
   In the court of the king, may porters trounce me,
   And in the battle's press, may I flee first,
   If he didn't lie who told you all those tales.

7. Lady, if I own a good, duck-hunting hawk
   Who's fine and moulted, good at catch but tame,
   Who can handle every other kind of bird—
   Swans and cranes, white herons, black ones too—
   Why would I want a mangy chicken-chaser,
   Fat and fidgety, who doesn't know how to fly?

8. You lying, jealous, poison-tongued flatterers,
   Since you've caused milordess all this trouble,
   I'll flatter you if you'll just leave us alone!

The vigor here is unmistakably De Born's. Fantastic conceit
is piled upon fantastic conceit, with humorous images intermixed,
until we arrive at the seventh stanza, where the woman is compared to a good, duck-hunting hawk. This sudden reduction,
the animal classification that recalls Duke William's comparison
of the qualities of two nags, shows the way in which poetic
artifice, even realistically detailed as here, is sliced through and
ultimately dismissed. The poem ends with an acid tornada and
Bertran shouting at the people around him. Even a love poem in
Bertran's hands becomes a critique of society. Granted that the
conceits here are more interesting for their detail than for their
dramatic impact, and the complaint against the *lauzengiers* is a
stock part of the Provensal love-verse tradition, still the poem is
dynamic and fresh in a way that many of the other cansos of
the latter part of the twelfth century are not.

Another of Bertran's love songs ranks among the foremost
in Provensal literature:[31]

1. Lady, since your heat is not for me
   And you've drifted from my side
   Without the slightest reason,
   I don't know where to search,
   For never again
   Shall such rich joy be garnered
   By me; and if I can't find another
   Of the same kind who meets my liking,
   Worth the same price as you I've lost,
   Never again will I have a lover.

2. And since I'll never find your like,
   One who's both beautiful and good,
   Whose body's richly full of joy,
   With lovely manners
   And ever gay,
   Whose worth is wealthy and ever true,
   I'll go around subtracting
   One pretty feature from every girl

To make my Lady Self-Conceived,
Who'll last me till I have you back.

3. That healthy, fresh complection
   I'll take, pretty Cembelis, from you,
   And also that sweetly loving look;
   And yet there's superabundance
   Of things I leave,
   For pretty things you're never lacking.
   Milordess Aelis, from you I beg
   Your graceful mode of conversation,
   For you could give milady help;
   Never will she be fool or mute.

4. And I wish the Viscountess of Chalais
   Would give me in full possession
   Her throat and both of her hands.
   And then I'll direct my career
   Without false turn,
   Flinging myself straight to Rochechouard
   To ask Milady Agnes' hair,
   For even Isolde, beloved of Tristan,
   Who is celebrated for all her parts,
   Never owned locks of higher praise.

5. And Audiart, though she wish me ill,
   I hope she'll give me a feature too,
   For she's put together in a noble way:
   No, she hasn't any fault,
   For her loving
   Never faltered, never turned bad.
   And from my Better-Than-Good I beg
   Her young, upright body of highest price,
   So fine that one can see in a glance
   How wonderful to hold her nude!

6. And also from my Lady Faidida
   I'd like that gorgeous set of teeth,
   Her welcome and that gentle response
   She bestows so generously
   In her abode.

My Beautiful Mirror, I bid she grant
Her gaiety and her beauty fair:
She knows how to always maintain
Good standing; she's most informed:
Never does she twist or change.

7. Pretty Lord [*Bels Senher*], from you I ask naught:
No, I'm as desirous of the one
Who's self-conceived as I am of you:
I feel a very avid
Love being born
Which has seized my entire heart;
But I'd rather just keep asking you
Than clench another with a kiss.
Why does Milordess refuse me thus,
Since she knows I love her so?

8. Papiols, take this song of mine
And run to my Lady Magnet [*Aziman*]:
Tell her love here's no longer known,
But has fallen from high to humble.

There is no doubt that any "amorous legends" about Bertran
de Born are as fictional as his own poem indicates.[32] He has been
connected with Maent (Maeut) de Montagnac, Aelis, Audiart,
and others, but when one reviews the corpus, the ladies are soon
relegated to the sidelines of the tourney. The poet was never
capable of writing sustained love songs in which the emotions
subdue the rhetorical devices; his heart was not in the boudoir,
but on the watchtower or in the countinghouse. It is no wonder
that Ezra Pound found him so compatible, both for his strong
imagistic control and for his interests in history.

The foregoing poem is memorable because it lays bare the
technique that most love poets have probably used, but which
few would admit: the mistress or object of adoration is a secret
composite drawn from the particulars observed around them.
The creative process thus mirrors that kind of abstraction from
particulars that Socrates talked about in the *Symposium* when
he suggested that one must rise from a love of material objects
and create his own personal notion of the beautiful and the good
as an object of worship. Here we see the process in act, although

in the seventh stanza, the masculine voice again cuts across the artifice and asks for the material reward; Alcibiades speaks, and the illusion vanishes. When the vision has melted, the poet calls the faithful jongleur-messenger Papiols and sends word to Lady Magnet that love has disappeared. Such is the case with the Bornesque love poem: emotion appears, only to evaporate. Yet the comment upon ideals and reality, upon self-conceived ladies and real situations, is pointed; the lust of the seventh stanza cannot operate with the phantom woman. Even in his love poetry, Bertran was a realist; that is probably why he has left us so little.

We shall close this consideration of the poet's works with the very moving plaint on the death of the Young King, Prince Henry. Although this poem is listed in Appel's edition among the doubtfully ascribed pieces, largely because it appears in only three manuscripts and in two is credited to Peire Vidal and Richart de Berbezilh, still the other one gives it to Bertran.[33] There is every reason to believe that Bertran, despite his previous antipathy toward the Plantagenets, keenly felt the general dismay that swept over England and Aquitaine when the young man died of fever in 1183 at the age of twenty-eight. His death occurred after he had ravaged the Limousin, including various chapels and sanctuaries, in one of his never-ending battles against his father.[34] Yet before looking at Bertran's lament, let us examine a portrait drawn from the chronicles. Giraldus Cambrensis, who was familiar with all of the major characters, described the Young King in the following way:[35]

Indeed he was unoffending and warmhearted, gentle and affable, kind and lovable, a stalwart avenger of any illtaken wrong, always more ready to pardon a wrongdoer than to convict him. . . . In arms and in military affairs he loomed erect with helmeted head, unreined, tough, fiercer than any wild beast, always triumphing more because of his own courage than because of luck, always revealing himself a Hector, son of Priam; except that the Trojan fought for father and fatherland, and this man, because of the counseling of the depraved, o grief! waged war against them. He had one sole vow, one chief desire, to exercise all of his strength for a single end: so that, like Julius Caesar of old, he could gain the time when that manly virtue of his would shine forth in all of its worthy merit.

This prose is dramatic, catching the prince in his dual role as peaceful gentleman and splendid warrior, but it in no way matches the solemn, moving dignity of Bertran's funereal measures:[36]

1. If all the grief and sorrow, the strife,
   The suffering, the pains, the many ills
   That men heard tell of in this woeful life
   Assembled, they would count as nil
   Compared to the death of the young English king,
   Who leaves behind youth and worth in tears
   In this dark world beset with shadowy fears,
   Lacking all joy, abounding in doleful spite.

2. Grievous and sad, sensing the bitter wrong,
   Stand his noble soldiers, left behind;
   His troubadours, his jongleurs sing no song,
   For death's bereft the warrior from mankind:
   Still they salute their young English king,
   Who makes the generous seem steeped in greed.
   He never did, nor will he now, take heed
   To repay this wicked world its tearful spite.

3. O boundless death, abounding yet in pain,
   Brag, brag you've got the finest cavalier
   Who ever stalked upon this broad terrain,
   Who, needing nothing, never knew his peer,
   For peer there never was to that English king.
   God, it's more just, if ever You would grant:
   Let *him* live, instead of all those tyrants
   Who never pay with worth—just doleful spite.

4. Since love now flees this jaded age, down-weighed
   By grief, I consider all its joys a lie,
   For nothing lasts that doesn't pass away,
   The way tomorrow feels today slip by.
   Let everyone admire the young English king!
   Who in all the world of valiant men was best.
   It's gone—that body full of lovingness,
   And all that are left are grief, discord, spite.

5. You Who desired to counter all this pain
   By entering this world with its many snares,
   And suffered death that we might live again—
   We cry out in Your just and humble name:
   Show mercy upon our young English king!
   Pardon, if pardon pleases, toward this end:
   That he may stand among his honored friends
   There where grief never goes—nor spite.

Both Giraldus and Bertran sense the tragedy of life in the death
of this sweet prince. As Giraldus puts it:[37]

> Good gods! If only brothers like this could have joined
> themselves to their father in a fraternal bond with filial
> affection, so that they could have been restrained by the
> double chain of benevolence and natural ties, then what a
> great, what an inestimable, outstanding, incomparable glory
> and victory they would have gained forever, for their seed
> and for their fathers! O how great a memory, a history truly
> worthy of being unraveled by the genius of Vergil!

But instead there was only loss.

There is nothing here that clashes with the rest of Bertran's
works. If the master of Altafort is vitriolic toward a jaded
society—every stanza ends with "spite," ira—he is nevertheless
absolutely faithful toward his lord, even at death. The courtiers
stand frozen in respect for the Earthly Messiah, who has passed
from the scene; with him go hope, valor, and virtue. Without a
court, the world disintegrates; society crumbles in the hands of
the vulgar; poetry, except for satire, withers. It is no accident
that the deaths of Prince Henry and Richard the Lion-Hearted
prepared the way for the tyrant John and England's loss of
Aquitaine. Philip Augustus did not miss the chance to swoop
into western France and bind the long-independent men of
Guyenne to his widening realm. Bertran lived long enough to
see the flowering of culture around him, and also its rape and
demise. The information contained in his biography that he
ended his life in the monastery of Dalon, as did Bernart de Ventadorn, may well be true.[38]

Despite Dante and his Comedy, Bertran de Born was no
crude warmonger. The man of Limousin was every bit as moral

as Marcabrun, but he was also practical and whimsical: his virtues were those of the court. Bertran did not mouth the easy, pious clichés of the chauvinist. Ezra Pound begins his Bornesque monologue "Sestina" with a curse, and such words were needed. Bertran paid the world around him in its own coin. If he was not a meek Christian, he deserves a better fate than to be thrown among discord-sowers. For with greater fullness of expression than any warrior in the *Song of Roland* exhibits, Bertran's voice rises over the welter of history to answer that perennial question: what is a man?

7

PEIRE CARDENAL

The Last of the Patricians

Just as Bertran de Born scourged the French nobility, constantly trying to recast them in the image of the bronze heroes of the past, Peire Cardenal incited the clergy to don anew sackcloth and hairshirts in imitation of the Christ and disciples whose words they were preaching but debasing. Both voices were doomed: their defeats mark the end of southern French political autonomy and the Old Provensal literary tradition. When Frédéric Mistral and the Felibrige circle tried to revive Provensal literature in the nineteenth century, they were dealing with a markedly changed language and were facing a gap across the ages that was too enormous to be bridged. For with the passing of Peire Cardenal (c. 1180–c. 1278), the dominant figure of the so-called Albigensian period, Provensal literature ceases to exist as a dynamic force.[1]

In order to understand the death of the great tradition, we may well learn something from history. Southern French culture, from Poitou to Provence and the Toulousain, had flourished brilliantly during the twelfth century, and this fruition is mirrored in the poetry just examined. Yet the movement of the culture was centrifugal, spiraling outward toward England, which owned a great deal of French soil because of Eleanor; toward Spain, which was extremely influential in the county of Toulouse; and toward northern France and its allies, who hedged in the counties on the east. In addition, the Papacy was greatly disturbed by this notoriously fun-loving, opulent, secular-oriented society.[2] This animosity erupted into open enmity shortly after the turn of the thirteenth century, when a fiery group of North French zealots set out to squelch the "material, heretical Cathars or Albigensians" of the South. We have already discussed this unorthodox movement and its kindred causes with reference to Jaufre Rudel, pointing out its limited influence in the early twelfth century. By this time, however, heretical sects were definitely protected in the Toulousain, the new heart of southern France. The counts of Foix, Toulouse, and Comminges may not have been Cathars or Waldensians themselves, but they certainly sympathized with any antipapal movements.[3]

In 1205 Pope Innocent III, ever casting an anxious eye upon insurgents, tried to check the increasing spread of Albigensianism by encouraging the energetic young Spaniard Dominic de Guzmán and Bishop Diego of Osma to go with a small band of preaching friars directly to southern French towns like Albi, where the heresy had taken root.[4] Dominic was hoping to prove that Christianity had not entirely lost its sense of grass-roots simplicity. William of Puylaurens notes in the prologue of his history, for example, that the heretics were often considered more holy than priests, even by loyal Christians; the South French often registered their contempt for a person by saying, "I'd rather be a priest!"[5] Dominic was thus trying to counter the all-too-familiar figure of the fat, worldly Chaucerian Monk, who is represented in Provensal literature by a poet called the Monk of Montaudon (c. 1180–c. 1210), who expressed his love of the material as follows:[6]

1. . . . And I like a man who speaks gently
And gives me gifts with a kindly heart,
A rich man who doesn't want to argue,
But says good words and pleasantly chats;
And I like sleep through storms and thunder,
And a big fat salmon in the afternoon.

2. And I like the gentle time of summer
When I can loaf by spring or by brook,
And the fields are green and flourish anew,
And the little birds are singing then,
And my girl friend sneaks up on the sly
And gives it to me one time quick! . . .

3. And I like a warmhearted salutation,
Without any latent stupidity;
And I like the comfort of my little girl,
Her kiss—and more if I can get it;
And I like to see my enemies lose,
Especially when it's I who win . . .

Although we are not even sure where Montaudon (if that was its actual name) was located, Cardenal certainly had this sort of figure in mind when he wrote:[7]

1. The clerics turn into shepherds,
Yet only to make the kill:
They radiate a saintliness
When they redon their garb;
They lead me to remember

How Lord Ysengrin* one day
Wanted to enter the sheepfold;
Yet because he feared the dogs,
He donned the fleece of a lamb,
And thereby had his jest:
How he butchered and devoured
Everything as he pleased!

2. The emperors and monarchs,
   Dukes, viscounts, and counts,
   Along with all their cavaliers,
   Are wont to rule the world.
   But now I see the possession
   Passing over to the priests,
   With snatching and betraying
   And plenty of hypocrisy,
   With foul play and preaching;
   And they treat you like a nuisance
   If you won't help play their game:
   You're done, as long as you delay.

3. The grander men they are,
   The fewer virtues shown,
   With more of foolishness
   And less of spoken truth,
   More strongly bent on lying,
   With less companionship,
   More strongly urged to erring
   With less of priestliness.
   Of false clerks I say this:
   Mankind has not heard tell
   From the very oldest times
   Worse enemies of God.

4. And when I'm in the refectory
   I don't consider it grand,
   For there at high table I see
   The scoundrels all ensconced;
   They're the first to dunk their bread.

* Fox figure from the *Roman de Renart*.

Ah, listen to the infamy!
To think they'd enter there,
And nobody will toss them out!
And never yet have I seen
One of those poor begging scamps
Sitting next to his wealthy frère.
No! of that we can excuse them,

5. Never need they have any fear,
   Those conquering Arab Sayids,
   For the abbots and the priors
   Will never rush against them
   Or try to seize their ground;
   No, that would cause discomfort;
   Instead, they direct their care
   Toward how they can own the world,
   How they can drive out the Emperor,
   Frederick,* from his safe retreat.
   Yet as soon as one attacks him,
   He certainly shows no joy!

6. Clergymen, he who reads
   Your hearts without guile and ill
   Is making a baleful mistake,
   For never did worse breed live.

Dominic did not succeed in his mission, despite some gains
in debating at Pamiers, where he converted Durand de Huesca;
in Fanjeaux, which became the center of his movement; in
Prouille, where he established a nunnery; and especially in Montréal, where the little book containing his beliefs bounced three
times out of the heretic fires.[8] The problem was not really
religious at heart. It has long been known that the Albigensian
Crusade was as much a political and economic movement as a
religious foray. Trouble flared when Peter of Castelnau, a papal
emissary, excommunicated Count Raymond VI of Toulouse
on several grounds, including the unproved charge of heresy.
Innocent had already warned Raymond: "we grieve that, for

---

* Frederick II; the poem has been dated about the year 1230, after the
major action of the Albigensian Crusade.

all that you nurture heretics, you are strongly suspected of heresy yourself."[9] While it is true that one of Raymond's five wives, Beatrice of Béziers, lived much of the latter part of her life in a Cathar convent, and although Raymond openly protected antipapal poets, Jews, Waldensians, and Albigensians, still the Count's real belief has never been established as anything but that of a lax but liberal Christian.[10] Like William of Aquitaine, the Count was given to love affairs, poetry, parties, and the joy of life. To the zealots of the North, men like Raymond and his associates (Count Raymond Roger of Foix and Viscount Raymond Roger Trencavel of Béziers) were life-loving materialists, and materialism in the minds of the Northerners was just a step from heresy.

When Peter of Castelnau was suddenly struck down by an assailant before crossing the River Rhone near St.-Gilles on January 14, 1208, the shock rippled from the Ile de France to Rome.[11] Up to that time the Southland had seemed a den of iniquity; it was now Hell itself. Innocent openly accused Raymond of responsibility for the deed: "not only because he publicly threatened Peter with death . . . but also . . . he admitted the actual killer to close intimacy and rewarded him with great gifts"; Innocent spoke freely of the Count as the agent of the devil.[12] As William of Puylaurens says: "Satan claimed in peace the greater part of this territory as his own domicile."[13]

The Pope tried desperately to enlist the support of Philip Augustus of France in crushing the King's southern liegemen: "And so *eya*, soldier of Christ! *eya*, most Christian prince! may the groans of the Church Universal move your most religious breast."[14] But affairs between Paris and Rome were already complicated by Philip's marital life.[15] Furthermore, the Frankish monarch had other more troublesome men on his mind: Emperor Otto IV in Germany and John Lackland in England.[16] Besides, the counts of Toulouse were faithful to the French throne, never causing trouble as long as they were left alone, and Philip needed them as buffers against the ambitious Peter II of Aragon and those other Spaniards across the Pyrenees. Only after the crucial battle of Bouvines in 1214, when the North French had decisively triumphed over Germans, Flemish, and English alike, did the Frankish king finally trouble himself with the problem of the Toulousain, and then largely through the efforts of his son, the future Louis VIII. But by that time the work of crushing heresies and attaching the Southland firmly to the Church and to the French crown had been accomplished by the controversial Simon de Montfort.

For if Innocent could not stir up the King, he did manage to infuriate many lesser lords who were committed to crushing their southern brothers for religious reasons or who were anxious to pick up some incidental spoils. From the first, Innocent made it clear that this war was a crusade, and to the victors belonged the possessions of the infidels. As he said to Philip: "We wish most of all that the goods of these very heretics be confiscated, either by you, toiling in your own person or relying on one granting necessary aid, or by the men of your own land who lift arms against these treacherous men who must be vanquished."[17] Since to a North Frenchman almost any Southerner was a heretic, the opportunities for gain were enormous. Aside from the still unblossomed, half-impoverished Count Simon de Montfort IV, who had inherited the earldom of Leicester in England from his mother but was unable to claim it fully because of King John, the Crusade numbered among its eminent standard-bearers Duke Eudes III of Burgundy, Count Hervé IV of Nevers, and the Archbishop Peter of Sens, along with numerous other prelates.[18] Unquestionably many of these men acted purely on grounds of faith and with a desire to eradicate wickedness as they defined it, but their conduct also leads one to draw other less noble conclusions. Simon himself prayed privately and delivered sermonlike speeches before many battles. He was an orator of the most effective kind, stirring his men to astounding deeds of conquest; but he was also capable of acts of great cruelty.[19]

On July 22, 1209, as the Crusaders stormed over the barricades around Béziers, Simon was one of the leaders in the massacre of thousands of helpless men, women, and children who had been deserted by their young, inexperienced ruler, Viscount Raymond Roger Trencavel, who had fled to the much more defensible Carcassonne. A letter written to Innocent by Abbot Arnaldus of Cîteaux and his assistant, the envoy Milo, tells how "in the space of almost two or three hours, after the moats and the walls were climbed over, the city of Béziers was captured and, not sparing rank or sex or age, our men put almost 20,000 people to the sword; and after this tremendous slaughter (*strage permaxima*) of enemies was carried out, the whole city was sacked and burned, as Divine Justice miraculously raged against it."[20] Caesarius of Heisterbach attributes to Arnaldus the legendary reply to the question of how to distinguish heretics from devout Christians for the massacre: "Kill them all! For God knows which ones belong to Him."[21] When Trencavel capitulated because of a shortage of water at Carcassonne after a two-week siege in August, the crusaders chose Simon as the new Viscount of Béziers and Carcassonne. He thus became a liegeman to both Peter II of Aragon, who held Carcassonne as a fief, and to Philip Augustus of France; his holdings were hastily confirmed by the Church.[22] For the next decade, the Crusade is primarily his story, for most of the other North Franks returned home, feeling that the cause had been won.

Simon, however, had broader designs. Spurred on by Innocent, he spent the next few years winning more ground in the territory of the suddenly deceased Trencavel, harassing Count Raymond Roger of Foix, Bernard of Comminges, and Gaston of Béarn; he even dared to raise a short but unsuccessful siege against the city of Toulouse.[23] In 1213, Raymond VI, who was eluding an open confrontation with his widely feared opponent by tactically siding with the crusaders after doing penance for his excommunication, called for help from his powerful neighbor and brother-in-law, Peter II of Aragon.[24] The haughty Spaniard suddenly found himself in a rather embarrassing position. Fresh from a stunning victory over the Moors at Las Navas de Tolosa, gained in league with Alfonso VIII of Castile, he was the darling of Innocent's eye, the perfect man for driving the infidels totally off the European mainland and for creating a vast Catholic country on the Iberian peninsula.[25] But now the crusader against the Moors was facing the crusader against the Albigensians, and Peter himself was eagerly eying the rich Toulousain hillsides and the tempting valleys of Languedoc. Innocent, realizing that Peter was far more important for future designs, instructed Simon to render homage to the Aragonese,[26] and Simon at first was ready to oblige, but later balked. Peter, deciding that the bold invader from the North had to be done away with, stormed over the Pyrenees, taking up a position near the small, poorly defensible château of Muret on the banks of the River Garonne, where he was joined by the Counts of Toulouse, Foix, and Comminges. This precipitous act had been dreaded by Innocent, who had warned the King: "no matter how much I love you as an individual, I could not spare or allow you to act contrary to the undertakings of the Christian faith."[27] The Pope realized that Peter's actions made Simon and his compatriots look like mere usurping mercenaries bent more on private gain than on religious principle.

Hopelessly outnumbered and finally facing the same kind of destiny that he had inflicted upon others, Simon feverishly lifted his men to his own high pitch of zeal.[28] As his army moved warily over the plain outside Muret, they were fully prepared to offer their lives to the God they had stoutly defended. But on that day, September 12, 1213, a miracle occurred. Against these staggering odds, Simon and his followers ran rampant over the men of Spain and the Gallic Southland. The Aragonese panicked and fled as the men of Montfort swept savagely but strategically into their ranks. The telling blow was the stabbing of Peter, whose corpse was stripped in the melee. As news of the King's death was bruited over the field, Simon then drove Raymond and the men of Toulouse, who were standing by, into flight, butchering the hundreds who could not swim across the river or escape in boats. For days the corpses drifted down the Garonne like wasted blossoms. With the young heir James I of Aragon already in his custody because of an earlier marriage pact, Simon towered as the undisputed master of the South.[29]

Even from this height, De Montfort was loath to attack impregnable Toulouse, which remained the heart of the opposition. Instead, he resumed his harassments and waited for papal recognition of his broad domain. Innocent dispatched Peter of Benevento with the mixed blessings of Rome, for complaints against Simon were now rife.[30] Count Raymond VI attempted to salvage as much as he could from a disastrous situation by greeting Peter with open arms, acknowledging papal authority, and tacitly agreeing to abdicate if his lands were restored to his son, the future Raymond VII. Meanwhile, Philip Augustus at last entered the fray by sending his son, Prince Louis, on a visit to the Languedoc, thus cleverly keeping the Kingdom of France's interest alive in an area where De Montfort, the Church, and Spain were all taking active roles.

During the Fourth Lateran Council, which convened in November 1215, Innocent was caught in a terrible dilemma, which the anonymous continuer of William of Tudela's *Song of the Crusade* describes in dramatic terms.[31] It is curious that this antipapal writer should have painted the Pope in endearing terms, far more effectively than did his formal eulogists. The poet describes how the Count of Foix eloquently defended himself and Count Raymond, who remained diplomatically silent in the

affair, against the slashing attacks of Bishop Folquet of Toulouse, an enigmatic figure who in his youth had been a writer
of love songs, but had since become the staunchest, most zealous
defender of the faith. Folquet, who with Guy de Montfort
pleaded the case for the absent Simon, eventually carried the
day. Raymond VI was exiled from his native land, which was
entrusted to the safekeeping of Simon, who was considered a legal
representative of the Church. But Innocent was deeply moved by
the potentially tragic fate of the future heir, Raymond VII, for
the young man had impressed all of the prelates because of his
handsome appearance, refined manner, and gifted tongue. It
was, in fact, difficult for any of the bishops who were not French
to see the Counts of Toulouse and Foix as conniving, Satanic
heretics; these outcasts looked too much like pitiful, dispossessed
gentlemen, unable to cope with a power-crazed general who had
usurped their domains in the name of Christ and charity. Innocent thus tempered his judgment by promising to restore Toulouse and the remainder of young Raymond's heritage after the
youth had come of age and had clearly demonstrated his good
will. Actually, the terms of this settlement were so vaguely defined and Raymond's position was so financially insecure that a
new field of contention was at once established; but Innocent's
death in July 1216 spared the prelate from seeing the worst of
that.

Meanwhile, Simon triumphantly visited Philip Augustus in
Paris and was invested with the feudatories of Toulouse, Béziers,
and Carcassonne. The King thus modified Innocent's wish, subtly
claiming through De Montfort a North French domination of
the South. All that was needed for Gallic union was Simon's
death, which was not long in coming. On the other hand, Count
Raymond VI and his son decided to return to their former
holdings, where the all-conquering Simon was almost universally
hated. Moving from Marseille, the father went to Aragon to
raise an army, while the son attacked the fortress of Beaucaire,
penning in a contingent of De Montfort's men and beating off
Simon's attempted siege. Thus a mere boy who was not yet of
age inflicted the first real defeat on the aged veteran, and the
tide began to turn against the crusaders.

In September 1217 Raymond VI returned with a hero's
welcome to his capital city and there organized a band of re-
sistance fighters composed of the Counts of Foix and Comminges,
the lesser lords of Albi and Gascony, his friends from Aragon,

and, most importantly, was sustained by the stout-hearted burgh-
ers themselves. Immediately Simon and his brother Guy sprang
to attack the city, hoping to take it while the ramparts were still
leveled under prior conditions of peace. But the Toulousains,
with a joyous frenzy that rivaled Simon's own religious exalta-
tion, began to ring their precious city with a new barricade; as
the *Song of the Crusade* tells it:[32]

> And then sound the bugles, then sound the horns;
> They rush over to the ropes and ready the trebuchet.
> And the barons of the city council carry their staffs,
> And they pass out food and good gifts and public doles;
> And the people carry picks and shovels and axes:
> They don't leave a single rod or a wedge or a hammer,
> Not a tub nor a caldron nor a vat nor a palisade;
> And they start to work on the portals and the wickets:
> Cavaliers and burghers all take the little stones,
> Ladies and demoiselles, the tiny boys and the girls,
> Young men and maidens, grand ones and lesser too,
> All of them singing ballads and songs and verse.

The siege began in October 1217 and did not end until
1218. Simon, in the fore as always, was struck down like a common infantryman as he tried to overcome the walls of the taunting capital on June 25, 1218, with a gigantic tower called a
"cat." As the *Song of the Crusade* describes the shattering
event:[33]

> Then came the rock straight where it ought to go
> And struck the Count over the helmet made of steel,
> And the eyes and the brains and the furthest of his teeth
> And his brows and his jaws it split into several bits;
> And the Count fell to earth, dead and bloody and black.

Ironically, the walls were supposedly "manned" at this point
by women. John of Garland sang of the death in terms more
heroic, but much less historically accurate, for the deed was
witnessed by many:[34]

> Simon fell down upon his helmet, that mighty mountain
> Of the Church collapsed, that defender of justice.

Not a single lament followed, lest the closed-in forces rejoice;
Under cover of night his corpse was lifted, the warrior left
the field.

With the death of Simon, North French influence suddenly
seemed to crumble, for his son, Amaury, lifted the siege and
hastily retreated. As Peter of Vaux-de-Cernay remarked of
Simon: "With him fallen, everything fell apart; with him dead,
everything died too."[35] Except for the brief skirmish of Prince
Louis and his peremptory massacre of the citizenry at Marmande
in 1219, fate now favored the South French forces led by Raymond VII, who won a stunning victory at Baziège. One by one
the great men of past deeds began to perish: St. Dominic (1221),
Raymond VI (1222), Philip of France (1223). By 1224 the men
of the Toulousain had won back almost everything that Simon
had gained, including Béziers, which was restored to the Trencavel family. Amaury de Montfort left the Languedoc in despair.

The new French monarch, Louis VIII, was astute enough
to see that the Southland was too rich, too strategically placed,
to be surrendered to quasi-autonomous rulers.[36] With the con-
tinuing sanctions of Rome, he led the French forces in triumph
down the Rhone, hearing with almost every step that another
ally was deserting the new arch-antagonist, Raymond VII. Only
at Avignon, where a series of cross-purposes led to a protracted
siege, was the army impeded. After that fractious city was
tamed, Louis walked unhindered and acknowledged as King
of Gaul all the way to the walls of Toulouse, which again
stiffened in the face of active harassment. But an illness con-
tracted during the siege of Avignon began to take effect, and
the King, heading northward, died en route in November of
1226.

The major work, however, was done: all that remained was
for Louis IX, the renowned St. Louis, to negotiate a peace
settlement with the excommunicated and abandoned Raymond
VII. In this he was assisted greatly by his mother, Blanche of
Castile. On April 12, 1229, the count accepted the humiliating
terms of the Treaty of Paris which included being publicly
scourged in the Cathedral of Notre Dame.

After the relatively peaceful decade of the 1230's, trouble
flared once again in the 1240's when Raymond gained the help
of Henry III of England, but Louis IX quickly put down the
revolt. All that remained of active contention was the eyrie re-

doubt of Montségur, which had long been the center of Albigensian activity, but now became a symbol of political rebellion.[37] There, high on a peak that was generally deemed impregnable, the leaders of the heretical faith valiantly withstood the protracted siege of the crusaders. But in 1244, access to the lofty keep was finally gained, and those heretics who would not embrace the teachings of Christianity were summarily burned at the stake.

The heresy itself gradually withered away, for the South French, tired of war and contention and constant scrutiny by the clergy, were eager to accept any conditions for peace. Yet the drain on South French resources, the crushing of local power, the brutal treatment of heretics, the cruel combat of brother against brother—these facets, so typical of any civil war, left a heritage of hatred that has not totally died out in southern France, even to the present day.

One of the most distressing after-effects of the war was the establishment of various boards of inquiry throughout the Toulousain. These so-called investigation centers, set up by Pope Gregory IX, were the forerunners of the boards of the Inquisition.[38] Rome thus seemed to be perpetrating a new kind of violence that dimmed even its earlier ironic position of declaring a crusade against Christians. We can hear the outcry against this kind of activity by Peire:[39]

1. Not a buzzard, not a vulture
   Can smell the stink of rotting flesh
   Like those clerics and those preachers
   On the sniff for earthly wealth.
   Right away they're rich men's servants,
   And when they sense disease's swipe,
   Then they cozen out bequeathings:
   The relatives have nothing left.

2. The Franks and the clergy get the praise
   For evil, since they're masters there;
   And the usurers and the traitors
   Own the age about half and half;
   For with their lying and their cheats
   They have so upset the world
   There's not a religious order left
   That hasn't mastered the lesson too.

3. Know what happens to all that loot
   Belonging to those who get it ill?
   Up there springs a mighty robber:
   Nothing will he leave behind.
   Name is Death; O, how he beats them!
   In just four ells of linen-cloth
   Off he rolls them to his mansion
   Where they find other evil galore.

4. Man, why perpetrate such folly,
   Why transgress those commandments
   Of God, Who is your rightful Lord
   And formed your body out of nothing?
   He who battles against his Master
   Would sell a good sow in the marketplace;
   Yes, his earnings will be those
   Won by that other villain, Judas.

5. Our true God, Who is full of sweetness,
   Master, be our guarantor!
   Keep us from the hellish tortures,
   Hold us sinners from torment safe;
   Unravel those out of the evils
   In which they're caught, in which bound:
   Yield them then Your truthful pardon
   In return for their true confessions.

Yet, curiously enough, although few scholars would try to
make a case for the religious side of the war, the Crusade *was*
successful in stamping out the exfoliating heresies. After the
conflict, the Church sent many emissaries like Dominic, men
with the firm but simple strength of St. Francis of Assisi, to serve
as models in a land that would not tolerate luxury-loving priests.
Furthermore, to combat the great secular love tradition in verse
that had gripped the imaginations of the southern French and
had spiralled outward into Germany, Spain, England, and Italy,
the Church vigorously supported the spread of Mariolatry after
centuries of being critical of its growth. Our Lady was needed
at a time when the many ladies of the poets were impoverished
and mute. It is no wonder that hymns to the Virgin dominate
that later collection of Provensal poems called the *Leys d'Amors*

(Laws for Love Poems),[40] a work that is more distinguished for its rhetorical comments than for its aesthetic achievement. In fact, Peire Cardenal, himself a man of the most devout religious feelings, wrote what is perhaps the most famous hymn to Mary in the Provensal language:[41]

1. Our true Virgin, our Maria,
    Our true life and our true faith,
    Our very truth, our very way,
    Our very virtue, creature true,
    Our true mother, our true friend,
    Our true love, our mercy true,
    By the action of thy very grace
    May thy heir inherit me!
    If it please thee, Lady, lend us peace:
    In thy son's name for me be it done!

2. Thou offerst penance for the folly
    By which Adam was taken over:
    Thou art the star that points the way
    To pilgrims in the Holy Land;
    Thou art the dawning light of day;
    Thy son is the resplendent sun
    Who warms it and sends us light,
    Truth-giver, of justice ever full.
    If it please thee, Lady . . .

3. Thou wast born over in Syria,
    Noble but poor in worldly goods,
    Humble and pure and pious
    In words and deeds and thoughts,
    Created with such mastery,
    Without an ill, with every good.
    Thou wast made so affable
    Even God put Himself in thee.
    If it please thee, Lady . . .

4. He who puts his trust in thee
    Will never need another defense,
    For though the world should perish,

Thou wouldst never pass away;
To thy prayers is humbled even
The Almighty—displease whom it may—
And thy son would never challenge
Thy true will at any time.
If it please thee, Lady . . .

5. David in prophetic measures
   Sang in a psalm* that he once wrote
   That on God's right hand was sitting—
   The King promised in His written law—
   A mighty queen we might see wearing
   Garments of orphrey and of vair:
   Thou art she; there is no doubting;
   No dissenter can test the point.
   If it please thee, Lady . . .

6. And since thou standest by God's side,
   See that He grant me peace alway.

This hymn, simple on the surface almost to the point of crudity, shows throughout a fine balance of Old Testament law set against New Testament grace, of the sternness of the lawyer set against the mercy of the defender, of the humble mother weighed against the powerful goddess, as Frederick Goldin has pointed out.[42]

What of this poet whose long life spans almost a century, this artist who with his own eyes witnessed the gradual decline of his native culture? His ancient biography, which seems more reliable than most others, says:[43]

Peire Cardenal came from Velay, from the city of Puy Nôtre-Dame. He came from honorable stock, and was the son of a knight and a lady. And when he was small, his father put him in the principal cathedral school at Puy so that he could become a canon, and there he studied literature and learned how to read and to sing. And when he reached the age of a man, he fell in love with the vain things of this world and acted gay and handsome and youthful. And he invented many a beautiful song with a good message. He

* Psalm 45; Vulg. 44.

also wrote some love songs, but few. He composed many sirventes, and they were beautiful and fine. In those sirventes he showed a lot of good sense and good examples for those who will pay attention. For greatly did he castigate the folly of this world, and much did he reproach false clerics, as his sirventes prove. And he visited the courts of kings and noble barons, taking with him his jongleur to sing his songs. And greatly was he honored and treated by my lord, the good King James of Aragon, and by many honored barons.

And I, Master Miguel de la Tor, the writer, make known of Peire Cardenal that when he passed away from this life, he had about one hundred years of age. And I, the aforesaid Miguel, have written down these sirventes and their moral lessons in the city of Nîmes.

Here in essence is the classic portrait of Cardenal: a somber, serious, brooding aristocrat—the Ghibelline par excellence. He rises like Farinata degli Uberti in Dante's *Inferno* out of the caskets around him, holding the hell of his century in great contempt. Even the name Cardenal (or Cardinal) could not be better chosen, with the religious overtone of "cardinal" and the supplementary meanings derived from Latin *cardo* (hinge), "cross-cutting, primary, essential."

We are not sure, despite what the vida says, that Peire was actually a man of great wealth, but we do know from his poems that he was sheltered in the courts of some of the richest men of his day. Only influential patrons could have saved him from the vengeance of his many powerful enemies. There is reason to believe, from a chart dated as early as 1204, that Peire performed secretarial services for Raymond VI of Toulouse, leader of the anticrusading forces.[44] There in Raymond's court was one of the last groups of Provensal literary men, composed of such figures as Raimon de Miraval, Aimeric de Peguilhan, and Aimeric de Belenoi.[45] These writers, though hardly original in their own right, were nevertheless composing the kind of good, dilutive poetry that is typical of any waning tradition. Certainly there was enough activity around to stimulate Peire and to supply him with an audience.

After Raymond VI's exile, Peire undoubtedly worked for the Count's son, Raymond VII. It is also quite possible that Peire knew Peter II of Aragon, the ill-fated ally of Toulouse, but this relationship has never been definitely established.⁴⁶ What did Peire do after his friends were defeated and the forces of inquisition were established in the Languedoc? Obviously, like that other outspoken critic of the Church, Guillem Figueira, he had to flee his residence. We can only speculate about his final days: perhaps they were spent with the Dauphin of Auvergne or with the benefactor Alphonse of Poitiers. Possibly Peire was maintained by Alfonso X, called the Wise, of Castile, and certainly, as the vida suggests, James I the Conqueror of Aragon was a patron and protector.⁴⁷ It is generally believed, without indisputable evidence, that Cardenal spent most of the years from 1230 to his death in Marseille, and that he died sometime in the late 1270's, probably in Montpellier.⁴⁸ The exact details are unimportant. Peire's exile from his native earth is all that one needs to prove the foreignness of the troubadours at the middle of the thirteenth century; by that time, they had become strangers in their own lands.

Peire Cardenal sums up the last, best parts of the energy of the Provensal lyric. All that was left was hard, deliberate scorn for a world gone mad. As Peire himself concludes in his famous fable:⁴⁹

1. There once was a city (I know not which)
   Where rain had fallen in such a way
   That all the inhabitants of the town
   Who were touched went suddenly mad.

2. They all went crazy, except for one:
   That one escaped (there was no more)
   For he was safe inside a house
   Asleep when all this was going on.

3. When he woke up after his sleep
   And saw that the rain had gone away,
   Outside he went among the folk.
   They all were acting completely mad.

4. One wore a cloak, another was nude;
   Another was spitting up at the sky;
   One threw stones, and another sticks;
   Another stood tearing at his gown.

5. One was striking, another hit back;
   Another was acting like a king
   And held himself regally in the hips;
   Another leaped through the market stalls.

6. One was threatening, another cursing;
   One was swearing, another laughed;
   One spoke, and didn't know what he said;
   Another made constant startled looks.

7. And the man who still had his wits
   Was wondrously struck by these fits
   And saw that they all were crazy,
   And he looked up, and he looked there,

8. To see if one wise man existed,
   And yet he could not spy a single one.
   And so he stood gaping at them all.
   And they showed greater wonder at him,

9. Amazed by his tranquillity.
   They thought he must have lost his mind
   Because he wasn't aping them,
   For to them it all appeared

10. That they were wise and full of wit
    And that he was utterly deranged.
    One strikes his cheek, the other his neck:
    He couldn't keep himself from tumbling.

11. One man presses, another shoves:
    He thinks he's going to flee the mass,
    But one man tears, another pulls;
    He takes the blows, rises—falls.

12. Then, lifting up with giant strides,
    He rushes home on double time
    Muddy and battered and halfway dead,
    And glad to be out of their clutches.

13. This little fable concerns this world:
    It's like the people you meet today.
    This age of ours is that very town
    That's full to the limit with lunatics.

14. For the greatest reason man can have
   Is to love and fear his God,
   And to hold to His commandments;
   But now that sense is wholly lost. . . .

Despite its cogent comment on the contemporary situation, the poem shows the weakness of the poetry of the day. The form is diffuse—at best a rollicking ballad in the original; the sentiment is overstated. Poetry, seeking an outlet in satire because genuine idealism is denied, becomes didactic, pedantic, and ultimately sterile. The poet seeks to destroy the hypocritical sententiae of his day, yet he merely turns up a new set of apothegms. Here Peire adds the heavy-handed, conceptual allegory that is far more akin to the North French *Roman de la rose* tradition than to the free-moving Provensal lyric.

Perhaps the finest poem that Peire wrote, one in which a dramatic situation is consistently maintained, is his famous complaint to God:[50]

1. I'd like to start a sirventes that's new,
   One I'll recite upon the Judgment Day
   To Him Who made me, formed me from the void.
   And if He plans to hold me in account,
   And if He wants to cast me to devilhood,
   Then I'll reply: "Master, mercy! no!
   For in a wicked age I groaned my years.
   And guard me now, I beg, from all those torturers."

2. Then I shall make His court all stand in awe
   As they attend the pleading of my case:
   For I'll say *He's* the guilty party then
   If He plans to cast His own to hellish pain.
   For He Who loses the things He ought to gain
   Rightfully wins a lack for His vileness;
   For He should be sweet, as well as generous,
   In holding on to souls who have transgressed.

3. Those devilish types He ought to dispossess
   And then He'd have a running stock of souls,
   And the clearing out would gladden all the world,
   And He Himself could give Himself His pardon:

Yes, willingly could He destroy them all,
Since everyone knows He owns the absolution.
"Beautiful Master Lord, go and dispossess
Those enemies who are vicious and are vile.

4. "Never should You deny the open door,
For Peter, who is porter there, receives
Shameful remarks: instead, every soul who treads
Past those portals should walk in with a grin.
For never was there a court one calls complete
Where one man laughed and yet another cried.
And though You are monarch powerful and bold,
Unless You open, I'll issue a complaint.

5. "I have no wish to voice You my despair;
Instead, I place in You all of my faith
In hope that You defend me from my sin:
It's *Your* burden to save me, corpse and soul.
Now let me offer You a pretty choice:
Either send me back where first I saw the day
Or pardon me for the wrongs that I have wrought.
Never would I have sinned had I not been born.

6. "If I suffer evil here and more in Hell,
By faith! that would surely be a sinful wrong,
And I'd have a rightful reason to reproach You,
For I've a thousand sufferings for every good."

7. —"Mercy I beg of you, Holy Lady Maria:
Offer good witness for me unto your son,
That He may lift this father and his children
And place them there in grace beside St. John."

During his lifetime Peire Cardenal complained about everything. I have not included his satiric attacks on women because
they are not in any way as witty as those of Marcabrun. Except
for the neatly turned conceits at the beginning of the previous
poem, humor of a gentle nature was not Cardenal's specialty.
Dourness dominates his work, and the laugh, whenever it does
come, is bitter. Yet when one surveys the age in which the poet
was living, with the destruction of so many beautiful traditions,

the silencing of music, and the stifling of creativity, what else can one expect?

Provensal literature began with rather crude, emotionless hymns and with a rhymed translation of Boethius; it ended with sugary songs to mythical ladies and with forceful hymns to the Great Lady. We are faced, in other words, with an ironic proposition: the Church helped to destroy the Provensal secular tradition, yet as that tradition waned, the Church received the benefit of some excellent hymnal composition. We have observed an interaction between church and state again and again in examining the lives and works of the foregoing poets. Yet, as D. W. Robertson, Jr., says, this interaction should not suggest absolute polarity.[51] Peire Cardenal attacked the Church as a political institution with the most acid-tipped barbs at his disposal; but at heart, as these last poems show, he was a pious Christian, not showing a single inarguable sign of being a Cathar or other heretic. Peire was one of the last of the patricians in an age of social dissolution, one of the last of the true poets in an age of sententious prose, one of the last of the traditional medieval believers before the dawn of Renaissance humanism. After him in southern France there is only the silence.

THE TROUBADOURS AND
MODERN SONG

When we survey these seven troubadours from a distance, we can clearly detect the origin, the florescence, and the decay of a great poetic tradition. South French troubadour verse arose from two obvious sources: the Christian ethos of the eleventh century and the instinctive urge of the people at large, both nobles and commoners, to create secular songs. The poetry is therefore not totally unlike jazz in its provenance, for this American music had its roots in Negro spirituals and in the free-styled rhythms of the slaves. The cries of *Eia* that punctuate the early Provensal songs are not unlike the *Hallelujah* of Negro lyrics. If the jazz seems much wilder in spirit and less ordered in its diction and structure, perhaps the difference is fairly obvious: the natives who were brought as slaves from Africa to the plantations of the New World had not achieved the level of literary excellence and metaphysical awareness that the song-makers of southern France had absorbed through the excellent monastic schools. The first great poet of Languedoc was a duke; William C. Handy and those others who escape the anonymous mist surrounding a great deal of Negro music were not educated men perpetuating a long-standing tradition in a conscious way; they were not, for example, aware of the Viennese musical theater that has profoundly affected the sentimental musical-comedy tradition in America. The Negro musicmakers sang primarily about the woes and torments of the self, but they also cried out about the JOY which would be theirs when it was their turn to "go marching in."

Let us not delude ourselves into thinking that the troubadours are divorced from the twentieth-century sensibility, that they exist in a void that has no bearing upon an age where self-doubt has mushroomed into worldwide *Angst.* Scholars of the nineteenth century seem to have cut these poets off from us at the very same time that they were embracing them; the troubadours were laid to rest with the inscription COURTLY LOVE. The poets merged into a faceless school. The brilliant, potentially dangerous ladies of southern France, fantastic women like Malbergion and Dangerosa and the Countess of Dia and the great Eleanor herself, dissolved into weeping, swooning damoiselles. Romantics like Sir Walter Scott and Alfred Lord Tennyson conjured up misty palaces where ladies trailing long veils swept down storied casements into the waiting arms of their guitar-strumming lovers; they ignored the simple fact that the lady in Provensal verse is as often a bitch-goddess as she is a sweet, sugary belle. Even more often, she remains perennially abstract, existing only as a generalized ideal that any reader can interpret as he chooses.

Similarly, books have been written about "the troubadours at home," even though the Provensal poets, like our modern beatniks, were often on the road, traveling as Bernart de Ventadorn did from his native castle to England, to Languedoc, and to Spain. The typical book about Provensal poetry contains beautiful photos of the familiar southern French landscape—the castles of the Loire, the Vale of Dordogne, the winding streets of Poitiers, the mighty battlements of Carcassonne—scenes which are all quite lovely, and all quite peripheral. The tiny idealized spring landscape that opens many Provensal love songs has no more direct bearing on the ruined castles that line the Rhone Valley than it does to the valleys of the Rhine or the Po or the Hudson. This landscape lives precisely because of its time-lessness and placelessness; the elements are genuinely fictive and not meant to be "real." The troubadours did not leave us tourist guidebooks any more than they left candid memoirs of their sex lives or propaganda pieces about the superiority of women.

They did, however, leave us their poetry, and this heritage binds them to us directly. Peire Cardenal cries out against the Church and conservatism in general in precisely the same way that Joan Baez and Bob Dylan are coherent spokesmen for modern liberal ideals. Bernart de Ventadorn manipulates the age-old tropes bequeathed him with the same sort of assured hand that Cole Porter and Lorenz Hart used in reworking the stock materials of their day. The Countess of Dia is quite comprehensible in the context of Billie Holliday and Helen Morgan;

her torch may be less intense, but it is held equally high. Even in the consciously artistic work of the Beatles and the Supremes and our other modern troubadours from Liverpool and Detroit and Nashville, we can hear the age-old love cries issuing forth in the same general atmosphere of hand-clapping, footstomping, and hilarity—call it "joy" or plain old "fun." The time-encrusted trope about the doctor and his medicine forms the basic motif of a popular rock-'n-roll song in which a man demands to know the cause of his suffering and is informed that it is "true love"— ah, the divine travesty! A rousing but melancholy song that shows a fine welding of hillbilly music to the Negro jazz beat, called "Sea of the Heartbreak," concerns a lover who is tossed endlessly about like a little ship at sea, just as Bernart and Publius Ovidius Naso had complained centuries earlier. Even in an age of deicide, the old lord-servant relationship is hymned in a variety of ways: "I'm just a prisoner of love"—although Freud has taught us to see sadomasochism in these situations, rather than prostration before a religious ideal. Modern songwriters go on calling their sweethearts "angels" at a time when interplanetary rockets seem to have uprooted most heavenly occupants.

How did the troubadours fix upon this store of images and attitudes that is still being sung about today? Because these elements are, to set Jung against Freud, an essential part of the human apparatus, and by no means monopolized by Christians or members of any other religion or culture. One has every reason to believe, without checking, that natives in the jungle and Eskimos tell their beloveds that they will follow them over hills and vales and any other appropriate parts of the local landscapes.

The music of the 1960's also seems close to the Provensal tradition because of its broad appeal. Everybody in southern France seems to have cared in some way about secular songs, even people like Marcabrun, who had a strong religious bent. We know from the chronicles cited earlier that the masses packed the halls in Poitiers to hear Duke William sing about the woes of captivity, and we know that the youthful songs of Abelard circulated freely in the markets and squares. Love songs would never have been frowned upon by the Inquisition if they had not been widespread and potentially troublesome.

As for the quality of the songs of the seven troubadours just examined, there is no need to apologize for their literary texture, which is usually polished, smooth, and sophisticated.

Unfortunately—and this loss can never be underestimated—we have no adequate knowledge of the element of rhythm in the transcription of the musical accompaniments for the songs, and the modern interpretations, as a result, are merely guesswork. Certainly the saccharine renditions of most of our interpreters of medieval music can bear almost no likeness to the original pieces. Here, for example, is a poem that illustrates the liveliness of Provensal verse; this love song by Richart de Berbezilh shows a deft manipulation of the clichés of medieval bestiaries in a way that insists upon lively music as an accompaniment:

1. Just like an elephant
   Who, when he falls, can't rise
   Till others have upthrust him
   With their cranelike cries,
   I'll take up his custom:
I know my troubles are pachodermly heavy
And if that Court at Puy with its tycoon
And all its loyal-loving lords and ladies
Don't lend a hand, I'll wallow in my swoon.
Lords and ladies, get pity for my pain
From her who makes laments and logic vain!

2. If you fine noble lovers
   Can't help my joy come back,
   Then poetry—I'll spurn it.
   It just can't fill my lack.
   Or else I'll become a hermit
Alone with no companion (for whom I'm burning).
My life's too full of misery and despair.
Joy's turned to grief, happiness to mourning.
My God, I'm not in any way like the bear!
When I'm abused or clubbed with a heavy bat,
I don't thrive, don't prosper—don't get fat.

3. O, I know Love's strong enough
   To help the tried but true man
   (Even if my love's more than "nice").
   Still, I never carried on like Simon
   Pretending to be Christ!
Wanting to soar to the very heavens above,

But shoved the other way for his sinful pride.
My pride is such a simple thing—just love.
Ergo, let pity give what love's denied,
For there's a place where reason conquers pity.
The place where reason fails is not so pretty.

    4. I'll shout to all the world
       About myself, prolix, profuse.
       If I could only imitate
       The phoenix (O, what's the use?),
       Who burns himself to procreate,
Then I'd burn all this misery and be purged.
I'd even burn those poems, bald untruths.
Then, in a chorus of sighs and tears I'd surge
Up where all virtue, loveliness, all youth
Reside—where pity's never in absentia,
Where all good forces hold annual convention.

    5. Song, be my middle-man
       Over there where I dare not go
       Nor even look, except cross-eyed.
       My penning in's so thorough
       That no one's on my side.
Better-Than-Woman, I ran from you two years
Wildly, like a deer running at chase.
Now I've come back, brimming over with tears,
Ready to die from the shouts of your huntress face.
Deerlike I come to you, lady, for your grace.
Do you care? Is love's memory so soon erased? . . .
    (*Atressi com l'olifanz,* ed. Hill and Bergin, pp. 115–17)

When we examine these sudden turns and lunges and thrusts, we find a source of delight that is all that is needed to justify a poetic tradition. The poetry has to be read, just as the music has to be played. Provensal literature was born in an atmosphere of *jeu d'esprit;* if the *jeu,* the game, is lacking, so is the spirit. Intellectuals who go around poking into this poetry, searching for doctrines of social emancipation and Neoplatonic idealism, are doomed to wring their hands in despair. Yet enough of all these laments; instead of complaining about the monotony and sameness of this verse, we should be thankful for its variety and its richness. Seven troubadours—how many movements, including those of our own day, can boast of an equally significant number?

NOTES
―――――――
INDEX

NOTES

All abbreviations of periodicals and serials are taken from the 1968 *PMLA International Bibliography*. In addition, I have used the familiar *PL* (*Patrologiae cursus completus: Series Latina*, ed. J. P. Migne, 221 vols. Paris, 1844–80) and *Recueil* (*Recueil des historiens des Gaules et de la France*, ed. Martin Bouquet, 24 vols. Paris, 1869–80).

WHERE DID THEY COME FROM?

1. The general thesis of C. S. Lewis, *The Allegory of Love* (repr. New York, 1958); also, Maurice Valency, *In Praise of Love* (New York, 1958).

2. This nineteenth-century term, which has become the slogan for Provensal poetry, was coined by Gaston Paris in his study of Chrétien de Troyes' *Conte de la Charette* in *Romania*, 12 (1883), 459–534, where the emphasis on courtliness suggested regal formality more than sentimental effusion. The term was subsequently turned into a perniciously convenient catch-all: Gaston Paris, *La Littérature française au moyen âge*, 6th ed. (Paris, 1922), p. 199; Alfred Jeanroy, *Les Origines de la poésie lyrique en France au moyen âge*, 3d ed. (Paris, 1925), p. xvi et passim.

3. See esp. E. Talbot Donaldson, *Ventures: Magazine of the Yale Graduate School, 5* (1965), 16–23, and D. W. Robertson, Jr., *A Preface to Chaucer* (Princeton, 1962), pp. 391–448. Both critics attack the supposed medieval basis for the concept: Andreas Capellanus, *De amore*, ed. S. Battaglia (Rome, 1902), and Jehan de Nostredame, *Les Vies des plus célèbres et anciens poètes provençaux*, ed. C. Chabaneau and J. Anglade (Paris, 1913). Nostredame, living in the sixteenth century, was too far removed from the period of florescence to be reliable; his editors have established not only his flaws but also his downright lies. Robertson exposes Capellanus' work as a pseudo-Ovidian, but actually religiously oriented handbook, rather than as a sociological document, as earlier scholars tried to interpret it. The translation by J. J. Parry under the title *The Art of Courtly Love* (New York, 1941) as a rendering of *De arte honeste amandi* did not help to rectify matters. The widespread phenomenon of "courtly" literature is discussed, not always coherently, by Peter Dronke, *Medieval Latin and the Rise of European Love-Lyric*, 2 vols. (Oxford, 1965–66).

4. The most insistent spokesman for placing the poetry in its proper intellectual milieu was Dimitri Scheludko; his essays, scattered through journals, include: *Archivum Romanicum, 11* (1927), 273–312; *ZFSL, 52* (1929), 1–38, 201–66; *ZRP, 54* (1934), 129–74; *NM, 36* (1935), 29–48; *ZFSL, 60* (1936), 257–334; *ZRP, 60* (1940), 191–234. See also Erich Auerbach, *PMLA, 56* (1941), 1179–196, modified in *Literary Language and Its Public* . . . (New York, 1965), pp. 67–81.

5. One especially abhors the bored attitude of Alfred Jeanroy, *La Poésie lyrique des troubadours*, 2 vols. (Toulouse, 1934), 2, 94 f.

6. See my *Cruelest Month* (New Haven, 1965), pp. 105–48.

7. Friedrich Diez, *Die Leben und Werke der Troubadours*, ed. Karl Bartsch, 2d ed. (Leipzig, 1882), and *Die Poesie der Troubadours*, 2d ed. (Leipzig, 1883); Joseph Anglade, *Histoire sommaire de la littérature méridionale au moyen âge* (Paris, 1921), and *Les Troubadours*, 2d ed. (Paris, 1919); for Jeanroy, see above, nn. 2 and 5. This tradition continues unchecked into recent works such as Ernst Hoepffner, *Les Troubadours dans leur vie et dans leurs oeuvres* (Paris, 1955).

8. J. A. Westrup, "Medieval Song," *Early Medieval Music up to 1300, 2: New Oxford History of Music*, ed. Dom Anselm Hughes, 2d ed. (Oxford, 1955), p. 237.

9. For a comparison of the influences of Augustinianism, Catharism, Waldensianism, etc., see Chap. 3: Jaufre Rudel.

10. See Karl Young, *The Drama of the Medieval Church*, 2 vols. (Oxford, 1933), *1*, 565, n. 1; Scheludko, *Archivum Romanicum*, 15 (1931), 137 ff. Seminal studies by Ernst Robert Curtius, *European Literature and the Latin Middle Ages*, tr. Willard R. Trask (New York, 1953); F. J. E. Raby, *A History of Christian-Latin Poetry*, 2d ed. (Oxford, 1953), pp. 219 ff.

11. *Les Origines et la formation de la littérature courtoise en Occident (500–1200)*, 3 vols. (Paris, 1944–63). See the excellent criticism by Antonio Viscardi, *ZRP*, *78* (1962), 269 ff.; *81* (1965), 454 ff.

12. *JS* (1891), 674 ff. Cf. the objections of P. S. Allen, *Mediaeval Latin Lyrics* (Chicago, 1931), p. 202, and Edmond Faral, *Romania*, *49* (1923), 237 ff.

13. *Provenzalische Chrestomathie*, ed. Carl Appel (Leipzig, 1895), no. 48.

14. For a just consideration of Ovid's contribution to world poetry, see Hermann Fränkel, *Ovid: A Poet Between Two Worlds* (Berkeley-Los Angeles, 1945).

15. For a study of the goddess Natura motif, relating Ovid and Claudian to Bernard Silvestris and the *Roman de la rose*, see Curtius, pp. 106–27.

16. Cf. Erich Auerbach, *RPh*, *4* (1950–51), 65–67.

17. The perceptive findings of comparative mythographers cannot be overlooked: Jessie L. Weston, *From Ritual to Romance* (Cambridge, Eng., 1920); James Frazer, *The Golden Bough*, 13 vols. (London, 1911–1936).

18. E.g., *Chansons de toile*, ed. H. Poulaille and R. Pernoud (Paris, 1946).

19. *De mundi universitate*, ed. C. S. Barach and J. Wrobel (Innsbruck, 1876); see Curtius, pp. 108–13.

20. The tedious Arabic-origin theory, which keeps popping back with its little store of strophic comparisons (the *zejel* or *zadjal*, especially), has been revived by the French-English anthropologist and novelist Robert S. Briffault, in his translated edition of *The Troubadours*, ed. Lawrence F. Koons (Bloomington, 1965). This work is extraordinary for the way it totally ignores Ovid's handling of the basic psychological situation of love and the recurrent tropes of love, and likewise for its bland neglect of Prudentius, Ambrose, and the whole of Catholic hymnology, which predates the Arabic stanzas held up as models for troubadour verse. Vague statements such as the following are meant to blot out a millenium of Church rhetoric and music: "Similar Church carols and

canticles in rhymed Latin are far less ancient than was at one time supposed" (p. 41).

Even if one forgot such seminal writers as Venantius Fortunatus, how could one explain the fact that not one important troubadour seems to have known Arabic? These poets were all schooled and preached to constantly in Latin, despite Briffault's absurd suggestion (p. 221, n. 18) that Latin was far removed from popular speech, and that Duke William, who signed Latin deeds and speaks about praying in Provensal and Latin, knew only enough of the older tongue to say his prayers (however much that might be!). When people from one culture adopt the ideas or modes from another, key words creep in, as the Japanese have adopted "Liverpool sound" to describe the music of the Beatles. Yet the only Arabic-inspired words in Provensal are either scurrilous, like *tafur* (dreadful), or highly technical and universal, like *algebra*. The troubadours stand as far removed from Avicenna and Averroes as they do from St. Thomas Aquinas and Albertus Magnus; they are Christian Neoplatonic in bent, as are many poets, including, no doubt, several Arabic poets. Yet proponents such as Briffault and Alois R. Nykl are so busy tearing down Provensal inventiveness and undermining Christian thought at the expense of their exotic favorites that they have never really performed the needed task of linking such works as Ibn Hazm's *Risāla* or *Dove's Neck Ring* to Ovid's *Art of Love* and Plato's *Symposium;* if Averroes perpetuates Aristotle, did not the poets also learn from the Greeks?

The Arabic influence on Italian poetry's philosophical vocabulary is undeniable, but on questions of form, tone, imagery, nothing more can be proved. Outstanding works treating this theory are: Ramón Menéndez Pidal, *Poesía árabe y poesía europea* (Madrid, 1941); *España, eslabón entre la Cristianidad y el Islam* (Madrid, 1956); Nykl, *Hispano-Arabic Poetry . . .* (Baltimore, 1946), and translation of *Risāla* (Paris, 1931); Samuel Singer, *Arabische und europäische Poesie im Mittelalter*, Abhand. der preussischen Akad. der Wissen.: Philos.-hist. Klasse, 13 (1918). For the quick but passing excitement over the Mozarabic *jarchas*, see S. M. Stern, *Al-Andalus*, 13 (1948), 299–346; Aurelio Roncaglia, *CN, 11* (1951), 213–49; Leo Spitzer, *CL, 4* (1952), 1–22.

The best-balanced study of Averroist sources, related primarily to Italian poetry, is Bruno Nardi's *Studi di filosofia medievale* (Rome, 1960). Although written long ago, one of the best critiques of the Arabic theory remains Alfred Pillet's work in *Schriften der Königsberger Gelehrten Gesellschaft: Geisteswis. Kl., 5*, pt. 4 (1928), 345–65. Note that the gifted Arabic scholar A. J. Arberry sees the influence in reversed terms in his *Arabic Poetry: A Primer for Students* (Cambridge, Eng., 1965), p. 27: "The causes which led to the development of the strophe in Spain and not in the East are obscure; the influence of popular songs in Romance has long been suspected, and is reinforced by the recent discovery that in the earliest *muwashshahs* the *envoi* was actually in Romance."

21. For an attempt to treat Arnaut's work and other Provensal poems in terms of interior stylistics, based largely on sound and rhythmic patterns, see Stephen G. Nichols, Jr., *The Disciplines of Criticism*, eds. P. Demetz, T. Greene, and L. Nelson, Jr. (New Haven, 1968), pp. 349–74.

1

DUKE WILLIAM IX OF AQUITAINE

1. Jean Boutière and A. H. Schutz, *Biographies des troubadours* (Toulouse, 1950), no. 25; similar to Geoffrey of Vigeois, *Recueil, 12,* 430: "*erat nempe vehemens amator foeminarum.*"

2. The errors are obvious: William's son, Duke William X, married Aénor, and their daughter Eleanor married the future Henry II of England, who was Duke of Normandy; the details about Eleanor's sons are correct. See Chapter 6: Bertran de Born.

3. The general history of the dynasty is well detailed by Alfred Richard, *Histoire des comtes de Poitou (778–1204),* 2 vols. (Paris, 1903). My account is also indebted to Jean Besly, *Histoire des comtes de Poictou et ducs de Guyenne* (Paris, 1647), esp. to his *Preuves.*

4. *Origines,* 2, pt. 2, 253.

5. He is called both Guido and Goffredus in *Chronicon S. Maxentii Pictavensis: Chroniques des églises d'Anjou,* ed. Paul Marchegay and Emile Mabille (Paris, 1869), p. 400 (anno 1058): "*Goffredus . . . relinquens filiam Audeberti comitis, uxorem suam, causa parentelae, aliam, Mateodam vocatam, accepit in conjugio*"; p. 404 (anno 1067): "*Per haec tempora duxit uxorem Guido comes Aldeardim, filiam Roberti ducis Burgundiae et neptam Ainrici regis Francorum, relicta Matode supradicta.*"

6. For details, see Richard, *1,* 380 f. In 1076 Pope Gregory VII still objected to "*propinqua consanguinitate*": Besly, pp. 363 f.

7. For birth, *Chron. S. Max. Pict.,* p. 405.

8. *Chron. S. Max. Pict.,* p. 403.

9. *Chron. S. Max. Pict.,* pp. 404, 406.

10. *Breve Chronicon S. Florentii Salmurensis: Chron. des églises d'Anjou,* ed. Marchegay and Mabille (Paris, 1869), p. 189; *Chron. S. Max. Pict.,* p. 408: "*Obiit Guido qui et Goffredus, comes Pictavorum; cui successit Guillelmus filius ejus, quindecim annorum existens.*"

11. See poem cited below by n. 92, sts. 2 and 4.

12. Cf. *Chron. S. Max. Pict.,* pp. 372 ff.

13. Bezzola, 2, pt. 2, 262, nn. 3, 4; Besly, p. 412: "*Cum itaque pater meus ex hoc mundo migrasset, satis puer ut plurimi norunt, ego remansi.*"

14. E. g., Ordericus Vitalis, *Historia ecclesiastica,* 10.20, ed. Augustus le Prévost, 5 vols. (Paris, 1838–55), *4,* 132. For a study of youth, see Erich Köhler, *Mélanges offerts à René Crozet . . . ,* 2 vols. (Poitiers, 1966), *1,* 569–83.

15. Richard, *1,* 389 ff.; Besly, pp. 413 f.

16. Besly, pp. 407, 409, 413.

17. Besly, pp. 392, 394, 413.

18. William of Malmesbury, *De gestis regum Anglorum,* 4.388, ed. William Stubbs, 2 vols. (London, 1887–89), 2, 455 f.; also, *Histoire générale de Languedoc:* 3, ed. C. Devic, J. Vaissete (Toulouse, 1872), 452 f.

19. Malmesbury, 4.344 ff. (2, 390–400).

20. *Chron. S. Max. Pict.*, p. 411; see bull issued in *PL 151*, 461 f.; for journey, *Vita*, PL *151*, 203.

21. Malmesbury, 4.388 (2, 457); *Chron. S. Max. Pict.*, p. 412.

22. Besly, pp. 408, 410; *Chron. S. Max. Pict.*, p. 411; *Hist. gén. de Lang.*, *3*, 452 f., 466, for discussion of legal details; 506 ff. for occupation of Toulousain.

23. Malmesbury, 4.369 (2, 425 ff.)

24. Ordericus, 10.5 (*4*, 25 f.), 10.12 (*4*, 80).

25. On Rufus' death, Malmesbury, 4.333 (2, 377–79); on William's usurpation and sale, *Hist. gén. de Lang.*, *3*, 542 ff.

26. Gaufridus Grossus, *Vita Beati Bernardi . . . de Tironio*, 6.48: *PL 172*, 1396; a somewhat less dramatic account by Hugo Flaviniacensis, *Recueil, 13*, 626.

27. Ordericus, 10.19 (*4*, 118).

28. *Chronicon Universale*, PL *154*, 979.

29. My account based primarily on Albert of Aix (Albericus Aquensis), *Historia Hierosolymitanae expeditionis*, PL *166*, 389 ff.; for the Archbishop, Anselm of Buis, 8.1 ff. (605 ff.). Albert is severely criticized by Heinrich von Sybel, *Geschichte des ersten Kreuzzugs*, 2d ed. (Leipzig, 1881), but he is more complete and more orderly than Malmesbury, 4.383 (2, 447 f.) and Ordericus, 10.19 (*4*, 118 ff.).

30. For Alexius, see Malmesbury, 4.349 (2, 400 f.); Ekkehard, *PL 154*, 981 f.

31. Albert, 8.4 (*PL 166*, 607).

32. Ordericus, 10.19 ff. (*4*, 122 ff.).

33. Albert, 8.6 (608 f.); Stephen Henry's story told more fully by Ordericus, 10.19 (*4*, 118 f.).

34. Albert, 8.5 (608). See Laurita and John Hill, *Raymond IV, Count of Toulouse* (Syracuse, 1962).

35. Ordericus, 10.19 (*4*, 122).

36. A dim view in Ekkehard, *PL 154* (981); Ordericus, 10.19 (*4*, 124 ff.). Journey in Albert, 8.7 (609 ff.). Cf. Steven Runciman, *A History of the Crusades, 2: The Kingdom of Jerusalem and the Frankish East, 1100–1187* (New York, repr. 1965), pp. 18 ff.

37. Albert, 8.17 (614 f.).

38. Albert, 8.24 (618); Runciman, 2, 25.

39. Albert, 8.24 (618); for later appearances, 8.41 ff. (623 ff.).

40. Albert, 8.25 (618).

41. Albert, 8.28 ff. (619 ff.).

42. Albert, 8.34 ff. (621 ff.).

43. Albert, 8.36 (622); this account differs radically from those of Malmesbury, 4.349 (2, 400 f.), and Ordericus, 10.19 (*4*, 122 ff.).

44. Albert, 8.38 (622 f.).

45. Albert, 8.40 (623); cf. Ordericus, 10.19 (*4*, 129): "*Pictavensis dux . . . pauper et mendicus vix Antiochiam pertingens cum sex sociis intrat.*" Malmesbury notes that only Hugh the Great, whose remains reached Tarsus, was missing from the great French leaders: 4.383 (2, 448).

46. Albert, 8.42 (624); cf. Runciman, 2, 56 ff.

47. Malmesbury, 4.383 (2, 448); Albert, 8.44 (624 f.).

48. Ordericus, 10.20 (4, 132).

49. William's priority was consistently maintained by Karl Vossler, *Miscellanea di studi in onore di Attilio Hortis*, 2 vols. (Trieste, 1910), *1*, 419 ff. More recently his creativity has been stressed by Antonio Viscardi, the most articulate critic of Bezzola's historicizing and of origin hunters: *ZRP*, *78* (1962), 269 ff.; *81* (1965), 454 ff.

50. Samples of her activities in Besly, pp. 416, 419 f.

51. Baldricus Dolensis, *Vita Beati Roberti de Arbrissello*, 3.16: PL *162*, 1051 ff.; see also *Vita Auctore Andrea*, PL *162*, 1061.

52. Goffridus Vindocinensis, *Epistolae*, 4.47 (PL *157*, 182): "*Feminarum quasdam, ut dicitur, nimis familiariter tecum habitare permittis, quibus privata verba saepius loqueris, et cum ipsis etiam, et inter ipsas noctu frequenter cubare non erubescis. . . Hoc si modo agis, vel aliquando egisti, novum et inauditum sed infructuosum genus martyrii invenisti. . . Tu autem contra rationem non mediocriter praesumpsisti, si qualibet occasione cubasti cum mulieribus, quas mundo furatus lucrari Domino debueras.*"

53. The relationships among William, Philippa, and Robert have been studied by Bezzola, *2*, pt. 2, 275 ff. Philippa's death is usually dated Nov. 28, 1117 or 1118 (Bezzola, *2*, pt. 2, 290, and Richard, *1*, 474); Robert's death is usually dated Feb. 23, 1117, but *Chron. S. Max. Pict.* says 1116 (p. 426). Philippa last appears on public rolls in 1115.

54. Ordericus, 11.16 (4, 217 f.); William of Tyre, *Recueil*, *12*, 518.

55. See below, n. 64.

56. On the name Dangerosa, see Richard, *1*, 472, citing PL *179*, 1384; on Malbergion, note the remarks of Besly, p. 2: Charlemagne "*établit des Comtes . . . pour mesnager les droicts, et le domaine de la Couronne, et administrer la iustice, estans obligez de tenir à cette fin les Mals ou Mallobergs ordinaires. On appelloit ainsi les auditoires publics, parce que suiuant les loix de France ils deuoient estre à l'abry, et à couuert l'Esté contre l'ardeur du Soleil, l'hyuer contre la pluye, et autres iniures de l'air: ce que le mot signifie. D'ou vient qu'au Palais de Poictiers, anciennement celui des Comtes, la principale tour . . . s'appelle encores auiourd'huy* Maubergeon." For picture, see *Enciclopedia Italiana*, 27 (1949), tav. 138, facing p. 601; it was restored and augmented by the Duke of Berry.

57. Ordericus, 12.21 (4, 378).

58. *Recueil*, *13*, 729.

59. Tyre, *Recueil*, *12*, 518; Argentré cited by Besly, p. 430.

60. *Epistolae*, 5.19: PL *157*, 202.

61. *Chron. S. Max. Pict.*, p. 428: "*comes Willelmus et dux Aquitanorum et rex Aragundiae pugnaverunt cum Abraham et aliis quatuor regibus Hispaniarum, in campo Cotanciae; et devicerunt et occiderunt quindecim millia Moabitarum et innumerabiles captivaverunt*"; Richardus Pictavensis, *Recueil*, *12*, 412 f. The suggestion of Briffault (*Troubadours*, p. 71) that William may have learned something from staying in courts in Spain, when the Duke went to that country only to put down the Moors, is as absurd as the author's hint that William may have learned composition from the monastery-bent Philippa, who had learned it from her first husband Sancho, who had learned it from the Arabs

(p. 53). A single quotation will demonstrate the author's inaccuracy: "Guilhem the younger was only fifteen when he succeeded his father who, according to his own desire, was buried in Spain, at Santiago da Compostela" (p. 53).

62. This year maintained by Bezzola, *2*, pt. 2, 267, and Richard, *1*, 493; in chronicles, *Chron. S. Max. Pict.*, p. 431; *Breve Chron. S. Flor.*, p. 190. However, 1127 has been upheld by numerous others, including Jeanroy and Besly, p. 452.

63. *Chron. S. Max. Pict.*, p. 432.

64. 5.439 (2, 510 f.).

65. All my translations based on *Les Chansons de Guillaume IX*, ed. Alfred Jeanroy (Paris, 1927); this poem, no. 5.

66. *Analecta Hymnica Medii Aevi*, *2:* ed. G. M. Dreves (repr. New York, 1961), no. 26, p. 38; the first part of this volume, the famed *Hymnal of the Abbey of Moissac* in southern France, contains some of the oldest hymns to the Virgin and saints, many placed by Dreves in the tenth century or before, thus paralleling or predating supposed Arabic precedents; the *Hymnal* is one of the earliest containing music (pp. 103 ff.). For a correlation of quantitative and qualitative meter, see F. J. E. Raby, *A History of Secular Latin Poetry in the Middle Ages*, 2 vols., 2nd ed. (Oxford, 1957), *1*, 304: "the quantitative iambic dimeter seems to have changed itself by an easy and, as it were, painless process into rhythmical form."

67. *An. Hymn.*, *2*, no. 18, p. 35; the stanzas show wide variations throughout the hymn, suggesting the enormous freedom offered the composer, yet also dramatically demonstrating the tendency *toward* rhyme, which seems at times inescapable (Latin case endings promote this uniformity).

68. *Les Troubadours* (Bourges, 1961), p. 127; *SM1* is now BN f. lat. 1139.

69. The dichotomy underlying William's work has always been apparent: Leo Pollmann, *ZRP*, 78 (1962), 357: "*Wir haben also in Wilhelm von Aquitanien ein kostbares Bindeglied kennengelernt, das von der Welt des der Liebe abgewandten Ritters heroischer Zeiten hinführt zur Welt höfischer Liebe*"; Theophil Spoerri, *Trivium*, 2 (1944), 276: "*Wilhelm begann auch mit der Opposition*"; Pio Rajna, *Mélanges Jeanroy* (Paris, 1928), pp. 349 ff., coined the phrase "*trovatore bifronte*", which has somehow stuck with the poet. Spoerri, however, saw more than mere opposition: a "*Schaffensprozess*."

70. First Tale, Third Day: Masetto da Lamporecchio insinuates himself into a convent, plays the deaf and dumb gardener, and seduces the nuns; Boccaccio thus travesties the *hortus conclusus* imagery that is traceable back to the Song of Songs. For a witty discussion of fabliaux, see Paul E. Bleichner, *PMLA*, 82 (1967), 33 f.

71. Ed. Jeanroy, no. 1.

72. *100 Selected Poems* (New York: Grove Press, 1959), no. 20, pp. 24 f.

73. Ed. Jeanroy, no. 8.

74. *Amores* 1.9.1.

75. Ed. Jeanroy, no. 10.

76. Traced in my *Cruelest Month* (New Haven, 1965); see also Ernst Robert Curtius, *European Literature and the Latin Middle Ages*, tr. W. R. Trask, Bollingen Series, 36 (New York, 1953), pp. 106 ff., 183 ff.

77. *Ars amoris*, 3.61–64.

78. Translated and analyzed in *The Cruelest Month*, pp. 9 ff.
79. See Raby, *Christian-Latin Poetry*, pp. 77 ff.
80. Ed. Karl Breul (Cambridge, Eng., 1915), no. 32 (*Levis exsurgit Zephirus*); the other poem, with a more difficult MS tradition, well edited by E. P. Vuolo, *CN, 10* (1950), 5 ff.
81. An excellent study of ambiguity in medieval literature by D. W. Robertson, Jr., *Speculum, 26* (1951), 24 ff.
82. Ed. Jeanroy, no. 1, 6.
83. Ed. Jeanroy, no. 6, 36.
84. See Edmond Faral, *Les Arts poétiques du XIIe et du XIIIe siècle* (Paris, 1962).
85. Developed by Scheludko, *AR, 15* (1931), 137 ff.
86. *PL 162*, 1052.
87. Ed. Jeanroy, no. 9.
88. This word has no real equivalent in modern English; "joy" is too formal to capture the colloquial flavor, which signified "fun," "a thrill," or in modern slang, "kicks"; yet these words do not have the religious connotation, except in an indirect Zen Buddhist-beatnik sense, that is still apparent in the modern English: "Joy to the world!" "Jesus, joy of man's desiring," etc. There is an unconvincing attempt to point up varying shades of meaning between *joi, gaug,* and *solatz* by Charles Camproux in *Mélanges István Frank*, Annales Universitatis Saravensis, 6 (Saarbrücken, 1957), pp. 100 ff. Equally unconvincing is A. J. Denomy in *MS, 11* (1949), 1–22; Moshé Lazar, *Amour courtois et "fin'amors"* (Paris, 1964), pp. 33–44.
89. E.g., *Carmina Burana*, ed. A. Hilka and O. Schumann (Heidelberg, 1941) *1*, pt. 2: no. 58, sts. 1 and 5; no. 74, st. 1.
90. Sappho, *Phainetai moi*; Catullus, *Ille mi par esse deo videtur*; for the philosophical development, see Aldo D. Scaglione, *Nature and Love in the Late Middle Ages* (Berkeley-Los Angeles, 1963), pp. 60 ff.
91. Ed. Jeanroy, no. 4; reprinted with permission in emended form from *Medieval Age*, ed. Angel Flores (New York: Dell, Laurel, 1963), pp. 174 f.
92. Ed. Jeanroy, no. 11.
93. Argued in Jeanroy's edition, p. 41, citing Diez, *Leben und Werke* (1829 ed.), pp. 15 f. One must, however, keep in mind Radulfus de Diceto (*Recueil, 13,* 729): "*Anno MCXII . . . Willelmus Comitis primogenitus matris injurias ulcisci proponens, insurrexit in patrem: inter quos lite protracta diutius, damnosum Aquitania transegit septennium.*" The historical authenticity has been challenged, for Radulfus was not among those closest to the scene.
94. *Cod. MS Monaster. Nov. Pictav.* in Besly, p. 452.

2

MARCABRUN

1. Boutière and Schutz, *Biographies*, no. 64. The name Marcabrun(s) occurs in the texts, although Marcabru, with the dropping of the terminal nasal, is normal in Old Provensal.

2. All my translations based on *Poésies complètes du troubadour Marcabru*, ed. J. M. L. Dejeanne, Bibl. mérid., 1st Ser., 12 (1909); this poem, no. 18. This edition supplemented by Kurt Lewent, *ZRP*, 37 (1913), 313–37, 427–51; Lewent's reading adopted in st. 4. Excellent selection and commentary by Martín de Riquer, *La Lirica de los trovadores, 1* (Barcelona, 1948), pp. 33–76. For a critical bibliography, see F. Pirot, *Le Moyen Age*, 73 (1967), 87–126.

3. Satiric and poetic traits of the Early Fathers treated most sympathetically by E. K. Rand, *Founders of the Middle Ages* (Cambridge, Mass., 1928).

4. Cf. Ovid, *Amores* 1.2.46 and Proverbs 6:27. Two leading researchers of Marcabrun's sources are Guido Errante, *Sulla lirica romanza delle origini* (New York, 1943), *Marcabru e le fonti sacre dell'antica lirica romanza* (Florence, 1948); and Dimitri Scheludko, *Archivum Romanicum, 15* (1931), esp. 178 ff.

5. Ed. Dejeanne, no. 36, who identifies the lord in the tornada as Count Alphonse Jourdain of Toulouse; although Bezzola's suggestion (*Origines, 2*, pt. 2, 322) of Alfonso VII of Castile makes better sense because of continuity with other poems. For a sample of the inability of intellectual historians to cope with Marcabrun's basic vocabulary of Joy, Measure, Gallantry, etc., see Lazar, *Amour courtois*, pp. 21–46; A. J. Denomy, *MS, 6* (1944), 175–260, and *MS, 7* (1945), 139–207. Cf. the considered opinion of James E. Shaw, *Guido Cavalcanti's Theory of Love* (Toronto, 1949), pp. 105–07.

6. A single connotation is impossible to establish, for the Germanic loan words were undergoing the same sort of transformation effected upon the Latin. If attested forms such as *drut liut* (beloved people) suggest a social, tribal sphere, there is still *drut-thiarna* (Beloved Virgin) to show the religious possibility. For the general problem, see Dennis H. Green, *The Carolingian Lord* (Cambridge, Eng., 1965).

   L.E. Kastner in *MLR, 28* (1933), 40, posits the basic meaning for *drut* as "faithful friend," but notes that the word soon acquired the connotation of *gaillard;* he identified the root as Celtic *druto* (Welsh *drut*), without establishing priority over the Teutonic form. The exact source is not so important as its international usage, for the word occurs in all of the major Romance languages; its cognates in modern Erse and Gaelic mean "whore."

7. Some of the most valuable essays relating secular to religious music: Hans Spanke, *ZFSL*, 54 (1930), 282–317, (1931), 385–422; 56 (1932), 450–78; Abhand. der Gesell. der Wissen. zu Göttingen: Philol.-hist. Kl., III Folge, 18 (1936), 24 (1940); and by Philipp August Becker, *ZFSL*, 56 (1932), 257–323. The effect of these earlier efforts is noticeable in the work of Jacques Chailley, *L'Ecole musicale de St. Martial de Limoges jusqu'à la fin du XIe siècle* (Paris, 1960). For listening, *History of Music in Sound: 2, Early Medieval Music up to 1300* (RCA Victor LM 6015 [2]).

8. Cited by Spanke, *ZFSL, 56* (1932), 472.

9. Ed. Dejeanne, no. 31; the text is uncertain almost throughout. I relate *buzina* in st. 4 to modern French *bousillage*. For an excellent discussion of Marcabrun's High and Low Love, see D. W. Robertson, Jr., *SP, 51* (1954), 539–60, esp. 557.

10. E.g., St. Bernard, *Sermones in Cantica, PL 183*, 794, 945 ff.

11. Ed. Dejeanne, no. 35. In st. 5, I read *garnizos* (loot) for *garssos* (traitors), with the overtone of arms or weaponry. In st. 6, I disagree

with the Hill-Bergin translation of *folpidor* as "place of torment," read-ing instead *volpidor* and connecting it with *volpilh, lâche;* the root *volp* (*vulpus*, fox) suggests a whorehouse in any case. Bezzola (2, pt. 2, 323) identifies the emperor as Alfonso VI of Castile and the Marquis (of Provence) as Count Raymond Beranger IV of Barcelona. The Count in st. 8 would be Duke William IX's son, the eighth Count of Poitou, who died in 1137. For an assessment, see Angelo Monteverdi, *La Poesia lirica provenzale* (Rome, 1950), 49 f.

12. *Lirica romanza*, pp. 406 f.: e.g., Isaiah 1:16, John 9:7, Psalms 50:9.

13. Ed. Dejeanne, no. 6; cf. Lewent, *ZRP*, 37 (1913), 320 f., some of whose emendations I have followed, as in st. 1.

14. Classical and medieval pastoral poetry related by Edmond Faral, *Romania, 49* (1923), 204 ff.

15. *Poetae Latini Aevi Carolini, 1*, 270–72; the attribution of the debate poem is doubted. For the origin of *tensos*, see Erich Köhler, *Troba-dorlyrik und höfischer Roman* (Berlin, 1962), 153 ff.

16. Ed. Dejeanne, no. 30; last 2 lines omitted from many MSS.; see Köhler, *Trobadorlyrik und höfischer Roman*, pp. 193 ff.; Alfred Pillet, *Schriften der Königsberger Gelehrten Gesellschaft: Geisteswissen. Kl., 5*, pt. 4 (1928), 345–65.

17. *De amore*, I.6A-G (ed. E. Trojel, repr. Munich, 1964), pp. 19–219. On the doctrine of similarity-seeking in love, see Albertus Magnus, *De animalibus*, XII.1.i., II.1.x; Thomas Aquinas, *Summa Theologica*, II.1, xxvii, art. 1.

18. Central to the notion of adhering to one's nature or reverting to a beastlike state is Boethius, *De consol. phil.*, IV.2: "*Est enim quod ordinem retinet servatque naturam; quod vero ab hac deficit, esse etiam quod in sua natura situm est derelinquit*"; IV.3: "*Quare versi in malitiam humanam quoque amisere naturam*"; we must remember that a trans. of Boethius is one of the earliest works in the literature. For Spitzer, see *Romania, 73* (1952), 79–82.

19. Ed. Dejeanne, no. 1; the last 2 lines are somewhat ambiguous. I follow Dejeanne's reading, doubting that *mas pauc mi tey* means "but [my man] cares little for me." The man's absence, not his negligence, seems to be the issue.

20. See Anna Granville Hatcher, *MLN, 79* (1964), 284–95, who points up the oppositions, but insists that the woman's plaintive song rises over the pastoral dialectic.

21. Ed. Breul, no. 32.

3

JAUFRE RUDEL

1. *Triumph of Love*, 4.52 f.

2. *La Princesse lointaine* (Paris, 1903); Bernhardt received the dedication.

3. Boutière and Schutz, *Biographies*, no. 60.

4. *Mélanges de littérature française du moyen âge*, pp. 498–538.

5. My translations based on edition of Alfred Jeanroy, (Paris, 1924); this poem, no. 5. My reading of st. 2, 1–2, based on Kurt Lewent, *MLN*, 76 (1961), 525 ff. Less valuable are the suggestions of Rita Lejeune, *Studi in onore di Angelo Monteverdi* (Modena, 1959), 403 ff.

6. Grace Frank, *MLN*, 57 (1942), 528–34; D. W. Robertson, Jr., *SP*, 49 (1952), 566–82. On the limits of allegory, see Theodore Silverstein, *PMLA, 82* (1967), 28 ff.

7. Richard of St. Victor, *In Cantica Canticorum, PL 196*, 475. Cols. 482–84 treat the Virgin's "whole and perfect beauty" (*integra et perfecta pulchritudine*); she is portrayed as the victor over Satan (484) in heroic terms.

8. Tr. M. Belgion, rev. ed. (New York, 1956); first published as *L'Amour et l'Occident* (Paris, 1946).

9. Note the witty remarks of Erich Auerbach on the *Ursprungsfrage* in general: *RPh, 4* (1950–51), 65–67.

10. See Borst's *Die Katharer* (Stuttgart, 1953). Primary sources: *Un Traité néo-manichéen du XIIIe siècle: le 'Liber de duobus principiis,'* ed. D. Dondaine, Inst. hist. Frat. Praedicat. (Rome, 1939); Richard Reitzenstein, *Die Vorgeschichte der christlichen Taufe* (Leipzig-Berlin, 1929): *Interrogatio Iohannis*, 297 ff.; René Nelli, *Écritures cathares: Textes précathares et cathares* (Paris, 1959); Durand de Huesca, *Une Somme anti-cathare: le 'Liber contra Manicheos,'* ed. Christine Thouzellier (Louvain, 1964).

11. *De fide catholica contra haereticos sui temporis, PL 210*, 308.

12. *PL 210, 309.*

13. See Borst, pp. 143 ff.

14. *PL 210, 351.*

15. *Ibid.* The attempt of Leo Pollmann to distinguish between *solatz* and *joi*, with religious and secular distinctions, is not very rewarding: *ZRP, 80* (1964), 256–68. Also too schematic is Eugen Lerch, *CN, 3* (1943), 214 ff.

16. *Le Nouveau Testament . . . en langue provençal, suivi d'un Rituel Cathare*, ed. Léon Clédat, Bibl. de la Fac. des Lettres de l'Univ. de Lyon, 4 (1887), xxiv. See the cogent remarks of A. J. Denomy, *MS, 7* (1945), 184; however, Denomy's inability to relate the poetry meaningfully to the Church (p. 179) seriously vitiates his work, as in his *Heresy of Courtly Love* (New York, 1947).

17. Ed. Clédat, pp. xviii f.

18. They were especially fond of Matthew and John (ed. Clédat, pp. xii, xvi f., xviii f.). For Christian equivalents, see Bernard of Morlas (Morlaix), *De contemptu mundi*, ed. H. C. Hoskier (London, 1929) and Innocent III, *PL 217*, 701–46. On the origin in Hellenistic times, E. R. Dodds, *Pagan and Christian in an Age of Anxiety* (Cambridge, Eng., 1965), pp. 1–36.

19. Borst, p. 164.

20. Ed. Jeanroy, no. 2.

21. Ed. Jeanroy, no. 4, st. 4; no. 8, st. 3.

22. Ed. Dejeanne, no. 30, st. 13, 6 and 8.

23. Locus classicus: Song of Songs 1.1. Synoptic comment: Cornelius a Lapide, *Commentarii in Sacram Scripturam*, 4 (Lyon-Paris, 1864), 715 ff., esp. 745.

24. *Sermones in Cantica, PL 183*, 877; also, 984 ff. Other love tropes touched upon in this seminal work are: the kiss (789 ff.); visions of love (790); supremacy of loved one (790 f.); mystical seclusion (794); lover as servant (794); beloved as medicine or doctor (794, 819–24, 945 ff.); lack of measure in love (825); drunkenness and madness (807 f., 833, 999); doctrine of faithful service (824); fruit as reward (825); beloved as light (846); vigil of love (856, 957 ff.); praise as proper language toward beloved (858). Also, Richard, *In C. C., PL 196*, 405 ff.; Bernard, *De diligendo Deo, PL 182*, 973 ff.

25. Ed. Jeanroy, no. 3.

26. *Symp.* 178 ff., 186 ff. Typical in poetry is Anacreon, Frag. 83, *Poetae Melici Graeci*, ed. Denys Page (Oxford, 1962), pp. 210 f., or the general feelings of entrapment in paradox expressed in Catullus 85 and Ovid, *Amores* 2.19.36 and 3.14.39. For an excellent assessment of Greek appreciation of mysticism, see E. R. Dodds, *The Greeks and the Irrational* (Berkeley-Los Angeles, 1951).

27. *L'Amour lointain de Jaufré Rudel et le sens de la poésie des troubadours*, UNCSRLL, 5 (1944). Less successful, because it reverses the process, is Myrrha Lot-Borodine's *De l'Amour profane à l'amour sacré*, preface E. Gilson (Paris, 1961). Too schematically Augustinian is Mario Casella, *ASI, 96*, pt. 2 (1938), 153 ff. See Diego Zorzi, *Valori religiosi nella letteratura provenzale: la spiritualità trinitaria* (Milan, 1954).

28. Ed. Jeanroy, no. 6.

29. Ed. L. W. Daly and W. Suchier, ISLL, 24, nos. 1 and 2 (1939), 134 ff. Antithesis as a dominant mode was suggested by Dimitri Scheludko, *Archivum Romanicum, 15* (1931), 155 ff.; for riddle literature, 164 ff. For a discussion in terms of psychological conflict, see Ronald N. Walpole, *RPh, 13* (1959–60), 429–41.

30. *PL 183*, 877.

31. Ed. Clédat, p. xiv.

32. *PL 183*, 952, citing Psalms 136:1 (Vulg.).

33. *PL 183*, 825, citing Luke 6:38.

34. Ed. Jeanroy, no. 1.

35. Ed. Dejeanne, no. 15, st. 7.

36. The attempt of Dronke (*Med. Latin and the Rise, 1*, 98 ff.) to link Raimbaut of Orange with the Neoplatonic tradition mistakes poetic obscurantism for philosophical absolutism, and shows no appreciation of Raimbaut's dark humor, a quality that pervades his work and sets him as far apart from Jaufre as from Guinizelli. Except for the decadents of the thirteenth century, such as Matfre Ermengaud, Rudel most clearly points the way to Italy; yet the path was long indeed. In his attempt to provide formal distinctions for some words of knowledge, A. H. Schutz in *Speculum, 33* (1958), 508 ff., concedes that "the troubadours were not philosophers" (p. 508), and deals largely with figures from the Albigensian period.

4

BERNART DE VENTADORN

1. *Purg.* XXVI. 115–20; *De vulg. eloq.* II.2.

2. Dimitri Scheludko, *Archivum Romanicum, 15* (1931), 137 ff., insisted on the Scholastic basis for this separation of styles, citing among others Geoffrey of Vinsauf (ed. Faral, pp. 284 f.): *"unus modus est utendi ornata facilitate, alius modus est utendi ornata difficultate."*

3. *Symp.* 178 f., 186 f.; see Dodds, *Greeks and Irrational,* pp. 64 ff.

4. All my translations from *B. von V.: Seine Lieder,* ed. Carl Appel (Halle, 1915); vida, pp. xi–xiv (left col.); selected version, Halle, 1926, using criticism of Kurt Lewent, *ZRP, 43* (1923), 657–74, and Oskar Schultz-Gora, *ZRP, 42* (1922), 350–70. I have consulted the literal translations in the edition of Stephen G. Nichols, Jr., John A. Galm, and others, which appears as UNCSRLL, 39 (1962). Earlier studies: Karl Vossler, *Der Minnesang des B. von V.* (Munich, 1918); Nicola Zingarelli, *Studi Medievali, 1* (1905), 309 ff. See Moshé Lazar, ed. and tr., *Bernard de Ventadour* (Paris, 1966).

5. Ed. Hill-Bergin, *Anthology,* no. 49, 19–24.

6. Henry is almost certainly the *"reis engles"* of no. 26, st. 7, 43; Eleanor the *"reina dels Normans"* of no. 33, st. 7, 45; another supporting poem, no. 21, st. 7; on the whole question, Appel, pp. xxxiii ff.

7. For a full-blown portrait, somewhat overstated, see Amy Kelly, *Eleanor of Aquitaine and the Four Kings* (Cambridge, Mass., 1950), pp. 109 ff. An important essay challenging these accepted terms by J. F. Benton, *Speculum, 36* (1961), 551–91; see also Antonio Viscardi, *Letterature d'oc e d'oil* (Milan, 1952), 141–43.

8. For Narbonne, ed. Appel, no. 23, 58; for Raymond, pp. xliv ff.

9. Ed. Appel, pp. xxxi ff. Cf. Bezzola, *Origines, 2,* pt. 2, 317, who favors Ebles II "the Singer."

10. E.g., Marcabrun, ed. Dejeanne, no. 31, st. 9; see above: Chap. 2, n. 9.

11. Ed. Appel, no. 2.

12. First studied systematically by Wilibald Schrötter, *Ovid und die Troubadours* (Halle, 1908); see my *Cruelest Month,* pp. 151 ff.

13. Ed. Appel, no. 37.

14. Ed. Appel, no. 44; Lewent's suggestions adopted in st. 1.

15. Ed. Appel, no. 30.

16. Ed. Appel, no. 15.

17. Ed. Appel, no. 28 (left col.); the opening word *pascor* can mean either "Easter" or "spring."

18. Ed. Appel, no. 26.

19. Ed. Appel, no. 4 (left col.).

20. Ed. Appel, no. 39.

5

THE COUNTESS OF DIA

1. See Oskar Schultz-Gora, *Die provenzalischen Dichterinnen* (Leipzig, 1888).
2. Jeanroy, *Poésie lyrique, 1,* 314, n. 1. There have also been suggestions that "Dia" is a given first name.
3. Boutière and Schutz, *Biographies,* no. 27.
4. "Die, Béatrice, comtesse de," *Larousse du XXe siècle, 2* (1929), 855. See the sentimental portrait of Sernin Santy, *Comtesse de Die* (Paris, 1893), who grasps for a historical subject. Cf. Jules Chevalier, *Bull. d'archéol. et de statist. de la Drôme, 27* (1893), 183–202; Jeanroy, *Poésie lyrique, 1,* 313 f. For a statement of the general insolubility of the problem, S. Stronski, *RLR, 50* (1907), 16 n. The very name Beatritz for the wife of William of Poitiers is unsupported: Chevalier, 190 f.
5. *Life and Works of the Troubadour Raimbaut d'Orange* (Minneapolis, 1952), pp. 27–30.
6. My translations based on Gabrielle Kussler-Ratyé, *Archivum Romanicum, 1* (1917), 161–82; this poem, no. 3.
7. Ed. Kussler-Ratyé, no. 4; I read "sin" for *error* in st. 1, although others prefer "fault" or "error."
8. E.g., Anglade, *Troubadours,* p. 151.
9. See the judgment of Dudley Fitts, foreword, *Sappho,* tr. Mary Barnard (Berkeley-Los Angeles, 1958), ix. The difference lies primarily in the Greek poetess' realistic description of natural imagery, which is absent from most of the Provensal work, where nature is presented in a conventional, stylized way. Frederic Will has spoken significantly of Sappho's "unlocalized objectivity," *CJ, 61* (1966), 260.
10. Ed. Kussler-Ratyé, no. 5; cf. *Sappho,* tr. Barnard, nos. 74, 82. My translation of the last stanza is somewhat free; reprinted with permission from *Medieval Age,* ed. Angel Flores (New York: Dell, Laurel, 1963), p. 184, with minor emendations.
11. Ed. Kussler-Ratyé, no. 2. The identification of Seguitz and Valenssa in st. 2 is troubled; see Oskar Schultz-Gora, *ZRP, 24* (1900), 122.

6

BERTRAN DE BORN

1. *Inferno,* XXVIII.118 ff.
2. Gaufredus Vosiensis, *Chronicon: Recueil, 12,* 421 ff., and *18,* 211 ff.
3. Collected by Léon Clédat, *Du Rôle historique de B. de B.* (Paris, 1879), pp. 22 ff., 92 f.
4. The most readable account, Amy Kelly's *Eleanor of Aquitaine and the Four Kings* (Cambridge, Mass., 1950) is often inaccurate or overstated.

5. *Historia rerum Anglicarum*, ed. Richard Howlett, Rolls Series, 82, pts. 1 and 2 (repr. 1964): 1.31 (*1*, 93), "*illa maxime moribus regiis offensa, et causante se monacho non regi nupsisse.*"

6. *Historia gloriosi regis Ludovici VII: Recueil, 12,* 127.

7. Newburgh, *Hist. rer. Ang.,* 1.31 (*1*, 93).

8. The traditional romantic picture described by Kelly, pp. 198–212; but cf. J. F. Benton, *Speculum, 36* (1961), 551–91.

9. *De principis instructione,* 3.8, ed. George F. Warner, Rolls Series, 21, pt. 8 (1891), p. 247, citing *Rem. Am.,* 323.

10. *De princ. instr.,* 2.3, p. 160.

11. *De princ. instr.,* 2.4 ff., pp. 163 ff.; *Hist. rer. Ang.,* 2.27 (*1*, 169 ff.).

12. *Hist. rer. Ang.,* 3.7 ff. (*1*, 233 ff.); 3.25 (*1*, 277 ff.).

13. *Hist. rer. Ang.,* 3.25 (*1*, 278): "*et maxime ex junioris filii defectione animo saucius, quem . . . speciali amplecteretur affectu*"; Giraldus, *De princ. instr.,* 3.25, p. 295.

14. *Hist. rer. Ang.,* 3.25 (*1*, 279); *De princ. instr.,* 3.28, pp. 305 f.

15. Kelly, pp. 313–440.

16. Geoffrey of Vigeois, *Recueil, 12,* 422.

17. *Recueil, 18,* 221.

18. All my translations based on editions of either Albert Stimming (2d ed. Halle, 1892) or Carl Appel (Halle, 1932); this poem, Stimming, no. 2. I have also consulted the Italian translations of Thomas G. Bergin (Varese, 1964). Affairs here dated in 1176 by Clédat (pp. 29 ff.), who cites Benedict of Peterborough, *Gesta regis Henrici secundi,* ed. William Stubbs, 2 vols. (London, 1867), *1,* 114, 120, but Stimming (p. 49), like Diez and editor Antoine Thomas (Toulouse, 1888), prefers 1182, as does L. E. Kastner: *MLR, 29* (1934), 144. My reading of st. 3 follows Stimming, but Kastner's suggestions, such as reading with Stronski *arenalh* as the name of a fortification (p. 146 f.), have often been used. For a sensitive defense of Bertran, drawn largely from his historical milieu, see Karen Wilk Klein, *SP, 65* (1968), 612–30.

19. Ed. Appel, no. 9, with emendations of Kastner: *MLR, 28* (1933), 37–42. According to Appel, the Count is Raymond V of Toulouse, and his foe is Alfonso II of Aragon. Others in st. 7: William VIII of Montpellier, lord of Montauberon; Viscount Roger II of Béziers and Carcassonne; Viscount Bernard Athon (Oto) VI of Nîmes; Viscount Peter of Narbonne; Count Roger Bernard I of Foix; Count Bernard IV of Comminges.

20. Kastner, *MLR, 28* (1933), 38, and Stimming, p. 49; however, Clédat prefers 1177 and Diez 1183.

21. See Appel, p. 92.

22. Ed. Stimming, no. 42; Appel (no. 40) has an additional tornada, about which, see Kastner, *MLR, 32* (1937), 217. Trans. reprinted with permission in emended form from *Medieval Age,* ed. Angel Flores (New York: Dell, 1963), pp. 186 f.

23. Noted by E. Talbot Donaldson, *PMLA, 69* (1954), 928 ff.

24. Reprinted with permission from "Near Perigord," *Personae: The Collected Poems of Ezra Pound* (New York: New Directions, 1926, 1954), p. 152.

25. Ed. Stimming, no. 26; reprinted with permission in emended form from *Anthology of Medieval Lyrics*, ed. Angel Flores (New York: Modern Library, 1962), pp. 56 f.

26. If Richard was actually king when the piece was composed, events would have to take place about the year 1195, as Clédat suggests (p. 86). According to Appel (p. 129), the opponent is Alfonso VIII of Castile.

27. Ed. Stimming, no. 40; cf. Kastner, *MLR*, 32 (1937), 212 ff. Reprinted with permission in emended form from *Anthology of Medieval Lyrics*, ed. Flores, pp. 59 f.

28. Ed. Stimming, no. 23; cf. Appel, no. 34, and Kastner, *MLR*, 32 (1937), 203–06, who are overly ingenious. In st. 5, "men of tourneys" is a desperate attempt to render MS *tornes* ("men of Tours"?), often emended to *cortes*, a bit too smoothly.

29. Clédat, pp. 77 f.; however, Stimming (p. 50) suggests 1191 and an even later date is possible, after Richard's ransoming. On Richard's rapid rewinning of lands lost to Philip, see Roger of Hoveden, *Chronica*, ed. William Stubbs, 4 vols., Rolls Series, 51: 3, 252 ff.; *Hist. rer. Ang.*, 5.1 ff. (2, 415 ff.).

30. Ed. Stimming, no. 31.

31. Ed. Stimming, no. 32.

32. E.g., the *razo* before Stimming, no. 33. See the introductory comments of Stanislaw Stronski, *Le Troubadour Folquet de Marseille* (Cracow, 1910); also his *Légende amoureuse de Bertran de Born* (Paris, 1914).

33. Ed. Appel, no. 43.

34. See Clédat, pp. 52 ff.; cf. Kelly, pp. 259–67. Even when Bertran is railing against young Henry (Appel, no. 10, st. 9), he shows an affection lacking in many of his poems about Richard.

35. *De princ. instr.*, 2.9, p. 174.

36. Ed. Stimming, no. 9; reprinted with permission from *Anthology of Medieval Lyrics*, ed. Flores, pp. 53 f.

37. *De princ. instr.*, 2.11, p. 179.

38. Ed. Stimming, p. 52.

7

PEIRE CARDENAL

1. Of the other figures of the thirteenth century, Guillem Figueira, ed. Emil Levy (Berlin, 1880), is similar to Peire in tone, but more restricted in output; he spent much of his life in self-exile in Italy. The Italian Sordello (c. 1225–70), who wrote in Provensal, shows the outward-going tendency of the tradition. Even Guiraut Riquier (1254–82), who left poems in a wide variety of genres, including some haunting pastorellas, spent at least ten years in Spain: *Las Cansos*, ed. Ulrich Mölk (Heidelberg, 1962).

2. Cardenal's satiric point of view has been closely related to Latin literature, including the work of clerics, by Karl Vossler: *Peire*

Cardinal . . . (Munich, 1916), pp. 127–56, esp. to Walter Map, the Archpoet, Golias, etc. See *Carmina Burana*, ed. W. Meyer, A. Hilka, and O. Schumann, *1*, pt. 1 (Heidelberg, 1930), no. 1 (against bribery), no. 6 (on decline of studies), nos. 8–11 (on simony and luxury); nos. 41–45 (against Rome). St. Bernard, who was one of the earliest prelates aware of the dangers in the South (*PL 182*, 434 ff.), and who preached there himself in the 1140's, attacked hypocrites in language similar to Peire's *Clergue si fan pastor* (see below, n. 7): "*Ipsi sunt, qui induentes sibi formam pietatis, et virtutem ejus penitus abnegantes, profanas novitates vocum et sensuum, tanquam melli venenum, verbis coelestibus intermiscent. Cavete proinde eos tanquam veneficos; et cognoscite in vestimentis ovium lupos rapaces.*"

3. See the opinion of Pierre Belperron, *La Croisade contre les Albigeois* (Paris, 1945), p. 106.

4. Peter of Vaux-de-Cernay (Petrus Sarnensis), *Hystoria albigensis*, 2.21, ed. P. Guébin and E. Lyon, 3 vols. (Paris, 1926–39), *1*, 23. Originally Dominic and Diego had desired to proselytize the pagans of Asia, but upon being refused papal dispensation, they became interested in the heresy. For a sympathetic portrait of Dominic, see Bede Jarrett, *Life of St. Dominic* (London, 1924).

5. *Chronique*, p. 119, ed. J. Beyssier: *Troisièmes Mélanges d'histoire du moyen âge*, ed. Achille Luchaire, 18 (Paris, 1904), 85–175.

6. *Die Dichtungen des Mönchs von Montaudon*, ed. Otto Klein (Marburg, 1885), no. 8a, pp. 51 f., vv. 7 ff.

7. All of my translations based on *Poésies complètes du troubadour P. C.*, ed. René Lavaud, Bibl. mérid., 2d Ser., 34 (1957); this poem, no. 29. In st. 4, I accept "dunk their bread" for *s'escaussir* (p. 176).

8. Recounted by Peter, *Hyst. alb.*, 2.54 (*1*, 47–49); the site of the miracle of the book is sometimes given as Fanjeaux; see Jarrett, pp. 29 f.

9. *PL 215*, 1167: *Epist.* 69 (1207).

10. Peter, *Hyst. alb.*, 2.28 ff. (*1*, 31 ff.); for the marital situation, 2.38 f. (*1*, 35 f.). Peter's charges are in many ways overstated; cf. Belperron, pp. 142 ff.

11. Recounted by Innocent in a letter addressed to the prelates of Arles, Narbonne, Aix, Vienne, and Embrun (*Epist.* 26, 1208): *PL 215*, 1354–58.

12. *PL 215*, 1354: "*concitavit adversus eum* [Peter] *diabolus ministrum suum, comitem Tolosanum.*" The adjectives "*lubricus*" and "*inconstans*" remind one of ecclesiastical descriptions of William IX.

13. *Chron.*, p. 120.

14. *PL 215*, 1358: *Epist.* 28 (1208); an earlier attempt in *215*, 1246 f.: *Epist.* 149 (1207).

15. *PL 215*, 1266: *Epist.* 176 (1207); see also *216*, 617 f.

16. Peter, *Hyst. alb.*, 3.72 (*1*, 73): "*Rex autem nuncio domini pape tale dedit responsum: quod duos magnos et graves habebat a lateribus leones, Otonem . . . et regem Anglie, Johannem.*" See Belperron, p. 148. The notion that Philip was totally unaware of the danger or the gain in the Languedoc is untenable.

17. *PL 215*, 1247: *Epist.* 149 (1207).

18. Listed by Peter, *Hyst. alb.*, 3.82 ff. (*1*, 81 ff.).

19. Praised by Peter, *Hyst. alb.*, 3.104–07 (*1*, 104–12); note his dramatic utterance before the battle of Muret, falling on his knees before the

Bishop of Uzès: *"Deo et vobis offero hodie animam et corpus meum"* (2, 150). His darker side is treated throughout by the anonymous continuer of William of Tudela's part of the *Chanson de la croisade contre les Albigeois*, ed. Paul Meyer, 2 vols. (Paris, 1875–79).

20. *PL 216*, 139: *Epist.* 108 (1209).

21. *Dialogus miraculorum*, 5.21, ed. Joseph Strange, 2 vols. (Cologne, 1851), *1*, 302: *"dixerunt Abbati: Quid faciemus, domine? Non possumus discernere inter bonos et malos. Timens tam Abbas quam reliqui, ne tantum timore mortis se catholicos simularent . . . fertur dixisse: Caedite eos. Novit enim Dominus qui sunt eius."*

22. *Chanson*, 694 ff., 779 ff. For Papal acknowledgment of Simon's holdings, *PL 216*, 152 f.: *Epist.* 123 (1209).

23. Peter, *Hyst. alb.*, 3.197–243 (*1*, 199–243); Puylaurens, *Chron.*, 17 ff., pp. 133 ff.

24. Peter, *Hyst. alb.*, 3.367 ff. (*2*, 65 ff.); Belperron, pp. 252 ff.

25. For Alfonso's account of battle, see *PL 216*, 699 ff.: *Epist.* 182 (1212); for Innocent's reaction, 703 f.: *Epist.* 183 (1212); for praise of Peter to Simon, 741 ff.: *Epist.* 213 (1212).

26. *PL 216*, 743 f.: *Epist.* 214 (1212).

27. *PL 216*, 851: *Epist.* 48 (1213).

28. Described by Peter, *Hyst. alb.*, 3.448–64 (*2*, 139–55). The battle is recounted memorably in *Chanson*, 2887 ff. Map in Belperron, p. 271.

29. Peter, *Hyst. alb.*, 3.211 (*1*, 209) about the year 1211: *"insuper rex tradidit comiti prefatum primogenitum suum custodiendum."* Also, Puylaurens, *Chron.*, 16, p. 132.

30. Puylaurens, *Chron.*, 23 f., pp. 139 f.

31. Ed. Meyer, 3152 ff.; for the young Raymond, 3180 ff.; Foix, 3200 ff.; Folquet, 3253 ff.; judgment favoring Simon, 3476 ff.; qualifications for young Raymond, 3568 ff.; the young man's plight, 3680 ff.

32. Ed. Meyer, 8169–80.

33. Ed. Meyer, 8451–55.

34. *De triumphis ecclesiae*, ed. Thomas Wright (London, 1856), p. 87.

35. *Hyst. alb.*, 3.611 (2, 315).

36. Last phases of Crusade summarized in Belperron, pp. 341–446. For Louis, see Puylaurens, *Chron.*, 30, p. 145; 33 and 34, pp. 148 ff.

37. See Zoé Oldenbourg, *Massacre at Montségur: A History of the Albigensian Crusade*, tr. Peter Green (New York, 1962), esp. pp. 316 ff., 340 ff. Also, Puylaurens, *Chron.*, 44, p. 165.

38. Puylaurens, *Chron.*, 41, pp. 159–61. For a localized study, see Richard W. Emery, *Heresy and Inquisition in Narbonne* (New York, 1941); general history, William Pelisso(n), *Chronicon*, ed. C. Molinier, Bibl. de Carcassonne, 6449 (1878).

39. Ed. Lavaud, no. 74.

40. Ed. Joseph Anglade, Bibl. mérid., 1st Ser., 17–20 (1919–20); the epitaph for the period might well be lines 725 ff., p. 68: "we submit/ Both individually and together/ To the faithful Church of Rome,/ From whom we all take governing and life/ For the Holy Spirit guides it."

41. Ed. Lavaud, no. 38.

42. *RPh*, 20 (1967), 466 f.

43. Camille Chabaneau, *Biographies des troubadours* (Toulouse, 1885), p. 62.

44. Chabaneau, p. 163, n. 8.

45. Edd. respectively Paul Andraud (Paris, 1902); Wm. P. Shepard and Frank M. Chambers (Evanston, Ill., 1950); Maria Dumitrescu (Paris, 1935). See Vossler, p. 2.

46. See Lavaud, p. 621.

47. See Lavaud, pp. 617–23. For James I, see objections of Jeanroy, *Poésie lyrique, 1,* 196 f. However, the excellent work of C. Fabre upon a double tornada omitted from most earlier editions of a sirventes has established the role of James: *Miscellany of Studies in Rom. Langs. and Lits. Presented to Leon E. Kastner,* edd. Mary Williams and James A. de Rothschild (Cambridge, Eng., 1932), pp. 241–43; for the approval of Alfons Hilka, *ZRP, 52* (1932), 799 f.

48. See Lavaud, p. 610; Jeanroy, *Poésie lyrique, 1,* 404. The earlier scholars put his death in the 1240's or before, but the vida, backed by Fabre (pp. 217 ff.), seems reliable. For the attribution of Montpellier, see Fabre, p. 242.

49. Ed. Lavaud, no. 80; I omit three more stanzas plus tornada.

50. Ed. Lavaud, no. 36.

51. *A Preface to Chaucer,* pp. 3–51.

INDEX

Abelard, 199
Ab la dolchor del temps novel (William), 48–49
Absalom, 145
A chantar m'er de so q'ieu no volria (Countess), 139–140
Achitophel, 145
Adam, 46, 48, 68, 103, 140, 188
Adela, Countess of Blois, 30
Ademar. *See* Aimar
Adrianople, 32
adultery, 17, 27–28, 35–38, 67, 71, 78, 117
Aelis (in Bertran), 167–168
Aénor, Anor, 36
Agnes (in Bertran), 167
Agnes (in William), 39–41, 44, 56
Agnes, St., 46–47
Agnes de Lastours (de Turribus), 149
Aíglina (in Marc.), 70
Aimar (son of Guigue VI), 133
Aimar V, Viscount of Limoges, 149–150
Aimeric I, Viscount of Châtelleraut, 35, 36
Aimeric de Belenoi, 190
Aimeric de Peguilhan, 190
A la fontana del vergier (Marc.), 84–85
Alain de Lille, 93–94, 96
Alain Fergant, Duke of Brittany, 36
Alanus de Insulis. *See* Alain de Lille
Albert, Count of Bianorate, 29
Albert of Aix (Albericus Aquensis), 29–32, 209–210 nn.
Albertus Magnus, 207 n.
Albi, 175, 183
Albigensian Crusade, 93, 175, 178–186
Albigensianism, 93. *See also* Catharism
Albigensian period, 175
Alcibiades, 169
Alcuin, 49, 79–80, 102
Aldrics of Vilar, 63
Alegret (in Bernart), 128
A l'entrade del tens clar (Anon.), 16
Alexius I Comnenus, Byz. Emp., 29, 31

Alfonso I (the Battler), King of Aragon, 37
Alfonso II, King of Aragon, 149, 153–154, 219 n.
Alfonso VI, King of Castile, 73, 214 n.
Alfonso VII, King of Castile, 67, 68
Alfonso VIII, King of Castile, 157–158, 181
Alfonso X, King of Castile, 191
Allegory; in Bible, 50, 78–79; in Marcabrun, 65–66, 85; in Alcuin, 79–80; in Jaufre, 92–93; in Peire, 193
Allen, P. S., 206 n.
Alphonse of Poitiers, 191
Altafort, 145, 147–150
Amars (in Marc.), 71
Amaury de Montfort, 185
Ambrose, St., 18, 49, 206 n.
Amics, en gran cossirier (Raimbaut-Countess?), 134–136
Amics Marchabrun, car digam (Marc.-Catola), 76–77
Amor, 42, 54, 65
amor fina, 70, 71, 94
Amors, Bon' (in Marc.), 69
Amors, e que. us es vejaire? (Bernart), 126–128
Anatolia, 30
Andraud, Paul, 223 n.
Andreas Capellanus, 83, 205 n.
Anglade, Joseph, 14, 206 n., 218 n., 222 n.
Anjou, 24, 25, 43, 56–57, 112
Ankara, 31
Anselm, Archbishop of Milan, 29–31
antifeminism, 34–35, 54, 95
Antioch, 31, 33, 74, 146
Apollo, 164
Appel, Carl, 217 n., 219–220 nn.
April Queen, 17
Aquitaine, 23–24, 63, 97, 149, 154, 171
Arabic literature, 18, 33, 34, 42
Arabic-origin theory, 206–207 nn.
Arabs, 15, 27, 74, 93, 96, 97, 98, 178. *See also* Moors
Aragon, 181–183
Arberry, A. J., 207 n.

Archpoet, 221 n.
Arenalh, 151, 219 n.
Aristotle, 159, 164, 207 n.
Arnaldus of Cîteaux, 180
Arnaut Daniel, 19, 109, 159
Arnold (jongleur), 161
Arramon Luc of Esparron, 152
Arsen (in William), 44, 56
Arthur, King, 46
Atressi com l'olifanz (Berbezilh), 200–201
Audiart (in Bertran), 167–168
Audiart of Beaugency, 24, 26, 36
Audiart. *See also* Hildegarde
Auerbach, Erich, 205 n., 206 n., 215 n.
Augustine, St., 15, 65, 71, 103
Aurora, 77
Auvergne, 26, 39, 191
Averroes, 207 n.
Avicenna, 54, 207 n.
Avignon, 185
Azalais of Porcairagues, 133

Baez, Joan, 198
Baldricus Dolensis, 34, 51, 210 n.
Baldwin I, King of Jerusalem, 33
Balzac, Honore de, 17
Barbasto, 25
Barcelona, 27
Barons (in Bertran), 149
Bartsch, Karl, 206 n.
Baudouin of Sebourg, 163
Baudri. *See* Baldricus
Bayard, 151, 152
Bazièe, 185
Beatles, 199
Beatrice (wife of Wm. I of Poitiers ?), 133
Beatrice of Béziers, 179
Beatritz (name applied to Countess), 133–134
Beaucaire, 183
Beaugency, 146
Becker, P. A., 213 n.
Bel m'es quan vei chamjar lo senhoratge (Bertran), 160–161
Belperron, Pierre, 221 n.
Bels Senher (in Bertran), 168
Be.m platz lo gais tems de pascor (Bertran), 154–156
Benedict of Peterborough, 219 n.
Benoît de Sainte-Maure, 147
Benton, J. F., 217 n., 219 n.

Berart of Mondidier, 163
Bergin, T. G., 8, 219 n.
Bernard IV, Count of Comminges, 153, 181, 219 n.
Bernard Athon (Oto) VI, Visc. of Nîmes, 153, 219 n.
Bernard of Clairvaux, St., 14–15, 92, 98, 103, 106
Bernard of Morlas (Morlaix), 215 n.
Bernard of Tiron, 28
Bernard Silvestris, 18, 206 n.
Bernard the Stranger, 33
Bernart de Ventadorn: 107–130; achievement, 109, 113; vida evaluated, 110–112; death, 112–113; critique of rhetoric, 115–118; related to William, 112, 113; to Marc., 113, 117; to Jaufre, 113; mentioned, 7, 13, 14, 147, 171, 198, 199
Bernhardt, Sarah, 89
Berry, 97, 98
Bertrade de Montfort, 28, 35, 67
Bertran (in Jaufre), 101
Bertran d'Argentré, 36, 210 n.
Bertran de Born: 143–172; known facts of life, 145–146; judged by Dante, 145, 159–160; related to Henry II, 146–149; possible connection with Eleanor, 147; related to The Barons, 149; family life, 149–152; used by Pound, 157, 159; related to epic tradition, 161–164; as love poet, 164–168; achievement, 171–172; related to William, 154, 166; to Marc., 163–164, 172; to Peire, 175
Bertran of St.-Gilles, 27
Besly, Jean, 208–211 nn.
Bethlehem, 105
Béziers, 43, 180–181, 183, 185
Bezzola, R. R., 15, 24, 208 n., 213 n., 214 n., 217 n.
Blacasset, 154
Blancheflor, 136–137
Blanche of Castile, 185
Blaye, 89
Bleichner, P. E., 211 n.
Blondel, 149
Boccaccio, Giovanni, 43, 59
Boethius, 98, 195
Bohemond I, Prince of Antioch, 30
Born, 149
Borst, Arno, 93, 215 n.
bos homes, 94
Boson of la Marche, 26

Boutière, Jean, 208 n., 212 n., 214 n., 218 n.
Bouvines, 179
Briffault, R. S., 206 n., 207 n., 210 n.
Brittany, 43, 97, 98
Brive, 157
Browning, Robert, 137
Bruna, Lady. *See* Marcabruna
Bulgaria, 15, 29, 32, 93
Byzantium. *See* Constantinople

Cabestanh, Cabestain, 19, 89
Caesarius of Heisterbach, 180–181
Cain, 73
Cambridge Songs, 49–50, 85
Camproux, Charles, 212 n.
Can la frej'aura venta (Bernart), 114–115
Can l'erba fresch'e.lh folha par (Bernart), 128–130
canso(n), 63
Can vei la lauzeta mover (Bernart), 7, 14
Carcassonne, 180–181, 183
Carmina Burana, 14, 53, 221 n.
Carolingian Revival, 24, 49–50, 79–80
Casella, Mario, 216 n.
Catalans, 153
Catharism, 92–96, 98, 100, 103, 106, 175
"Cathar Ritual in Provensal," 94–95
Celts, 24
Cembelis (in Bertran), 167
Cercamon, 19, 63
Chabaneau, Camille, 233 n.
Chailley, Jacques, 213 n.
Chalais, Viscountess of (in Bertran), 167
Châlus, 149
Chambers, F. M., 223 n.
chanson de geste. See epic literature
Chanson de Roland. See Song of Roland
Chantars no pot gaire valer (Bernart), 122–123
charity, 50, 65, 71, 75, 83–84
Charlemagne, 34, 75, 102, 161
Chaucer, Geoffrey, 137, 156, 176
Chevalier, Jules, 218 n.
Chinon, 148
chivalry, 47, 74–75, 156
Chizé, 25

Chloe, 46
Chrétien de Troyes, 147, 205 n.
Christ. *See* Jesus Christ
Chronicon S. Maxentii Pictavensis, 208–211 nn.
Church: related to William VIII, 24–25; to William IX, 27–28, 34–38, 43, 46–47, 58–59; to chivalry, 75; to major heresies, 93–96; influence on rhetoric, 49–51; upheld by Marc., 67–68, 71–72, 83–84; attitude toward love, 113; toward marriage, 117; toward lyrics, 199; action in Albigensian Crusade, 175–185; end of Provensal tradition, 194–195
Cino da Pistoia, 159
Cistercians, 93, 112
Claudian, 206 n.
Clédat, Leon, 215 n., 218–220 nn.
Clergue si fan pastor (Peire), 176–178
Clermont, Council of, 26
companho, 24, 54
Companho, faray un vers . . . covinen (William), 43–44
Compostela, 37
"Comtesa de Dia," 133
Confolens, 44
Conrad, Constable of Germany, 29–31
consolamentum, 94
consolati, 94
consolation, 98
Constantine de Born, 149–150
Constantinople, 29–30, 32, 146
contemptus mundi, 95
Corinna, 113
Countess of Dia: 131–141; role in history, 133; vida, 133; evaluation of vida, 133–134; related to Raimbaut III of Orange, 133–136; evaluation of rhetoric, 137–138; related to Sappho, 138–139; mentioned, 198
"courtly love," 13, 198, 205 n.
courts, medieval, 15, 17, 24, 33–34, 43
Crusade, Albigensian. *See* Albigensian Crusade
Crusade, First, 26–27, 29, 30
Crusade, Second, 104, 146
Crusade, Third, 148
crusades, 26, 37, 75, 85, 105–106
Crusades of 1101, 28–33, 57
crusade song, 58, 72–74

Cummings, E. E., 44
Cupid, 54, 65
cupidity, 71, 94
Curtius, E. R., 206 n., 211 n.

Dalon, 111, 112, 145, 171
Damascus, 73
Damoetas, 79
dance song, 16–17
Dangerosa, 35–38, 198
Danishmends, 30
Dante Alighieri, 51, 106, 109, 137, 145, 147, 149, 156–157, 159–160, 171, 190
Daphnis, 46, 79
Daurostre, 46
Davenson, Henri, 41
David, 65, 77, 145, 189
debate poem, 75, 79–80
Dejeanne, J. M. L., 213–214 nn., 217 n.
Delilah, 76
Denomy, A. J., 212 n., 213 n., 215 n.
De Rougemont, 92
Detroit, 199
devinalh. See riddle poem
Dickinson, Emily, 133
Die, 133
Diego, Bishop of Osma, 175
Diez, Friedrich, 58, 206 n., 212 n., 219 n.
Dirai vos senes duptansa (Marc.), 64–65
Disputation of Pippin with Albinus (Alcuin), 102
Dodds, E. R., 215–217 nn.
Dominic, St., 175–176, 178, 185, 187
Domna, puois de me no.us chal (Bertran), 166–168
domneiar, 23, 164
Donaldson, E. T., 205 n., 219 n.
Dordogne, 112
Drôme River, 133
Dronke, Peter, 205 n., 216 n.
drudaria, 67
drut, 67, 153
Dumitrescu, Maria, 223 n.
Durand de Huesca, 178
Dylan, Bob, 198

Ebles (in Bernart), 121
Ebles (in Marc.), 70, 72
Ebles II (the Singer), Visc. of Ventadorn, 72, 112

Ebles III, Visc. of Ventadorn, 112, 149
Ebles IV, Visc. of Ventadorn, 149
Ebles Manzer, 25
Eden, Garden of, 50
eia, eya, 16, 68, 197
Ekkehard of Aura, 29, 209 n.
Eleanor of Aquitaine, 23, 36–37, 110–112, 146–149, 175, 198
Elias VI (Talleyrand), Count of Périgord, 149–151
Emery, R. W., 222 n.
Emma (in William), 39–41
epic literature, 29, 34, 46, 49, 154, 161, 163, 172
Ermengarde of Anjou, 36, 45, 50
Ermengarde of Narbonne, 112
Errante, Guido, 74, 213–214 nn.
Estat ai en greu cossirier (Countess), 136–137
Etienne. See Stephen
Eudes III, Duke of Burgundy, 180
Eve, 140, 164
excommunication, 27–28, 35, 38, 58

fabliau, 42–43
Fabre, C., 223 n.
Faidida (in Bertran), 167
Fanjeaux, 178
Farai chansoneta nueva (William), 45–46
Farai un vers de dreyt nien (William), 55–56
Farai un vers, pos mi sonelh (William), 39–41
Faral, Edmond, 212 n., 214 n.
Farinata degli Uberti, 190
Felibrige movement, 175
Ferran (in Bernart), 128
Filhol (in Jaufre), 97
fin'amors. See amor fina
Fin ioi me don' alegranssa (Countess), 138–139
Fitts, Dudley, 218 n.
Floris, 136–137
Flores, Angel, 8, 212 n., 218–220 nn.
Foix, 153, 157
Folquet of Toulouse, Bishop (earlier, Folquet de Marseilha), 183
Fontevrault, 34–35, 51, 148
Foulques IV (the Rough), Count of Anjou, 28, 35, 56–57
Foulques V, Count of Anjou, 35
Francis of Assisi, St., 187

Frank, Grace, 215 n.
Fränkel, Hermann, 206 n.
Franks, 23–24, 55, 74, 83, 106, 146, 186
Frazer, James, 206 n.
Frederick II, Emp., 178
Freud, Sigmund, 199

Galfridus, Gaufredus. See Geoffrey
Gall, Monastery of St., 42
Gallus, 79
Galm, J. A., 217 n.
Garonne River, 181, 182
Garsenda, Countess of Provence, 133
Gascony, 25, 28, 57, 63, 153, 183
Gaston of Béarn, 181
Genesis, 49
Geoffrey of Brittany, 23, 147
Geoffrey of Taunay, 26
Geoffrey of Vendôme, 26, 35, 37, 210 n.
Geoffrey of Vigeois (Gaufredus Vosiensis), 145, 149, 208 n., 217–220 nn.
Geoffrey of Vinsauf, 50
Geoffrey the Fat (Gaufridus Grossus), 27, 209 n.
George, St., 46, 47
Germanicopolis, 31
Gervais of Melkley, 50–51
Gimel, 44
Giraldus Cambrensis, 147, 148, 169, 171, 219–220 nn.
Girard, Bishop of Angoulême, 38, 58
Gisors, 163, 164
Gnosticism, 93
godfather (in Jaufre), 91, 92, 95, 103
Godfrey of Lorraine, 30
Goffridus, Goffredus. See Geoffrey
Goldin, Frederick, 189
Golias, 221 n.
Good Neighbor (in William), 48, 51
Good Reward (in Jaufre), 104–105
Gourdon, 150
Green, D. H., 213 n.
Gregorian chant, 14, 15
Gregory IX, Pope, 186
Guido of Biandrate, 29
Guigue VI, Dauphin of Viennois, 133

Guilhem de Saint Gregori, 154
Guilhem, Guillem. See also William
Guillem Augier, 154
Guillem Figueira, 191, 220 n.
Guinizelli, Guido, 216 n.
Guiraut de Bornelh, 109, 111, 134, 159
Guiraut Riquer, 220 n.
Guy de Montfort, 183, 184

Handy, W. C., 197
Hart, Lorenz, 198
Hatcher, A. G., 214 n.
Hautefort. See Altafort
Hector, 169
Henry IV, Holy Roman Emp., 30
Henry VI, Holy Roman Emp., 149
Henry II, King of England, 23, 110–112, 126, 145–148, 164
Henry III, King of England, 185
Henry, Prince (Young King), 23, 145, 147–148, 169–171
Heraclea, 31, 32
Hervé IV, Count of Nevers, 180
Hildegarde (unknown Countess of Poitou), 36
Hilka, Alfons, 223 n.
Hill, John and Laurita, 209 n.
histriones, 28
Hoepffner, Ernst, 206 n.
Holliday, Billie, 198
Holy Land, 26, 27, 72, 91–92, 98, 104, 146, 188
Homer, 49
homosexuality, 18, 80
Hopkins, Gerard Manley, 75
Horace, 164
Huesca, 27
Hugh, Count of Montebello, 29
Hugh Catola, 75–77
Hugh of Lusignan, 26
Hugh the Great, Count of Vermandois, 31
Hugo Brun (in Jaufre), 97
Hugo Flaviniacensis, 209 n.
hymns, Church, 14, 16, 18, 41–42, 47, 49–50, 53, 68, 71, 75, 206 n.

iambic dimeter, 41, 75
Iam, dulcis amica, venito, 50
Ibn Hazm, 207 n.
Ida, Margravine of Austria, 32–33

Ieu m'escondisc, domna, que mal no mier (Bertran), 164–166
Innocent III, Pope, 175, 178–185
Inquisition, 186, 199
Isolde, 119, 167
Itier de Born, 149

James I (the Conqueror), King of Aragon, 182, 190–191
Jarrett, Bede, 221 n.
Jaufre Rudel: 87–106; vida and evaluation, 89–92; interpreted by allegorizers, 92; related to Catharism, 92–96; to Christian Neoplatonism, 101–104; to William, 56, 95, 97, 100; to Marc., 83, 97, 105; to Bernart, 113; on crusade, 105–106; achievement, 106
jazz, 68, 197, 199
Jeanroy, Alfred, 14, 58, 205–206 nn., 211–212 nn., 215–216 nn., 218 n., 223 n.
Jehan de Nostredame, 205 n.
Jeremiah, 164
Jerusalem, 27, 33
Jesus Christ, 57, 68, 71, 75, 84, 94, 95, 98, 103, 105, 175
Jews, 75, 93, 96, 97, 98, 158, 159, 179
John, First Epistle of, 95
John, St., 194
John I (Lackland), King of England, 147–148, 171, 179, 180
John of Garland, 50, 184
joi, 18, 25, 53
Josephat, vale of, 72
joven, 25
Juan of Compostela, shrine of San, 37
Judas, 187
Julius Caesar, 169
Jung, Carl, 199
Juvenal, 74, 152

Kastner, L. E., 213 n., 219–220 nn.
Keats, John, 46
Kelly, Amy, 217–218 nn., 220 n.
Kilij Arslan, Sultan, 31–32
Klein, K. W., 219 n.
Knights of the Hospital, 135
Köhler, Erich, 208 n., 214 n.
Kussler-Ratyé, Gabrielle, 218 n.
Kyrie eleison, 14

Lancan vei per mei la landa (Bernart), 125–126
Lanfranc Cigala, 154
Lanquan li jorn son lonc en May (Jaufre), 90–91
Las Navas de Tolosa, 181
Lateran Council, Fourth, 182–183
Latin language, related to Old Provensal 7, 14, 15, 41–42, 47–48, 51, 57, 116
L'autrier jost' una sebissa (Marc.), 80–83
Lavaud, René, 221–222 nn.
Lazar, Moshé, 217 n.
Leda, 77
Leicester, 180
Lejeune, Rita, 215 n.
Le Mans, 148
Leonard, St., 39, 43, 151
Leopold II, Duke of Austria, 149
Lerch, Eugen, 215 n.
letter, Provensal lyric as, 51
Levis exsurgit Zephirus, 50, 85
Levy, Emil, 220 n.
Lewent, Kurt, 8, 213–215 nn., 217 n.
Lewis, C. S., 205 n.
Leys d'Amors, 187–188
Limoges, 56
Limousin, 23, 39, 110, 148, 150
L'iverns vai e.l temps S'aizina (Marc.), 68–71
Liverpool, 199
Lo coms ma mandat e mogut (Bertran), 152–153
Lo gens tems de pascor (Bernart), 123–125
Lombarda, 133
Lombards, 29–31, 151
longe, lonh, 104
Lot-Borodine, Myrrha, 216 n.
Lo tems vai e ven e vire (Bernart), 120–121
Louis VII, King of France, 84, 111–112, 146–148, 179
Louis VIII, King of France, 182, 185
Louis IX, King of France, 185

Maent (Maeut) de Montagnac, 168
Magnet, Lady (in Bernart), 126
Magnet, Lady (in Bertran), 168, 169
Maia, 93
Mainz, 149
Malbergion, 36, 38, 67, 198

Manicheanism, 56, 93. *See also* Catharism
manna, 82, 83, 97
Marcabrun: 61–86; vidas, 63; death, 63; basic qualities, 65–66; related to Church, 67–68, 71–72, 74–75; to William, 63, 66, 67, 72, 75, 83; to Jaufre, 83, 95, 97, 105; to Bernart, 113, 117; to Bertran, 163–164, 172; to Peire, 194; achievement, 85–86; mentioned, 18, 199
Marcabruna, 63, 65
Marcion, 93
Maria of Ventadorn, 133
Marie of Champagne, 112
Mariolatry, 187
Marseille, 183, 191
Martial, St., 55, 135
Martial of Limoges, monastery of St., 42
Martin, monastery of St., 41–42
Mary, Virgin, 14–15, 46–47, 53, 92, 95, 103–105, 115, 187–189, 194–195
Matfre Ermengaud, 216 n.
Matthew of Vendôme, 50
Maubergeonne, tower of, 36
May Queen, 17
Meliboeus, 79
Mélissinde, 89
Menalcas, 79, 80
Meyer, Paul, 222 n.
midons, 53. *See also* Milordess
Miei sirventes vuolh far de.ls reis amdos (Bertran), 157–158
Miguel de la Tor, 190
Miller, Henry, 43
Milo, envoy, 180
Milordess, origin of, 52–54, 95, 113
Mistral, Frédéric, 175
modern song, 197–201
Moissac, hymnal of, 211 n.
Mölk, Ulrich, 220 n.
Monk (in Chaucer), 176
Monk of Montaudon, 134, 176
Montaigu, 153
Montauberon, 153, 219 n.
Montaudon, 176
Monteverdi, Angelo, 214 n.
Montierneuf, 25, 26, 37, 58
Montmorillon, 37
Montpellier, 191
Montréal, 178
Montségur, 186
Moors, 20, 24, 37, 74, 75, 181
Morgan, Helen, 198
Moses, 94

Mout jauzens me prenc en amar (William), 52–53
Mozart, W. A., 109
Muret, 181, 182
music, 14, 42, 68, 97, 206 n., 213 n.

Narbonne, 112
Nardi, Bruno, 207 n.
Nashville, 199
Natura, 17, 18, 85, 206 n.
nature opening, 46, 49–50, 198
Nelli, René, 215 n.
Nichols, S. G., Jr., 7, 207 n., 217 n.
Nicomedia, 29, 31, 32
Nieul, 44
Nîmes, 190
Niort, 37, 74
Normandy, 43, 55, 110–112, 126, 164
North French literature, 17, 29, 42, 154, 193
No sap chantar qui so non di (Jaufre), 100–101
Nykl, A. R., 207 n.

O admirabile Veneris idolum, 68
obscurantism. *See trobar clus*
Oc e Non. See Richard I
octosyllabics, 41
Ogier the Dane, 162, 163
Oldenbourg, Zoé, 222 n.
Oliver, 161
Orange, 133
Ordericus Vitalis, 28–30, 33–34, 36, 58, 72, 208–210 nn.
O Roma nobilis, orbis et domina, 68
Otto IV, Holy Roman Emp., 179
Otto Altaspada, 29
Ovid: related to William, 45, 47, 49–51, 54, 56; to Marc., 65, 76–78; to Bernart, 113; to Countess, 138, 139; mentioned, 7, 15, 17, 18, 147, 194

Pamiers, 178
Pamperdut, 63
Papiols, 163, 169
Paris, 90, 183
Paris, Gaston, 16, 205 n.
Paris, Treaty of, 185
Parry, J. J., 205 n.

Paschal II, Pope, 27
pascor, 156
passio hereos, 54
pastoral poetry: classical Latin, 79; medieval Latin, 79–80; Provensal, 80–86
pastoreta, 80–86
Pattison, W. T., 133–134
Paul, St., 66
Pax in nomine Domini! (Marc.), 72–74
Peire (co-author of tenso with Bernart), 112
Peire Cardenal: 173–201; vida, 189–190; evaluation of vida, 190–191; background of Albigensian Crusade, 175–186; related to Church, 176–178, 186–189, 193–195; to Marcabrun, 194; to Bertran, 175; achievement, 201; mentioned, 198
Peire d'Alvernhe, 111, 112
Peire Vidal, 19, 89, 169
Pelisso(n), William, 222 n.
perfecti, 94
Périgord, 23, 148, 150
Périgueux, 150–152
Per l'aura freida que guida (Marc.), 66–67
Peter, Archbishop of Sens, 180
Peter II, Bishop of Poitiers, 26, 35, 38, 50, 72
Peter II, King of Aragon, 179, 181–182, 190
Peter, St., 194
Peter of Benevento, 182
Peter of Castelnau, 178, 179
Peter of Lara, Visc. of Narbonne, 153, 219 n.
Peter of Vaux-de-Cernay (Petrus Sarnensis), 185, 221–222 nn.
Petrarca, Francesco, 89
Petronilla, abbess of Fontevrault, 34
Petronius Arbiter, 43
Peytieux, Mount, 133
Philip I, King of France, 23, 27, 35
Philip II, King of France, 148–149, 163–164, 171, 179–185
Philippa de Born, 146
Philippa of Toulouse (Mahaut, Matilda), 27, 28, 30, 34–38, 45, 47, 50
Picts, 24
Pidal, R. M., 207 n.
Pillet, Alfred, 207 n., 214 n.
Pippin, 102
Pirot, F., 213 n.
Pisa, 118

plaint, *planh*, 169–171
Plato, 54, 100, 109, 113, 168, 207 n.
Poitiers, 23–24, 27–28, 36, 42, 74, 95, 112, 146–148, 199
Poitiers, Council of, 27–28
Poitou, 23, 24, 34, 43, 56, 57, 97, 98, 151
Pollmann, Leo, 211 n., 215 n.
Pons de Capduelh, 154
Pop Bogomil, 93
popular-origin theory, 16–17, 41–43, 206 n.
Porter, Cole, 198
Pos de chantar m'es pres talentz (William), 56–57
Pound, Ezra, 18, 109, 152, 157, 159, 168, 172, 219 n.
precs, 116
Priam, 169
Pro ai del chan essenhadors (Jaufre), 98–100
Prouille, 178
Proverbs, book of, 65–66, 78–79
Prudentius, 49, 206 n.
Psalms, 49
pure love. See *amor fina*
Puy, court of (in Berbezilh), 200
Puy Nôtre-Dame, 189

Quan lo rius de la fontana (Jaufre), 96–97
Quan lo rossinhols el folhos (Jaufre), 104–105
Quan. See also *Can*
Quercy, 101, 150

Raby, F. J. E., 206 n., 211–212 nn.
Racine, Jean, 109
Radulfus de Diceto, 36, 212 n.
Raimbaut de Vaqueiras, 134
Raimbaut III of Orange, 18, 133–134
Raimbaut IV of Orange, 134
Raimon de Miraval, 190
Rajna, Pio, 211 n.
Rand, E. K., 213 n.
Raymond IV, Count of Toulouse, 26–27, 30–33
Raymond V, Count of Toulouse, 110, 112, 149, 152–154, 219 n.
Raymond VI, Count of Toulouse, 178–185
Raymond VII, Count of Toulouse, 182–185

Raymond Beranger IV, Count of Barcelona, Marquis of Provence, 74, 214 n.
Raymond Roger, Count of Foix, 179, 181–183
Raymond Roger Trencavel, Visc. of Béziers and Carcassonne, 179–181
refined love. See *amor fina*
Reims, Council of, 36
Reitzenstein, Richard, 215 n.
Rhone River, 133, 179, 185
rhyme, 16, 18, 41, 56
Richard I (the Lion-Hearted), King of England, 23, 147–152, 157–158, 161, 163–164, 171
Richard, Alfred, 7, 208 n., 211 n.
Richard of St. Victor, 92
Richardus Pictavensis, 210 n.
Richart de Berbezilh, 169, 200
riddle poem, 54, 100–102
Riquer, Martin de, 213 n.
Robert d'Arbrissel, 28, 34–36, 47, 51, 148
Robertson, D. W., Jr., 195, 205 n., 212 n., 213 n., 215 n.
Robert the Old, Duke of Burgundy, 24
Rochechouard, 157, 167
Roger II, Visc. of Béziers and Carcassonne, 153, 219 n.
Roger Bernard I, Count of Foix, 153, 219 n.
Roger of Hoveden, 220 n.
Roland, 34, 154, 161
romance, medieval, related to romanticism, 46–47, 89, 92
Roman de la rose, 193, 206 n.
Roman de Renart, 177
Romans, 17, 24, 75, 93, 113, 139
Roncaglia, Aurelio, 207 n.
Rosamond Clifford, 147
Rostand, Edmond, 89
Rougemont, Denis de. See De Rougemont
Rousseau, Jean Jacques, 46
Runciman, Steven, 31, 209 n.

Sade, Marquis de, 43
Saint-Gilles, 179
Salisbury, 148
Salve, festa dies, 49
Samson, 76
Sancho I (Ramírez), King of Aragon, 27

Sancho, Regent of Provence, 153
Sancho Panza, 152
Santy, Sernin, 218 n.
Sappho, 54, 133, 138
Saracens, 91, 96–98
Satan, 94–96, 118, 179
Scaglione, A. D., 212 n.
Scheludko, Dimitri, 205–206 nn., 212–213 nn., 216–217 nn.
Schrötter, Wilibald, 217 n.
Schultz-Gora, Oskar, 217–218 nn.
Schutz, A. H., 208 n., 212 n., 214 n., 216 n., 218 n.
Scott, Sir Walter, 138, 198
Sedulius Scottus, 49
Seguin (Seguitz), 140, 218 n.
Self-Conceived Lady (in Bertran), 167–168
Shaw, J. E., 213 n.
Shepard, W. P., 223 n.
Silverstein, Theodore, 215 n.
Simon de Montfort, 180–185, 200
Singer, Samuel, 207 n.
sirventes, 63, 150
Si tuit li dol e.lh plor e.lh marrimen (Bertran), 170–171
Socrates, 168
solatz, solace, 98, 116
Solomon, 64, 65, 77, 78
Solomon, Temple of, 74
Song of Roland, 75, 86, 154, 172
Song of Songs, 49–50, 92, 103, 118
Song of the Crusade, 182, 184
Sordello, 220 n.
Spain, 25–27, 37, 74, 75, 149, 154, 175, 179
Spanke, Hans, 213 n.
Spitzer, Leo, 83, 100, 214 n., 216 n.
Spoerri, Theophil, 211 n.
spring opening. See nature opening
spring rites, 16–17
stanzaic patterns, 41–42
Stephen, Count of Burgundy, 30–31
Stephen Henry, Count of Blois, 30–31
Stern, S. M., 207 n.
Stimming, Albert, 219–220 nn.
Stronski, Stanislaw, 218–220 nn.
Supremes, 199
Syria, 188

Talleyrand, Talairan. See Elias VI
Tancred, Prince of Galilee, 30, 31, 33

Tant ai mo cor ple de joya (Bernart), 118–120
Tarascon, 153
Tartarassa ni voutor (Peire), 186–187
Tennyson, Alfred Lord, 198
tenso, 75, 134–136
Tertullian, 65
Thomas, Antoine, 219 n.
Thomas à Becket, 147, 148
Thomas Aquinas, 113, 207 n.
Tityrus, 79
tornada, 41
Tortosa, 33
Toulousain, 23, 26–27, 35, 93, 95, 152–154, 175, 178–186
Toulouse, 153, 181–185
Tripoli, 89
Tripoli, Countess of, 89–90
Tristan (hero), 119, 167
Tristan (in Bernart), 128
trobaire, 15
trobairitz, 133–134
trobar clus, 18, 97, 109, 133
trobar leu, pla, 109
trope, 15, 43, 199
Turks, 24, 26, 27, 30–33
Turpin, 29

Uc of Saint Circ, 111
Uc, Ugo. *See also* Hugh, Hugo
Una civ tatz fo, no sai cals (Peire), 191–193
Un sirventes novel vueill comensar (Peire), 193–194
Un sirventes on motz no falh (Bertran), 150–152
Urban II, Pope, 26, 75

Valence, 133
Valency, Maurice, 205 n.
Valenssa, Valence, 140, 218 n.
vanto, 117
Velay, 189
Venantius Fortunatus, 49, 207 n.
Ventadorn (Ventadour), 110–112
Ventadorn, Viscount and Viscountess of (in Bernart's vidas), 110–112
Venus, 17
Vera vergena, Maria (Peire), 188–189
Vergil, 49, 50, 79, 128, 171

vers, 63
Vienna, 149, 197
Vigil of Venus, 49
Villon, François, 59, 162
virtus, 75, 86, 159–160
Viscardi, Antonio, 206 n., 210 n., 217 n.
Volontiers feira sirventes (Bertran), 162–163
Von Sybel, Heinrich, 209 n.
Vossler, Karl, 210 n., 217 n., 220 n., 223 n.

Wace, 147
Waldensians, 93, 175, 179
Walpole, R. N., 216 n.
Walter Map, 221 n.
Waltharius, 34
Welf IV, Duke of Bavaria, 32
Weston, Jessie L., 206 n.
Westrup, J. A., 206 n.
Wife of Bath, 138
Will, Frederic, 218 n.
William II, Count of Nevers, 31
William IV, Count of Toulouse, 26–27
William I, Count of Valentinois, 133
William VIII (Gui-Geoffroi), Duke of Aquitaine, 23–25
William IX, Duke of Aquitaine: 21–59; vida, 23; family background, 23–25; character, 25; adolescence, 25–27; relations with Church, 27–28, 35–38; marriage to Philippa, 27; on Crusades of 1101, 28–33; married life and adulterous affairs, 34–36; death, 58–59; related to Marc., 63, 66, 67, 72, 75, 83; to Jaufre, 56, 95, 97, 100; to Bernart, 112–113; to Countess, 138; to Bertran, 154, 166; mentioned, 146, 179, 197, 199
William X, Duke of Aquitaine, 36, 56–58, 74, 146, 214 n.
William II (Rufus), King of England, 27
William IV, Visc. of Angoulême, 149
William VIII, Visc. of Montpellier, 153, 219 n.
William of Gourdon, 150–151
William of Malmesbury, 37–38, 47, 58, 72, 208–210 nn.

William of Newburgh, 146, 148, 219–220 nn.
William of Orange, 134
William of Peitieus, 133–134
William of Puylaurens, 176, 179, 221–222 nn.
William of Tudela, 182
William of Tyre, 36, 210 n.
Winchester, 148
witchcraft, 56

Young, Karl, 206 n.
Young King. *See* Henry, Prince
Ysengrin, 177

zadjal, zejel, 206 n.
Zingarelli, Nicola, 217 n.
Zola, Emile, 17
Zorzi, Diego, 216 n.